HARVARD HISTORICAL STUDIES, 120

*Published under the auspices
of the Department of History
from the income of the
Paul Revere Frothingham Bequest
Robert Louis Stroock Fund
Henry Warren Torrey Fund*

D1714041

THE
Humanist-Scholastic
Debate
IN THE
RENAISSANCE & REFORMATION

ERIKA RUMMEL

Harvard University Press
Cambridge, Massachusetts
London, England

First Harvard University Press paperback edition, 1998

Library of Congress Cataloging-in-Publication Data
Rummel, Erika, 1942–
The humanist-scholastic debate in the Renaissance and Reformation
/ Erika Rummel.
p.   cm.—(Harvard historical studies ; 120)
Includes bibliographical references and index.
ISBN 0-674-42250-3 (cloth)
ISBN 0-674-42251-1 (pbk.)
1. Rhetoric.   2. Debates and debating.   3. Humanism—History.
4. Scholasticism—History.   I. Title.   II. Series: Harvard
historical studies ; v. 120.
PN175.R86   1995
803.53´09´031—dc20   94-34983

Acknowledgments

I THANK THE MANY FRIENDS and colleagues who have provided me with advice at various stages of writing this book and have generously shared their research with me. I owe a special debt to James Estes, James Farge, Paul Grendler, James Hankins, and Charles Trinkaus, who gave me assistance ranging from encouragement and scholarly advice to the more mundane tasks of proofreading and manuscript preparation. I profited a great deal from their expertise. I gratefully acknowledge the financial assistance of the Killam Foundation and the institutional support of Wilfrid Laurier University. Thanks are also due to the Board of *The Collected Works of Erasmus*, who allowed me the use of their Toronto office conveniently located at the library of St. Michael's College, and to the Herzog August Bibliothek in Wolfenbüttel, Germany, where I was a research fellow during two summers.

Contents

THE HUMANIST-SCHOLASTIC DEBATE
IN THE RENAISSANCE AND REFORMATION

CHAPTER ONE

The Protagonists
and the Issues

IN 1513 A DISPUTE AROSE at the University of Erfurt between the poet Tillmann Conradi and certain "inarticulate sophists" that was seen by at least one observer—Mutianus Rufus—as an instance of a larger controversy.[1] Explaining the context to a correspondent, he wrote:

Latin letters made their debut here recently, after a difficult journey that ended safely thanks to the industry of a few. The young generation received them, eager for pure speech. A felicitous development, I said, hoping for a gradual increase in intellectual vigor and for the deliverance of Greek and Latin literature from their lowly station. With barbarism driven out of our midst, I hoped for a general flourishing of studies supported by learned teachers and a good supply of books. I encouraged individual students to leave behind the old grammar teachers and acquire a splendid education. I found some who took my good advice. Some gave proof of their eloquence in the legal profession; others, inspired by poetic ardor and in admiration of the dignity of poetry, wrote verse; still others purified their style and attempted to speak and write with utmost elegance. I was filled with joy therefore and congratulated the students. But alas for the attitude of the barbarians! Oh, capital crime! The *magistri nostri* spoiled this blessing, to the immense detriment of the student body. While I praise the *magistri* for their keen minds, their zeal, labor, vigilance, religious devotion, and integrity, I condemn them for their inflexibility, envy, and ill will—fatal flaws in the human character. They will not abandon their mean studies, they refuse to look favorably on a better doctrine, they begrudge youth the privilege of studying the best arts and command that everyone board their ship of fools.[2]

While Mutianus correctly describes the conflict at Erfurt as a new development in the wake of the recent importation of humanism into Northern Europe, the controversy between the champions of humanistic studies and the defenders of the scholastic method was of longer standing. It had a prelude in Italy in the fifteenth century and went through several permutations before running its course in Northern Europe. In the preliminary phase, epitomized by the exchange between Giovanni Pico della Mirandola and Ermolao Barbaro, the debate breathed the atmosphere of a literary salon. Soon, however, it acquired a sharper edge. Humanists had begun to apply their language skills to sacred texts, infringing on an area that was traditionally regarded as the monopoly of theologians. Questions concerning qualification and entitlement came to the foreground as the debate was taken up at universities in Northern Europe. Theologians and philologists jockeyed for position, vied for students, and disputed the territorial boundaries of their respective disciplines. Another shift occurred in the first half of the sixteenth century, when the controversy entered the sphere of doctrinal dispute and was subsumed into the Reformation debate. In this last phase the question of authority touched not only on professional competence and academic qualifications but also, and increasingly, on vocation, apostolic mandate, and magisterium.

In the first, unfocused stage of the debate inaugurated by Petrarch at the end of the fourteenth century, humanism and scholasticism were both new to Italy. Each movement soon attracted champions and detractors. Mutual recriminations followed. The scholastics were faulted for their addiction to Aristotle, for their barbarous Latin, and for obscurantism; the humanists for shallow estheticism and an admiration for classical civilization that bordered on paganism. The polemics meandered from question to question. Did truth need the embellishment of rhetoric? Did the study of classical literature corrupt Christian minds? Was rhetoric deceptive or could it serve a moral purpose? Were poets frivolous fools or inspired visionaries?

The nature of the discussion was shaped by the literary genres adopted by the participants in the early debate. Few of them used the scholastic method of inquiry; most employed a less structured approach, with a rhetorical thrust. The epistles of Petrarch, Salutati, Pico, and Barbaro and the stylized dialogues of Leonardo Bruni and Giovanni Pontano belonged to genres that encouraged variegation and blunted or even concealed the author's point of view. They demanded a feigned naturalness, the "graceful, nonchalant spontaneity" of Castiglione's gentleman.[3] Renaissance handbooks (and classical manuals before them) counseled letter-writers to refrain from unduly long, technical, and complex argumentation. After all, the personal letter replaced, and therefore ideally reflected, the spoken word. Petrarch accordingly went to some lengths to establish the informal nature of his diatribe against scholasticism, *On His Own Ignorance*, which takes the form of an epistle. It was not a book, Petrarch insisted, but "a conversation." It had "neither the bulk nor the disposition nor the style nor, above all, the gravity of a book."[4] The rambling introduction and conclusion bracketing the more coherently argued central part are calculated to reinforce the author's claim.

In a similar vein, Bruni claimed that his *Dialogues* were a faithful record of past conversations, but the exchange was carefully stage-managed to produce a "natural" effect and disguise literary criticism as spontaneous conversation.[5] The necessity of maintaining a literary conceit prevents the author from pursuing a tightly constructed, sustained, linear argument. It invites the mingling of topics and allows for the voicing of contrasting opinions. Indeed, the rules of the art absolve the author from developing a logical argument or presenting a logically derived conclusion. He is permitted to terminate the argument with civilities: the polite and perfunctory agreement of the participants in a dialogue or, in the case of an epistle, polite deference to the opinion of the addressee. The principles of epideictic oratory, which seeks to display the author's rhetorical skills rather than establish the truth, inform Bruni's *Dialogues* as well as the famous exchange between Pico and Barbaro. Pico's defense of scholasticism is no rigorous debate but an elaborate construct. The "barbarian" whom he enlists to defend scholasticism pleads his case in perfectly elegant language, mocking the purpose of his speech. Such playfulness, such delight in literary acrobatics, characterizes the first stage of the debate. It is largely absent from contributions in the sixteenth century, when the protagonists tended to display an earnest, not to say dour, attitude.

An interesting sidelight on the conflict between humanists and scholastics is provided by the *laudes disciplinae*, which formed the core of graduation addresses and inaugural lectures at universities. They too were a form of epideictic oratory, and therefore free of the constraints imposed by dialectical argumentation. Such speeches, Cornelius Agrippa of Nettesheim observed, operated in a sphere that was outside the rules governing the demonstration of truth, *citra veritatis statuendae regulam*.[6] The

rules of epideictic oratory did not require the author to explore or answer all possible counterarguments to his thesis; he was merely expected
to be agreeable and say what the occasion demanded regardless of personal convictions. Thus it was possible for Stephan Hoest (and perhaps
incumbent upon him as rector of the University of Heidelberg in the
1450s) to praise the *via antiqua* and the *via moderna* on two separate occasions and humanism on a third.[7] In the later phases of the debate, when
the question of the relative merits of the humanistic and scholastic methods had ceased to be an academic question and had become a matter of
ideology, such detachment or ambivalence became unacceptable or was
regarded as duplicity. "It is not permitted these days to open one's mouth
about things that earlier one could debate on either side," Erasmus
wrote in a moment of nostalgia for the polite insincerities of another
age.[8] It took time, however, for all concerned to take cognizance of this
development and write in accordance with the new standards of "political correctness"—to borrow a contemporary term. For a while confusion reigned, as scholastic theologians refused to distinguish declamations from disquisitions, and humanists refused to have their literary
productions examined *ad theologorum rigorem*.[9]

The conflict, which began in Italy as a literary debate, continued as
interfaculty feuding at universities, where humanists and theologians
were in competitive positions. Polarized by the Reformation, the parties
turned the feuds into dogmatic disputes. Epideictic oratory was an inappropriate and unsatisfactory medium to discuss the professional and
dogmatic issues that dominated the later phases of the debate. Protagonists began to favor different genres to express their opinions. They put
forward their views in designated apologiae or in apologetic prefaces to
books expected to arouse controversy. Their model was no longer familiar conversation elevated to a literary level, but the argumentation associated in classical handbooks with political and forensic oratory or with
Aristotelian dialectic. This type of argumentation obliged the author to
present reasoned arguments and called for an authoritative tone rather
than charm. The polemicists generally dispensed with niceties such as
creating a literary setting, suppressing the opponent's name, or casting
the debate as third-person accounts. We still find compositions that recall an earlier, more innocent age: Erasmus' *Antibarbari*, a literary debate
in utramque partem held in a classic garden setting, was drafted in the
1490s and published in 1520; Juan Luis Vives' charming allegorical *Somnium* appeared in 1521. But such compositions were now the exceptions.
In the early debate protagonists had left themselves room to maneuver—
if we assume that the medium was the message and that they chose the

literary genre that would allow for fluidity of thought. In later stages the respective positions hardened. On the whole, the polemics of the six-teenth century were aggressive and unforgiving in tone. Unvarnished bluntness came to characterize the dispute. A magisterial tone pervaded the writings of the scholastic theologians; invective was the weapon of choice in the humanistic camp.

Feelings ran high and were expressed in uncompromising terms, often without the palliative of courteous speech. There are many examples of incendiary language used by both humanists and scholastics. When the poet Jacob Locher became entangled in a controversy at the University of Ingolstadt, he composed an outrageous piece, *An Invidious Comparison between the Sterile Mule and the Muse Bedewed with Charm*, full of scatolog-ical outbursts and violent imagery.[10] In 1519 Willem Nesen issued this appeal to fellow humanists: "If men of letters know what's good for them, they'll sharpen their pens and overwhelm [the theologians] with a myriad of books. They don't deserve mercy. They are beasts, not human beings." This was also the opinion of Johann Reuchlin, who called the theologians "more inhuman than brute beasts . . . rather like pigs or sows delighting in their own filth and treading on the pearls of others." Ulrich von Hutten likewise advocated war against the theologians. "I don't think we should listen to those who want us to avoid unpopularity," he wrote defiantly. "I am not afraid [of the theologians] . . . Let them hate me, and I'll do my best to make them fear me too." Elsewhere he de-clared: "I have in mind to declare war on those depraved hypocrites. Believe me, unless they are unmanned, there will never be an end to the strife." Eobanus Hessus used similar military metaphors in a letter supporting Reuchlin: "You will win. We shall triumph."[11] The belliger-ent attitude of the humanists is acknowledged and lampooned by Ortvi-nus Gratius in his *Lamentations*. "They will wage war on the theolo-gians," one of his characters writes; another is said to have escaped the fury of the humanists with difficulty: "I feared for my life . . . I barely made it home alive."[12] But there is no lack of militancy on the part of the scholastic theologians either. They, too, indulged in name-calling, labeling the humanists pagans, heretics, sophists, dreamers, and fools. Some, like the Louvain theologian Frans Titelmans, were polite but cut-ting in their remarks; others were scurrilous in their abuse. Nicolaus Baechem, a member of the Commission for the Extirpation of Heresy in Brabant, called the humanists Erasmus and Lefèvre "cranes, asses, beasts, blockheads, and Antichrists."[13] The Paris theologian Pierre Cousturier used more creative language to characterize the hated philol-ogists. He described Jacques Lefèvre as a "sciolist, a manikin, a philoso-

5

phaster, a translationist."[14] Hermannus Buschius reports that humanists were routinely abused in these terms: "Poets are rascals, orators pigs, and their writings the food of demons."[15]

The second phase of the debate in which such uncivil exchanges became the norm is dominated by disputes over academic qualifications. One tends to think of versatility and all-round learning as the trademark of Renaissance Man, and no doubt this was promoted as an ideal, but when it came to practicing an art professionally, scholars tended to take a compartmentalized view of the disciplines. When humanists began to apply their skills to sacred texts, theologians closed ranks to defend their territory from encroachment. Their concern is lampooned in an anonymous skit in which a Cologne theologian rebuffs the humanists: "Go and fret over your Latin, spin out verses, deliver grand speeches, publish books on how to write Latin . . . but what business of yours is it to correct the Magnificat?"[16] In an effort to protect their monopoly, the theologians began scrutinizing the professional qualifications of their humanistic challengers and alleged that they lacked the necessary credentials. Noël Béda vigorously complained about *humanistae theologizantes*, theologizing humanists, and in 1534 made a formal representation to the Parlement of Paris, alleging that the lecturers at the nascent Collège de France were exceeding their mandate by using biblical texts in their language courses.[17] Béda claimed that commenting on the Bible was the exclusive privilege of the faculty of theology and its members. The issue was by no means a new one. Half a century earlier the Italian humanist Aurelio Brandolini had protested against the view that biblical studies were the exclusive preserve of men who held a doctorate in theology.[18] In Spain, the renowned philologist Elio Nebrija vigorously defended his rights against critics who wanted him to abandon biblical studies because he had no formal training in theology: "No one can curtail my sphere of interest and keep me from coursing through the rest of the arts and sciences."[19] In Germany, Johann Eck dismissed Oecolampadius as a "grammatisch theologus," but Hutten sneered at the protectionism of the theologians in the preface to *Nemo:* "Nowadays one must be a *doctor,* but it isn't necessary to be *doctus;* in fact that counts for nothing."[20]

The battle was not only about academic qualifications, however, but also about methodology. In this vein, Pierre Cousturier complained that he could not have a professional argument with a humanist because he was dealing "with grammarians who knew nothing of dialectic."[21] Edward Lee had the same difficulty. His opponents, he said, were "arguing about grammatical points, whereas I am speaking of theological matters."[22] A Spanish theologian stated the principle behind these complaints: "In matters of theology one must speak and write theologically," by which he meant "in the style of scholastic theologians."[23] The Leipzig theologian Johann Seitz explained the need for technical terminology: "There are important reasons for subjecting theological language [*theologicus loquendi modus*] to rules from which one must not depart. If you do not observe them, the irregular form of speech . . . may lead to heresy."[24] In his proem to *De locis theologicis* (Salamanca, 1563) Melchior Cano accordingly declared: "Let no one expect polished language from me . . . My aim is to please the scholastics. I dare not depart from the terminology of the schools and their peculiar form of speech."[25] Humanists, however, refused to be put into the straitjacket of scholastic terminology. Mutianus Rufus protested: "We are denied the right to free discussion. We must speak *ad regulam*, according to their rule."[26] Johann Sturm accommodated the scholastics reluctantly, noting in the preface to his *Partitiones dialecticarum* (Lyons, 1554): "I used many expressions that could have been phrased in better Latin because I did not wish to exacerbate the dialecticians by departing too far from the custom of the scholastics."[27] If the scholastics complained that the humanists were unable or unwilling to use proper dialectical reasoning, they in turn complained that scholastics knew no Latin and relied on "a few tricks and loopholes to ensnare or elude their opponents."[28] Pedro Mexia lampooned the scholastic method in his *Diálogos o Coloquios* (Seville, 1562), in which one character explains: "Disputing and being obstinate are one and the same thing, for disputation and obstinacy is nothing but one person holding one view and another holding the contrary view and the two wrangling about it. One can't have arts or sciences without it. And that's how it is. And I don't see how anyone can condemn such a necessary thing . . . all the philosophers and all the saints used it, and today it is used by all the schools and universities in the whole world."[29]

Beyond the language and format of argumentation, the dispute extended to the question of prooftexts to be cited in support of an argument. Here, too, the parties had difficulties finding common ground. The scholastic preference for and reliance on medieval authorities is summed up by Jacques Masson, who wrote that "the genuine sense of Scripture is found in its purest form in the expositions and commentaries" of the scholastic doctors.[30] Gabriel Biel in his *Correctorium* had expressed it more poetically: referring tyros to the Bible was like "casting infants into the great and spacious sea." Scripture was "too difficult and almost unusable" for beginners; they were better off with Peter Lombard's *Sentences*, where everything was laid out for them in order and

7

discussed *scholastico more*.[31] The humanists, by contrast, adopted the slogan *Ad fontes!*, turning their attention to the scriptural text in the original and relying on the explications of patristic writers who, they argued, were able to give more faithful interpretations because of their proximity to the source in time. Medieval theologians, they felt, had departed from the primitive faith of the church.[32]

Methodological considerations were no doubt a significant factor in the controversy, but humanists suggested, somewhat maliciously, that less exalted motives were involved in the dispute. The scholastics, they said, were less concerned about standards, qualifications, or method than about their livelihood. Buschius alleged that they fought against the teachers of the humanities because "they wanted to be the only ones to profit financially from the crowd of students."[33] In the *Letters of Obscure Men*, one fictive theologian, acknowledging the competition, complains that he cannot get a university position and is forced to drudge as a secretary. "The poets," he says, "are the bane of the universities." They lure away students from the study of theology and leave its professors without a following. Erasmus likewise attributes the tensions between the two camps to the scholastics' fear of lecturing "to empty benches."[34]

In the early sixteenth century the controversy escalated in tandem with the Reformation debate. The humanists, for some time stereotyped as poets and grammarians meddling in theology, were now often labeled Lutherans; the scholastics, stereotyped as barbarians and quibblers, were now perceived as reactionary papists and corrupters of the true Church of Christ. This motif appears, for example, in the *Dialogue of the Bilinguals and Trilinguals*, a lampoon on the faculty of theology at Louvain, published in 1520. The opening scene of the skit shows the theologians in the act of burying the Muse alive. "What has she done to deserve that?" one of the onlookers asks. He is told that "her crime is an atrocious one . . . she has been condemned for heresy."[35] The same motif also appears in an anonymous farce on the theologians of Paris dating from the early 1530s, in which the "théologastres" declare in a mixture of French and crude Latin: "Great evils are upon us. Everyone now is reading Greek . . . and even Hebrew. I haven't read a word of it, but I know well that whoever speaks Greek is suspect of heresy." Elsewhere in the skit they explicitly link the biblical humanists with Luther: "Erasmus, Lefèvre, Luther, and you [Berquin]—truly, you are nothing but heretical fellows."[36] The suspicions and accusations satirized in the two skits are voiced in earnest by the papal legate Girolamo Aleandro. He fumed against "the captious tribe of grammatists and poetasters" who equated deviating from the Church with learning.[37] The same view prevailed in Gotha and Erfurt, for Mutianus Rufus reports his adversaries as saying: "Urbanus [Rhegius], Spalatin, and Mutianus are poets, speak Greek, and hold impious views on sacred matters."[38] The Louvain theologian Titelmans perpetuated the view, observing that language studies had made heretics out of men like Hutten, Oecolampadius, and Melanchthon.[39] Similarly, Jacob Proost reported that the Louvain theologians Masson and Baechem had called him a heretic and a champion of heresies like Erasmus and Luther, because he was studying Greek.[40]

The accused humanists counterattacked. "Scholastic theology," Agrippa von Nettesheim wrote, "has deteriorated into sophistry. These new peddlers of theosophy ... have transformed a sublime discipline into a war of words."[41] It was ignorance of humanistic studies that had caused the corruption of the Christian faith, wrote Franz Burchard in an oration, a work of which Melanchthon thought so highly that he published it as an appendix to one of his own works. Updating the original debate over rhetoric and philosophy, Burchard rewrote Barbaro's reply to Pico in 1534, changing the terms of reference to reflect the controversy over biblical humanism which dominated his own time. Burchard's contribution demonstrates how the terms of the debate had changed. The discussion no longer revolved around style and the ability of the scholastics to express themselves in pure and elegant Latin. It concerned their ability to understand and interpret the Word of God. The scholastics, Burchard wrote, "were incapable of handling the controversies and ideas of antiquity. In consequence they have spread in the Church many impious and pernicious opinions."[42] The debate moved from esthetics to ideology. The tone had changed, too. Ermolao Barbaro had explicitly noted the contrived nature of his debate with Pico. His literary adversary might quarrel with him "in word but agreed at heart." He acknowledged Pico's stratagem and praised his cleverness: "What more cunning scheme could you have hit upon than to try by the highest eloquence to defend the accused who confess themselves injurious to eloquence?"[43] Nor was his reply to Pico in earnest; rather, he was "jesting on this amusing subject."[44] Burchard by contrast is entirely in earnest, and, far from praising Pico's conceit, mildly reproves the Italian humanist: "I would that you might have elected to try out your power and inventiveness in another way ... I would not have the [scholastics] armed with the authority of your name, nor equipped with your weapons against the most eminent art."[45] His own disquisition is written from the heart and written for his contemporaries.

Titelmans' and Aleandro's linking of the humanities with Lutheranism, and Burchard's linking of scholasticism with the decline of the true faith, are typical of the last phase of the controversy, when it became part of the Reformation debate. Some saw a conspiracy in the theologians' facile equation of humanism with Lutheranism, but there had been, at least at the outset of the Reformation, an affinity of objectives: the quest for an unadulterated biblical text and a historically correct interpretation. Soon, however, philologists found themselves in conflict with the traditional Church. Faced with contradictions between their scholarly findings and the interpretations of the Church which claimed teaching authority, they had three options: break with the established Church, divorce secular from sacred studies, or attempt a synthesis of science and faith. Agrippa of Nettesheim claimed that fear of criticism and persecution drove many scholars underground: "The scholastic tyranny certainly drove quite a few away from the humanities and caused many who had embarked on them to turn back. It was such a deterrent even for those who loved the humanities and persevered in their studies, that they disguised their erudition and allowed the fruit of their labors to die with them, depriving posterity of the benefit."[46] To reconcile scholarship with obedience to the Church required a difficult balancing act. Erasmus' personal solution to the dilemma of the humanist caught between philological and theological exigencies was *pia curiositas*, by which he meant an intellectual curiosity circumscribed by considerations for the authority of the Church, and a scholarship subject to the decrees of the Church.[47] While Erasmus was thus successful in fusing the persona of the believer (and, as he saw himself, of the orthodox theologian) with that of the philologist, his Christian humanism, to give it its modern name, remained a hybrid. "It was not a resting place for the European spirit," R. R. Bolgar wrote, and was "too full of unresolved contradictions to count as satisfactory."[48] Thus Erasmus' solution inspired many but was adopted by few. The general tendency was toward polarization rather than fusion of the two currents, and as a consequence, a certain regrouping took place within the humanistic camp. Some distanced themselves from biblical studies and retreated to the field of secular scholarship; others discovered their religious vocation, abandoned secular studies, and became theologians and reformers. This process of redefining priorities has been noted by modern historians. For example, Cornelis Augustijn remarked that Luther was the catalyst that separated the champions of the New Learning into humanists proper and biblical scholars, and Lewis Spitz observed: "It is astonishing to see how many of the younger humanists . . . changed their professions to take up theology and enter the parish ministry."[49]

Throughout this preliminary sketch of the conflict I have referred to the protagonists as "humanists" and "scholastics," applying the sort of "simple dualisms" deplored by J. Overfield, who argues that "many 'humanists' saw value in certain aspects of scholasticism . . . many 'scholastics' cultivated an interest in ancient literature."[50] Overfield is right to advise caution, but caution need not keep us from searching for patterns.[51] To adapt Voltaire's dictum: if humanist and scholastic purists did not exist, it would be necessary to invent them for structural purposes. Indeed, they *have* been invented for us by the polemicists who were looking for suitable bêtes noires. Their clichés provide a starting point for our investigation of the scholastic and humanistic *typoi*.

In noncombative usage, the term *humanista* denoted a student or teacher of *studia humanitatis*, that is, a curriculum focusing on language skills. In the rhetoric of controversy, however, humanists were nothing but philologists, nothing but "grammarians, speechifiers, and Greeklings."[52] In the derogatory terms of the dispute, *studia humanitatis* were downgraded to *poetria*, poetical stuff. "You poets," said Baechem, "are all imagination and lies."[53] The textbook definition of scholasticism is "a system of inquiry based on Aristotelian logic combined with Christian doctrine," but in the radicalized language of the debate, scholastics were "barbarian thickheads" and "Scoti, Scauri, and Bardi," that is, "benighted, hobbling fools."[54] The battle lines were drawn and the stereotypes established: all scholastic theologians were obscurantists who had never read classical authors, wrote atrocious Latin, and were interested only in esoteric quibbles, while all humanists were grammarians and wordspinners, interested in form rather than substance, pseudo-Christians whose brains had been addled by reading pagan literature.

From the rough outline of characters drawn for us by the combatants, we proceed to finer distinctions. Style, though a frequent subject of dispute, turns out to be an unreliable criterion for determining cultural affiliation. Classical usage, or the absence of it, appears to be more indicative of chronological and geographical incidentals than of *Weltanschauung*. After 1530 especially, style becomes meaningless as an indicator, because classicizing Latin was increasingly becoming the norm in scholarly writing. A better criterion to distinguish humanists from scholastics is their methodology. Champions of scholasticism favor syllogisms and other forms of inference familiar from dialectical textbooks. Their disquisitions are usually tightly structured and often arranged in numbered points or captioned paragraphs. The scholastics, E. Panofsky wrote, "felt compelled to make the orderliness and logic of their thought palpably explicit."[55] Humanists, by contrast, opted for more informal presentations. "There is no formal argument here," Buschius proudly pointed out in his *Vallum humanitatis*, "no artful conclusions, no barbarous syllogism."[56] Humanists tended instead to use rhetorical devices—similes, metaphors, historical examples—to give their works the character of essays or orations.

Although humanists did not, as their accusers claimed, disdain tradition and authority, they were inclined to examine the source texts rather than their interpretations. When citing or expounding biblical passages, moreover, they often took a philological approach, arguing on the basis of grammatical rules, etymology, and classical usage. The scholastic arguments are logical rather than philological. In support they often quote a slate of authorities, from scriptural texts to Latin Fathers and medieval theologians. References to classical authorities other than Aristotle are limited. Humanists, as a rule, cite a much larger range of classical and patristic authors and either shy away from medieval authorities altogether or qualify their use. Thus Mutianus Rufus calls Albertus Magnus and authors like him *futiles auctoritate*, weak in authority, reporting that his critics in turn rejected the testimony of classical Latin and Greek authors, calling any reference to them as a case of *impertinenter allegare*, an irrelevant citation.[57]

The two movements also differ in their orientation, with scholastics aiming at the perfection of doctrinal theories and humanists focusing on the implementation of doctrine in the life of the believer. The humanists were, as Lewis Spitz put it, "action-oriented and people-directed."[58]

The best criterion for labeling a writer "scholastic" or "humanistic" is also the most intangible: intellectual curiosity. In her book, *Philosophie und Philologie*, Hanna-Barbara Gerl suggests that the scholastic is best defined in terms of his approach to investigating problems (*Perspektive der Fragestellung*). Unlike the humanist, he is often unwilling to consider the whole range of questions.[59] The scholastic inclines toward *Verengung*, a narrowing of the range of investigation. He tends to be a specialist; the humanist aims at being a universal scholar. The contrast is not a modern construct. Already in the fifteenth century Bartolommeo della Fonte noted that philology, the master science of the humanists, was all-embracing, whereas other disciplines, like theology, "have established limits."[60] In the sixteenth century, Marc-Antoine Muret made a similar observation. Physicians, lawyers, and other professionals studied well-defined subjects, only the humanists tasted the "whole variety of the liberal arts."[61] Such observations should not lead us to the simplistic conclusion that scholastics had closed minds and humanists open ones. Rather, it was, at the psychological level, a conflict between *Seelenwinkel und Weltall*, as Heiko Oberman has felicitously expressed it,[62] and on the intellectual/academic level a question of circumscribing the terms of investigation. To put it another way, scholastics argued for more restrictive terms, which they equated with greater mental rigor; humanists for a more generous interpretation, which they saw as a step toward the Renaissance ideal of the *uomo universale*.

If we run into occasional difficulties applying these criteria to the protagonists in the debate, it is not only because they were eclectics but also because of a conscious effort on the part of some polemicists to beat the other party at its game. Thus we find scholastics quoting classical authors to show that they were not as innocent of the New Learning as their opponents depicted them; and humanists using syllogisms to prove that they too knew how to use dialectical reasoning. Erasmus—the quintessential humanist—answers the syllogisms of his adversary, the Franciscan Luis Carvajal, with syllogisms of his own and boasts that he learned dialectic as a child of eleven; Wimpina, the defender of scholastic theology at the University of Ingolstadt, let it be known that he, too, had once composed verses. More often than not, however, cross-over attempts remain amateurish and the "impostor" is promptly unmasked by the opponent.[63]

More confusing is the appropriation—or rather misappropriation—of humanistic slogans by scholastics during a period of internal reform that took place in the early sixteenth century. Johann Eck, for example, prefaced his books, which were to replace the standard texts at the universities of Freiburg, Tübingen, and Ingolstadt, with promises of "eliminating barbarism" and "sweeping away the filth of the sophists."[64] His efforts and similar initiatives at other universities were, however, mere housekeeping—repairs to the façade but not to the structure of the scholastic edifice. In spite of the modern catchphrases Eck spouted, his approach remained firmly traditional.[65]

Finally, there were the "traitors," humanists suborned by the other party to fight the enemy with their own weapons. Maarten van Dorp was widely regarded as a *collaborateur* and nicknamed Phenacus ("Trickster"); Euricius Cordus was accused of selling out to the enemy. Agrippa of Nettesheim referred to such ghostwriters as "parasites of the scholastics."[66]

Since individual criteria are subject to many qualifications, it is safer to judge the affiliation of writers by rating them not on a single point, but according to a set of characteristics. One may consider, for example, a writer's position on a number of key issues: the value of classical education for Christians, the importance of style in philosophical/theological writings, the role of languages and philology in the interpretation of Holy Writ. Generally speaking, humanists supported classical learning, gave weight to stylistic considerations, and emphasized the importance of linguistic skills in biblical studies; scholastics took the opposite view. However, the protagonists were usually too sophisticated to speak in unqualified terms. Thus humanists supported classical learning, *acknowledging however* that pagan authors lacked the light of faith; scholastics cautioned against classical learning, *acknowledging however* that pagan wisdom could be adapted to Christian purposes. Both parties used the biblical metaphors of "spoiling the Egyptians" and "trimming the nails and cutting the hair of the pagan woman" to justify their qualified approach to classical studies. Similarly, the humanists depicted the study of languages as a necessary but not a sufficient condition of understanding Scripture; scholastics admitted the usefulness of such studies but declared them optional. With respect to style, scholastics usually insisted on the importance of technical theological language and the immutability of biblical idiom; humanists allowed for technical terms where they were unavoidable, but otherwise insisted on compliance with common scholarly usage, or as it was often put, the usage of *probati autores*, standard classical authors.

In categorizing the protagonists we should look on cultural affiliation much as we do on political affiliations today: people cast their votes without being card-carrying party members, and in Canada we speak of "small-l liberals" as opposed to Liberal party faithfuls. The designations "scholastic" and "humanistic" admit of similar qualifications. For purposes of a meaningful discussion of the conflict we must adopt a set of criteria. Training and style of the protagonists are the least reliable indicators; attitude and approach are more telltale. The questions to ask therefore are not whether a scholar was able to cite the classics, but what value he put on them; not whether he knew Greek or was able to distinguish between classical and nonclassical usage, but whether he thought such skills were relevant to the theologian; not whether he knew certain texts but whether he had a historical understanding of them. Thus the cultural affiliation of a writer should be determined by means of probing his attitude and searching for a consistent pattern and sustained views. As Charles Trinkaus put it: "In any given figure, what may be set up as a type is more an identification of a major direction and not a model to which he in most instances should be held tightly to conform."[67]

It remains to examine the origins of the controversy in the Renaissance. The roots of the humanist-scholastic conflict were complex. It was fed and sustained by a general resentment against the New Learning, which was based first of all on a natural resistance to change; secondly, it arose out of fear that the pagan authors championed by the humanists might contaminate Christian thought; and finally, it rested on the belief that the rhetorical splendor of classical diction did not agree with the concept of Christian humility. To these misgivings were added concerns specific to the academic milieu, such as rivalry between the faculties and disagreement over methodological principles, and concerns specific to the Reformation: the notion that humanism was synonymous with Lutheranism.

Among the factors informing the controversy, resistance to change was the most pervasive. In the sixteenth century traditionalism was a more powerful force than it is today, when we have become inured or at any rate resigned to rapid shifts in customs and values, and when we are pressed by advertising to equate innovation with progress. For long periods in history, however, the word "new" had negative connotations and the desire for innovation was seen as a sign of rebelliousness and insubordination. In classical Latin, *cupidus rerum novarum*, literally "keen on new things," was an idiom for "revolutionary." This concept had not changed much by the end of the sixteenth century, when Artegall in the *Faerie Queene* remarks, "All change is perillous."[68] The humanists, who were the challengers in Northern Europe, were frequently confronted with the charge that they were "keen on new things," that is, that they were revolutionaries. In the context of our controversy, the charge of innovation is constantly brought into play. In the 1450s Manetti complained that his critics evaluated scholarship by the same standards as wine: the older the better.[69] In 1530—almost a hundred years later—Frans Titelmans was still harping on the same theme, accusing Valla, Lefèvre, and Erasmus of "turning up their noses at the old and pursuing the new."[70]

Just as powerful as the resistance to change was the entrenched view of classical authors as purveyors of corrupt pagan morality. Jerome's famous dream, in which he was flogged for his attachment to Cicero, is the classic expression of a phobia still prevalent in the Renaissance. Misgivings about classical authors extended to both the content and the form of their writings. The content, it was felt, did not agree with Christian doctrine, and polished speech did not accord with the simplicity of heart recommended by the Gospel. In the context of the debate which set the advocates of a *theologia rhetorica* against the defenders of scholastic idiom, Alberto Pio proclaimed that it was better to speak like a barbarian and hold doctrinally correct views than to speak polished Latin and hold questionable views. Similarly, the German Franciscan Nicolaus Ferber von Herborn declared that he wanted nothing to do with polished speech: "I prefer to be a simpleton and a barbarian so that I may enter the kingdom of God."[71]

The three ingredients that prompted strong opposition to humanism—resistance to change, fear of pagan contamination, and the rejection of sophisticated language—are well represented in Erasmus' dialogue *The Antibarbarians*. There the critics of the New Learning complain "that those first-rate authors through whom our forefathers have become immensely learned . . . are being shamefully pushed aside for the introduction of some unheard-of abominable monsters of paganism—Horace, Virgil, and Ovid—. . . [authors] who please those whose ears were always itching for something new." The champions of the New Learning object that their enemies "have some perception that there is an incompatibility between pure religion and consummate learning . . . If they smell out someone with learning of a more polished kind, they hold him in abhorrence. 'Beware,' they say,' he's a poet, he's no Christian.'"[72]

These, then, were the popular prejudices which formed the subtext of the controversies. Superimposed on them in the later stages of the debate are professional concerns, interfaculty rivalries leading to quarrels over competency, and in the final phase, disputes about orthodoxy.

The controversy, which spanned some two hundred years, issued in numerous polemics and has attracted considerable scholarly attention. Much of it, however, is concentrated on the first phase. Subsequent phases have been, if not neglected, at any rate treated as extensions of the original debate rather than as distinct phenomena with a rationale of their own. Failure to recognize the complexities characterizing the debate and to take into account its permutations over the passage of time has led to remarkable discrepancies in modern interpretations. For some time it was fashionable for Renaissance historians to stress the total incompatibility of the humanist and scholastic positions. More recently, however, revisionist views have been voiced, for example by Paul Oskar Kristeller, who declared in *Renaissance Thought* that historians "under the influence of a modern aversion to scholasticism . . . exaggerate the opposition of the humanists to scholasticism" and expressed the view that their controversies were by and large "personal feuds, intellectual tournaments, or rhetorical exercises."[73] Kristeller's statements are expressed in deliberately unequivocal terms, but certain qualifications are implied by the context. It is clear that the forcefulness of his remarks was mustered to combat the notion that humanism succeeded scholasticism *as a philosophy*.[74] His point is valid within these limits and aptly characterizes the first phase of the debate. However, some scholars citing Kristeller have given his views a wider application than warranted. In his most recent study of humanism and the Reformation, Lewis Spitz, for example, declares without qualifications—implicit or explicit—that "the struggle between scholasticism and humanism during the Renaissance [has] been wildly exaggerated."[75] Even more categorical is Winfried Trusen's statement: "It is an accepted fact, I believe, that there was no principal enmity between humanists and scholastics in Germany."[76] James Overfield goes one step further, faulting not only the interpretation of modern historians but the eyewitnesses themselves. The humanist-scholastic controversies, he writes, were not "the titanic and never-ending struggles *imagined* [my italics] by the humanists"; they were "limited in time and place and only briefly effective."[77] Laetitia Boehm, on the other hand, recognizes the significance of the controversies and implies that there was an Italian and a German phase: "The opposition to scholasticism, taken over from Italy, forms a *leitmotif*, especially of early German humanism."[78] Charles Nauert likewise sounds a note of caution regarding the revisionist stand. He accepts the premise "that the idea of an irrepressible conflict needs to be demonstrated, not taken for granted," but concludes, after investigating the evidence, that humanists and modern historiographers are not guilty of exaggerating the truth. Rather, modern scholars "may in fact be underestimating the distaste of the German humanists for scholasticism," and "Northern humanists of the early sixteenth century did express distaste for scholasticism frequently enough that it must count as one of their chief characteristics."[79] Nauert and Boehm point the reader in the right direction by introducing a differentiation between the age of the Reformation in Northern Europe, where humanists faced well-established and prestigious theological faculties, and Early Renaissance Italy, where scholasticism was an import and there was no strong theological presence at the universities.[80]

A closer inquiry into the later phases of the humanist-scholastic debate allows us to put into perspective the traditional view that emphasizes the antagonism between the parties, and the revisionist view that claims, in its most extreme formulation, that the controversies "were mere episodes in a long period of peaceful coexistence."[81] The latter view has some validity for the early Renaissance, which was characterized by doctrinal and academic latitudinarianism. However, two developments put an end to the prospects of a peaceful coexistence: a stricter delineation of academic competency, which separated "Queen Theology" from her "handmaid" philology;[82] and the exacerbation of the debate during the Reformation, which made it difficult for scholars to plead detachment. The age that saw the rise of Luther was so poisoned with suspicion that, as Vives put it, "one could neither speak nor remain silent without risk"; and it was so encumbered with sensibilities that Erasmus exclaimed: "I would never have thought it possible for people to be so thin-skinned and morose!"[83] The traditional interpretation of the humanist-scholastic debate as a fundamental rift is appropriately applied to this later phase in the debate, when the Reformation controversy radicalized the polemic and lifted controversy from the level of an academic debate enlivened by the fire of rhetoric to the level of a visceral dispute marked by the fires of the Inquisition.

CHAPTER TWO

Paradigms of the Debate

NEITHER THE LANGUAGE nor the issues of the debate in the Renaissance was entirely new. The controversy had roots in both classical antiquity and early Christian thought. It revived elements of the Platonic debate over the respective merits of rhetoric and philosophy, translated Lucian's satirical review of the philosophical schools into terms relevant to the Renaissance, reinterpreted the Pauline disparagement of Pharisaical legalism, and borrowed from patristic sermons and commentaries.

"Sophist" was used as a mutual term of reproach in the Renaissance debate. Clearly, the concept was derived from Plato's dialogues, which reflect the animosity of his generation against a new type of professional: the sophist, or teacher of rhetoric. In the *Gorgias,* named after the protagonist, a prominent rhetorician, Socrates inquires into the nature of rhetoric. He invites Gorgias to define his art, but the sophist delivers a eulogy instead:

> If you only knew how rhetoric comprehends and holds under her sway all the inferior arts. Let me offer you a striking example of this. On several occasions I have been with my brother Herodicus or some other physician to see one of his patients, who would not allow the physician to give him medicine, or apply a knife or hot iron to him; and I have persuaded him to do for me what he would not do for the physician just by the use of rhetoric . . ., and in a contest with a man of any other profession, the rhetorician more than anyone would have the power of getting himself chosen, for he can speak more persuasively to the multitude than any of them, and on any subject. Such is the nature and power of the art of rhetoric. And yet, Socrates, rhetoric should be used like any other com-

petitive art, not against everybody—the rhetorician ought not to abuse his strength any more than a pugilist or pancratiast or other athlete.

Socrates fails to be impressed by this eulogy and, returning to his original question, offers his own definition of rhetoric, beginning in his customary enigmatic manner: "It is a part of a not very creditable whole." Prodded by Gorgias to elaborate, he continues: "In my opinion, then, Gorgias, the whole of which rhetoric is a part is not an art at all but the habit of a bold and ready wit, which knows how to manage mankind; this habit I sum up under the word 'flattery'; and it appears to me to have many other parts, one of which is cookery, . . . another part is rhetoric, and the art of attiring and sophistry are two others." Because rhetoricians did not use a scientifically verifiable, rational approach (that is, an "art" or *techne*) and produced only belief, not knowledge, their skill was useless in the pursuit of the truth, Socrates contended, and Gorgias' offer to teach his students justice "if they do not know it" was futile.[1]

While Plato invests Gorgias with a certain respectability, depicting him as morally responsible and well-meaning though naively unaware of the limitations of his art, he shows less mercy toward another, more sinister type of sophist, who relies on rhetoric rather than on logic, or rather, on logical fallacies. He is characterized as "a dissembler, who in private and in short speeches compels the person who is conversing with him to contradict himself," "an imitator of the wise," and a "juggler of words."[2] This is the type represented by Euthydemus in the dialogue named after him. Giving a public exhibition of his skill in argumentation, Euthydemus poses the question "Are those who learn smart or ignorant?" His teenage victim answers ingenuously: "Those who learn are smart." This leads to a rapid-fire exchange:[3]

—When you were a learner, did you know the things you were learning?
—No.
—Were you smart then?
—No.
—And if you were not smart, you were ignorant?
—Yes . . .
—Then it is the ignorant who learn, and not the smart, as you suppose.

Just as the young man is ready to concede defeat, Dionysodorus, Euthydemus' brother and sidekick, steps in to "rescue" the victim and prove that he was right after all.

—But when the teacher lectured on a subject, was it the smart or
the ignorant who learned the subject of the lecture?
—The smart.
—Then it is the smart who learn and not the ignorant.

The sophists' mental gymnastics are greeted with applause by a group
of bystanders, but Socrates soon reveals the tricks of their trade—in this
case playing on the meaning of complex and ill-defined terms.

Unlike Gorgias, whom Socrates chided for using rhetoric in problem
solving, Euthydemus and his brother are criticized less for their
method—a variant on the Socratic method of inquiry—than for their
frivolity. "Such things are the sport of the sciences," Socrates comments.
Euthydemus' display of verbal skills "makes a wonderful show of accurate reasoning" but serves no philosophical purpose. Sophists of his kind
do not wish to instruct; they aim merely at a technical knockout of the
sparring partner.[4]

When the Platonic debate resurfaced in the Renaissance, the two-
faceted image of the sophist—voluble rhetorician/ quibbling trickster—
was retained. Thus the curious ambivalence of Marsilio Ficino, who
sometimes interprets "sophist" in terms suggesting a mercenary humanist, and at other times, a scholastic dialectician.[5] In his epitome of Plato's
Protagoras, for example, Ficino cautions against "imbibing the poison of
false opinions and wicked morals from sophists, of whom they think
highly because of their reputed wisdom and artful eloquence"—*fucata
eloquentia* is a catchword generally used by the enemies of the humanists
to disparage the study of rhetoric and contrast its artificial splendor with
the natural simplicity becoming to a Christian.[6] In his epitome of *Euthydemus,* however, Ficino speaks of the sophists as practitioners of a perverted dialectic much like that taught in his own day.[7] In his epitome of
the *Sophist* he points out, moreover, that Plato distinguished two kinds
of sophists: the pseudo-dialectician and the blustering rhetorician, "the
sophist who strenuously contradicts his partner in every point and holds
forth everywhere, seeming to know everything . . . whereas he possesses
an opinion rather than knowledge," and his counterpart, "the magician
and imitator who fashions deceptive word-images of everything that is
true, thus deceiving the ears of the inexperienced listener." He hastens
to assure his readers, however, that Plato, "by far the most eloquent
writer," does not condemn "legitimate eloquence."[8]

A similar ambivalence prevails in the works of Erasmus. In his handbook, *Foundations of the Abundant Style,* he speaks respectfully of the
sophists as the founders of abundant style *(copia):* "Now in case anyone

should feel inclined to despise [*copia*] as some newfangled discovery recently brought into the world within the four walls of my own study, I
would have him know . . . that a number of famous sophists blazed a
trail, showing how to compress and abridge what was being said, which
cannot be done without at the same time demonstrating how to expand
it."[9] Elsewhere, however, Erasmus contrasts the "rash garrulity" of the
sophist with the sober speech of Socrates, "the speech of a studious and
penetrating mind."[10] Transferring the Platonic image of the sophist to
the debate of his own time, he generally uses it to condemn scholastic
wrangles. Thus he declares in the *Ratio* that "it is better to be less of a
sophist and wiser in the ways of the Gospel and the Epistles." In the
same treatise he disparages "dialectic, or rather sophistry, as it is taught
nowadays."[11]

Erasmus' contemporary, Eobanus Hessus, likewise speaks of two types
of sophists, the orator and the pseudo-logician. On the one hand, there
are the ancient sophists "who excelled in declamation" and "whose presence might perhaps be desirable"; on the other, there are the modern
sophists, "our dialecticians and theologians."[12]

Given the iridescent quality of the sophist in Plato's dialogues, which
carried over into Renaissance usage, it is not surprising to find "sophist"
applied as a term of mutual reproach in the humanist-scholastic debate.
Humanists foisted the pseudo-logician image on the scholastics, condemning what they saw as the quibbles and tricks of a dialectician; scholastics applied to the humanists the image of the orator who impresses
with words rather than substance. Thus Petrarch speaks indignantly of
theologians transformed into dialecticians, "and sophists at that"; Bruni
describes the dialectical method as "confounded by British sophism,"
and Vives condemns the scholastic theologians at Paris for teaching a
"sophistic discipline," a logic "stuffed with the vain devices of sophistry."[13] Similarly, Agrippa of Nettesheim inveighs against "the modern
school of sophists" who blather about "formalities, hecceities, instances,
restrictions . . . and the rest of those intolerable and vain words that are
taught in the *Parva logicalia*."[14] The connection between scholasticism
and sophism is frequently made by German pamphleteers of the sixteenth century. We find references linking the study of Aristotle with
"Sophisterei" and "Sophisten," and scholastic doctors described as
"learned sophists . . . the offspring of the Great Whore called the School
of Paris."[15]

Scholastics in turn applied the designation "sophist" to the humanists.
Pierre Cousturier used the term to indicate that they were pretenders to
knowledge, "sophists and philosophasters."[16] Jacques Masson's discus-

sion of the term "sophist" in his dialogue *De tribus linguis* affords another
example of the Platonic concept being adapted to the debate by a defender of scholasticism. His distinction between the true theologian and
his imitators—biblical humanists and quibbling dialecticians—corre-
sponds to Plato's true Socratic philosopher and his imitators—rhetoricians and eristic sophists. In Masson's dialogue Ioannes, the true theologian, disputes with Petrus, the humanist. Refuting Petrus' argument that
theologians need Greek to read the sources of Christian doctrine in the
original, Ioannes engages him in a "Socratic" dialogue, thus establishing
his persona:

> *IO:* Let us assume, then, that a knowledge of languages is necessary.
> But let us see whether it is necessary for everyone.
>
> *PE:* Yes, it is.
>
> *IO:* Bread, shoes, clothing—are they needed by everyone or not?
>
> *PE:* By everyone, of course.
>
> *IO:* Will all therefore become bakers, shoemakers, and tailors?
>
> *PE:* Don't be ridiculous. These are servile tasks. They are done by
> servants and tradesmen. Language skills belong to the field of
> liberal studies and are appropriate to free citizens and noble
> minds. They are not only necessary but also respectable skills.
>
> *IO:* Mathematics, metaphysics, and music are in this category, are
> they not?
>
> *PE:* Yes.
>
> *IO:* Why, then, do we not exhort everyone to become musicians,
> following Socrates' example, who learned to play the flute when
> he was already an old man?

Petrus is obliged to concede that a knowledge of languages is not needed
by everyone and shifts his position to new premises:

> *PE:* Language skills are necessary for professional teachers at any
> rate, for every teacher must know the language in which his sub-
> ject is being taught or which is spoken by the founding father of
> the subject . . .
>
> *IO:* Do you accept the report that some hundred years ago a Ger-
> man invented the cannon, unknown to our ancestors?
>
> *PE:* All right.
>
> *IO:* If an Arab, a Greek, an Italian, or a Spaniard wanted to learn
> this noble art, will he first of all take care to learn German so that
> he may know the inventor's language?
>
> *PE:* It would be more efficient to hire an interpreter who speaks the
> language, as do the merchants.

IO: I think you have seen Ioannes the royal musician and Iosquin de Près.

PE: Many times. Their hymns are sung everywhere in all the churches.

IO: Do they know Greek [the language of the mythological founder of music]?

PE: You are joking. They barely know Latin.

IO: Then you see that one can know the art without knowing its founders or their language. And a subject matter first treated in Greek or Hebrew [that is, Christian doctrine] is not lost on someone who does not know Greek or Hebrew, as you just claimed with more rhetorical flair than truth.

Having established the parallel between himself, the genuine theologian, and Socrates, the genuine philosopher, by this role-playing exercise, Ioannes proceeds to set himself apart from the "sophists," that is, the imitators. There are two classes of sophists, he explains:

those who think they are profound theologians if they synthesize and analyze useless quibbles and frivolous matters, whereas they are a thousand miles away from being true theologians. They speak instantly of instances, infinitely of the infinite, they think up monstrous cases and, despising God and man, dive into their inventions, dream of nothing but fables, think little of poets, orators, theologians of old and (I shudder to say it) even canonical Scripture itself . . .; secondly, there are others, not much better than these, who perceive that the first kind are mad, but think they themselves are sane. They see no wisdom among the first and suppose it must be wholly among themselves (for wisdom must be somewhere!). They are the ones who equate theology with rhetoric, and say that without rhetoric theology is uncultured, frigid, weak, lowly, and quite unworthy of human beings. They say that rhetoric or poetry has given us the princes of the old theology . . . and never cease to demand from the theologian a knowledge of grammar, languages, and rhetoric.[17]

Masson's concept of the two types of sophists and the usage of other polemicists is clearly indebted to Plato's characterization of the Athenian sophists. Another classical source that has left its imprint on the humanist-scholastic debate is Lucian, a second-century Greek satirist who enjoyed enormous popularity in the Renaissance.[18] Manuscripts of his work were brought into Italy in the early fifteenth century and translated by prominent humanists like Guarino and Poggio. Northern humanists manifested a similar interest in the Greek author. Latin versions of Lucianic dialogues were published by Agricola, Reuchlin, Erasmus, More, Mosellanus, and Melanchthon, among others. Of particular significance in our context are the express parallels drawn by some translators between Lucian's satirical remarks on the philosophers and their own criticism of the scholastics.

The prefaces of Lucian's humanist editors and translators indicate that the publications served a programmatic purpose. Readers were expected to look beyond the historical setting and apply Lucian's words to their own time. It was no coincidence that Willibald Pirckheimer published Lucian's *Fisherman* together with his own defense of Reuchlin; he wished thereby to draw attention to the parallels between the pseudo-philosophers lampooned by the Greek satirist and the pseudo-theologians of Cologne described by himself.[19] Similarly, Erasmus used the opportunity of publishing a translation of Lucian's *Banquet* to criticize contemporary conditions. He declared in the preface: "We see the schools of philosophers and theologians squabbling among themselves like children, and waging internecine war no less [than Lucian's characters]; in fact those who profess religion fight as bloody battles among themselves as ever Lucian reported from that banquet, whether it were truth or fiction."[20] When Vincentius Obsopoeus published a translation of *Hermotimus* (Haguenau, 1527), he too noted the parallels between the Lucianic philosophers and the scholastic theologians of his own time, but while the Greeks had been the decadent disciples of great philosophers like Plato and Aristotle, he said, the contemporary scholastics were the wretched disciples of fools like "Ockham, Scotus, Thomas, and among the more recent arrivals, men like Eck."[21] In the same vein Heldelinus, a student of Melanchthon and editor of Lucian's *Jupiter tragoedus* (Basel, 1532), observed in his preface: "Sometimes these dialogues depict manners and people not at all unlike those of our own time." In Mycillus' edition of Lucian's *Opera omnia* (1538) we read that the manners and actions of his contemporaries were "quite similar to those described by Lucian when he ridicules the vain pretensions to virtue and knowledge among the philosophers of his own time."[22]

While the translators of Lucian invited readers to discover the relevance of the ancient text for themselves, other humanists demonstrated it by adapting Lucianic motifs to the social and political situation of their own time. The sketches Lucian wrote were easily adapted to suit the humanistic cause. In his *Runaways*, for example, Philosophy complains of unwanted hangers-on, the "sophist tribe" with their "useless and superfluous wisdom, in their own opinion invincible—those clever, baffling, absurd replies and perplexing, maze-like queries." In the *Dialogues of the Dead*, Menippus invites Hermes to unmask a philosopher, "or rather an impostor" full of "ignorance, contentiousness, vanity, unanswerable puzzles, thorny argumentations, and complicated conceptions." In the *Icaromenippus*, Menippus relates his encounter with the philosophers: "But my dear man, what if I should tell you all they said about Ideas and incorporeal entities, or their theories about the finite and the infinite? On the latter point also they had a childish dispute, some of them setting a limit to the universe and others considering it to be unlimited."[23]

Humanistic adaptations make use of similar characters and situations. In the *Intercoenales* of Leon Battista Alberti, for example, we find the image of the contentious, quibbling philosopher presented in a Lucianic manner. Giovanni Pontano recreated the Lucianic *Dialogues of the Dead* in his *Charon*. In an obvious reference to the contemporary debate, the god Mercury tells the ferryman of the underworld how a philosopher was worsted by an orator. While the latter represents the humanist position, the former is a thinly disguised scholastic dialectician. He is depicted as an obscurantist, ignorant of belles lettres, an Aristotelian who mangles the text of the Greek philosopher, treating him "like a shoemaker, pulling a thread through his teeth." He is a clever fellow, so that "willy nilly you must agree" with him, but he is practicing a corrupt form of dialectic introduced "first by the Germans and then adopted by the French."[24] Poggio Bracciolini actually invoked Lucian in *Contro l'ipocrisia*, a diatribe against the mendicant orders: "If Lucian were alive, he would place [the mendicants] among his philosophers."[25] A connection between Lucian and Erasmus was made by readers of his *Colloquies*. In his invectives against the Church, Erasmus appeared "to want to rival Lucian," Juan Sepúlveda wrote. Similarly, Erasmus Alberus declared that his namesake was "a regular Lucian and scoffer at religion," and Petrus Canisius observed that the Erasmians were "impious fellows sharing a joke with their Lucian" at the expense of the clergy.[26] One Erasmian, Eobanus Hessus, imitated Lucian's *Runaways* in a dialogue of the same title, in which he applies the Greek satirist's criticism of the Cynics to preachers hostile to the humanities.[27] Cristóbal de Villalón also wrote his *Castanets (Crotalon)* in the style of Lucianic dialogues, transferring what Lucian says about the philosophical schools of antiquity to the scholastic schools of nominalists and realists.[28]

Juan Luis Vives imitated Lucian in the *Dream*, published as a comical sideshow to Cicero's *Dream of Scipio* (Basel, 1521).[29] This little *jeu d'esprit* takes us to the court of Sleep, whose deliberations are interrupted by "certain Parisian sophists" (35). Most annoyed by their noisy quarreling, Sleep has them ejected. Their language, he says, "is not human, and certainly not divine, but mere uproar and disruption of all peace . . . As the god sank back he mumbled something—I am not sure whether it was *eis korakas*, 'off to the crows,' or *eis kolakas*, 'off to the boot-lickers' in Greek, or *in cloacas*, 'down the drain' in Latin" (35–37). The sophists depart together with certain dreams that have befriended them, but they are unsure where to go next. "There was nothing of which they were more ignorant than the world in which they lived . . . they had all heavenly items at their fingertips. But as they could not tell how many miles Saint Denis was from Paris or how to get to Notre Dame from the Petit Pont, they prayed and besought the dreams to act as their guides" (37). As a result of associating so closely with the dreams the sophists begin to resemble them. The younger generation, especially, "reshaped and reformed themselves entirely from head to foot, within and without" (41). Finally they become indistinguishable from dreams and consequently are able to deceive Sleep's guards and slip back into his palace.

It may well be that the use to which Lucian was put by Renaissance humanists contributed to his reputation as a corruptor of youth and an "atheist"—a reproach which, as Christopher Robinson claims in his comprehensive study of the reception of Lucian, was first voiced in the Renaissance by traditionalists and stood in stark contrast to the praise accorded to the author in antiquity.[30]

Well-read humanists found in the classics a rich supply of images with which to taunt the scholastics. By the middle of the sixteenth century, they had become commonplaces of humanistic literature. Marius Nizolius provided a kind of master list of classical *loci* in his *De veris principiis* of 1551:

> It appears that our generation is not the first to condemn dialectic; it has been condemned since ancient times . . . To review briefly what dialectic (so revered by the common herd and the ignorant) is like, I shall list here a few Greek and Latin testimonies and verdicts on dialectic. Among the Greeks, Zeno, the well-known leader of the Stoics, says that the skills of the dialecticians are like weights that weigh neither wheat nor some other valuable commodity, but only straw and dung. Ariston of Chios says that dialectic is like mud on the road, useless and tripping up the traveler. The same author also compares the speech of the dialecticians to spiderwebs: fine but useless. Indeed, he likewise asserts that to engage deeply in the study of dialectic is like eating crabs; it is necessary to go through

many shells because there is so little meat in them. Nor is there any shortage of Greeks who compare dialectic partly to the moon, because it never ceases to wax and wane, partly to a polyp that devours its own carefully nursed arms (for dialecticians, as they improve, refute their own arguments), partly to gamblers at dice, for like them, the dialecticians cheat each other with relish. As for the Latins, I shall say nothing of Cicero, who at one point calls dialectic inane elegance, at another a thorny type of speech or thorny speeches, and uses other uncomplimentary epithets. The author who wrote the *Rhetorica ad Herennium,* whether he was Cicero or Cornificius or someone else, speaks candidly of dialectic and the dialecticians in the second book, saying that their precepts are of no help to the orator whatsoever, indeed they are an impediment . . . Seneca condemns and rejects dialectic and dialecticians passim . . . calling them foolish for wanting to waste their whole life on stuff and nonsense, acting as if they were serious matters.[31]

Nizolius' extensive list of commonplaces shows that humanists were well aware of the classical antecedents of the debate. The polemicists could also turn to Christian sources for inspiration, however. The Pauline letters in particular provided fertile ground. The first Epistle to Timothy is full of warnings against "vain talk" (1.6), "profane and vain babbling" (6.20), "doting about questions and battles of words whereof come envy, strife, railings, evil surmisings, perverse disputings" (6.4–5). The Pauline rebukes were frequently adapted by humanists and applied to the scholastic dialecticians. Erasmus' *Annotations* on Timothy are an example of this process:

> [Paul speaks of] "vain talk," *mataiologia* in Greek, which is, as far as the pronunciation is concerned, not far from *theologia,* although the two things are very different. Therefore we must take care not to practice theology in such a manner that we fall into *mataiologia,* fighting endlessly about frivolous nonsense . . . What shall I say about the superfluous (not to say, impious) questions we pose about the power of God and about the power of the Roman Pontiff?

Here Erasmus proceeds to list some fifty questions that can be traced to scholastic handbooks, concluding: "and on this kind of theology, which is anything but simple, they waste their whole life, while professing apostolic simplicity . . . what has the profession of an apostolic life to do with pagan philosophy and vain curiosity? They solemnly consecrate their lips to the Gospel, and they splutter nothing but Averroes and Aristotle!" In the same work Erasmus comments on Paul's warning to those "doting about questions and battles of words": "[Doting] means laboring under a mental illness, a word that applies remarkably well to those sophistical theologians who disdain what they should learn and waste their whole wretched life on the most foolish labyrinths of subtleties and nonsense."[32] Similarly, Lefèvre d'Etaples comments on Paul's warning against "battles of words" and "vain questions": "I wish that our time did not spawn such men and the present age were free of such monsters."[33]

The scholastic theologians, in turn, took comfort in the hierarchy established by Paul in I Corinthians, which places the gift of prophecy above the gift of tongues: "Those who speak in tongues may build themselves up, but those who prophesy build up the community ... those who prophesy are of greater importance than those who speak in tongues" (1 Cor 14:4–5). Jacques Masson seized on these passages in his polemic against Petrus Mosellanus, who had just inaugurated Greek lectures in Augsburg: "The gift of languages should be appreciated, but exegesis is more valuable, and prophecy excels both ... this appears to be the meaning of Paul when he castigates the Corinthians for their excessive inclination toward the gift of tongues."[34]

Both humanists and scholastics took refuge in the writings of the Fathers to defend their respective positions. Jerome's dream of being flogged for his inordinate love of Cicero was often quoted by the scholastics; his famous dictum "it is one thing to be a prophet, another to be a translator" was quoted with equal frequency by the humanists in defense of their biblical studies. St. Augustine's balanced comments on the subject of language studies in *De doctrina Christiana* was mined by both parties for suitable snippets supporting their own point of view.[35] Passages in the Fathers rejecting human learning and contrasting it with the wisdom of the pious were also used by both parties in the debate—by the humanists to rebuke the subtle reasoning of scholastics; by the scholastics to condemn the application of philological, that is, human skills to the revealed text. On the whole, however, patristic writings provided more ammunition to the humanists than to their adversaries. It is not surprising, therefore, that Otto Brunfels conceived the idea of publishing, in 1520, a list of patristic commonplaces in support of the humanistic argument. "They will provide you with a starting point," he wrote in the dedicatory letter to Capito, "and give you the courage to inveigh against the sophists more bitterly." Entitled *Refutation of Sophistry and Vain Questions*,[36] the book offered a selection of passages from the Greek and Latin Fathers. Just how closely Brunfels associated the patristic position with that of the biblical humanists of his own day can be seen from his going, without transition, from the works of the Fathers to Lefèvre d'Etaples' writings. "I pass over Erasmus," he continues, "because there is no place in his work where he does not inculcate this [i.e. the anti-scholastic position]." For further material he refers readers to classical writers, Plato and Lucian predictably among them.[37]

Surprisingly, Brunfels does not mention the "first humanist" and father of the debate in the Renaissance, Petrarch, who composed the first polemic to focus exclusively on the topic.[38] His tract, *On His Own Ignorance*,[39] reflects the historical roots of the debate in the characterization of the scholastic method as mental gymnastics rather than a genuine search for the truth; the view that dialectic has no moral application and therefore must not become a lifetime pursuit; the description of the dialectician as contentious, quibbling sophists; and the rejection of the notion that subtle speculation could further an understanding of the Word of God. An element in Petrarch's critique which had no antecedents in classical or biblical sources, but came to dominate the debate in the Renaissance, was anti-Aristotelianism. Aristotle's doctrine, the mainstay of medieval scholasticism, formed the core of the curriculum taught at the universities of Paris and Oxford. Although his authority was impugned from time to time, and aspects of his doctrine, especially in metaphysics and natural philosophy, were subject to prohibitions and censorship, Aristotelian logic prevailed. Neither the mystics of the fourteenth century, who urged a turning away from arid dialectics to the spiritual fervor of the Fathers, nor the humanists who waged a prolonged campaign against the dialecticians in the fifteenth and sixteenth centuries, were able to oust Aristotelian logic completely from European universities.

A second feature of Petrarch's critique that is typical of the Renaissance debate is his hostility to the use of dialectic in theology. He castigates jurists, physicians, and philosophers for using the scholastic method, but it was the application of dialectic to *res divinae* that caused him the greatest concern. In this respect he foreshadows the course of the humanist-scholastic debate, which eventually came to focus on method in theology. In a letter to Francesco Nelli, prior of S. Apostoli in Florence, he laments the adverse effects of the scholastic method recently imported from Paris and Oxford: "You see how far things have gone: those who profess a knowledge of divine things have been transformed from theologians into dialecticians, not to say sophists." He reiterated this concern in a letter to his brother Gherardo: "Our vanity has corrupted learning and turned theology into dialectics." His remarks are even more pointed in the *Epistolae seniles*: "I do not know whence comes this new race of theologians who do not spare even the doctors of the Church and soon will turn on the apostles ... [and the Fathers]. Augustine, they say, saw much and knew little . . . One of those practicing the modern method of philosophizing said: keep your insignificant little doctors of the Church. I have my own model . . .—if only you could bring yourself to read Averroes you could see for yourself how far he surpasses your foolish babblers."[40]

We find Platonic and Pauline elements in Petrarch's criticism of the dialectical method. Like Paul, who rejects contentiousness, Petrarch objects to the dialectical method as being by nature adversarial. The dialectician is always sparring for a fight. "He would rather fight than win . . . he takes the greatest pleasure in arguing; he is not looking for the truth but for a fight." Dialectical disputations tended to deteriorate into squabbles and cavils,[41] with the participants behaving like "cawing crows."[42] The dialectical method not only promoted an unchristian righteousness, it had no intrinsic value. It was a "windy" science, nothing but empty "chatter" and "noise," lacking the gravity and serious purpose that was the mark of a bona fide philosophical discussion. The "vain and petty questions" of the dialecticians made no contribution to knowledge and had no moral application.

Taking up what was to become a standard defense of scholasticism, Petrarch acknowledged that dialectical disputation "stimulates the intellect, points the way to the truth, shows how to avoid fallacies, and, last but not least, makes for an acute and ready mind," but he denied that such mental exercises deserved long-term or exclusive attention. "While it is to some purpose to deal with dialectic in passing, it is not equally laudable to stay with it; indeed, it would be folly for a traveler to forget his final destination because the route is pretty."[43]

Petrarch measured the usefulness of a discipline by its moral impact. The study of dialectic was not edifying, he contended. It was a science that dealt with "words" rather than "things," that is, it had no connection with life. The victories to be won in a scholastic disputation were therefore shallow and demonstrated verbal dexterity rather than moral insight. Its excellence was intellectual rather than ethical, and therefore deficient. Exhorting an acquaintance to study philosophy, Petrarch specified that he should apply himself not to "that wordy, windy scholastic philosophy in which scholars take ridiculous pride, but that true philosophy . . . which lies in things rather than words."[44] To his brother he wrote in a similar vein. True philosophy was not taught in the highways and byways—"the supreme good is not trite." The petty questions of the scholastics were better left alone: "Ignorance of such things generally carries no risk, and ignorance is perhaps safer than knowledge," for in scholastic disputations "good morals are neglected, the very thing in which that noble philosophy which cannot deceive consists, is despised, and all effort is concentrated on empty words."[45]

Although Petrarch quotes Cicero in support of the view that philosophy should "heal the spirit, take away vain solicitude, and issue in freedom from desire as well as fear,"[46] the Christian dimension of his approach to learning is understood and expressed in other contexts. Moral improvement had been the principal aim of Petrarch's own studies and, echoing Augustine's style in the *Confessions*, he devoutly prayed for success in this quest: "But Thou, my God, Lord of learning, beside whom there is no other, whom I must and will prefer to Aristotle and all philosophers, to the poets and all those who proudly speak such exceeding words, to all writings, all doctrines, and all else . . . for I do not wish merely for a good name, which Solomon prefers to precious ointments, but for the thing itself: I want to be good, that I may love Thee and deserve to be loved by Thee in turn . . . for one of the feeble ones who believes in Thee is more blessed than Plato, than Aristotle, than Varro, than Cicero, who in all their knowledge did not know Thee . . . and whose learned ignorance has been made manifest."[47]

There is a strong mystical element in Petrarch's criticism of dialectic and his emphasis on the moral dimension of philosophy. He drew his inspiration from the Bible, which declares that "piety is wisdom,"[48] and from Gregory, Hugh of St. Victor, and Bernard of Clairvaux, who developed this theme in their writings.[49] The wisdom recommended in Scripture was not an intellectual virtue. One must "not so much know but love the virtues." This love, however, comes from God: "I know well that this cannot come about without Christ's teaching and help; no one can become wise or virtuous or good unless he has taken a deep draught, not from that fabulous spring of Pegasus in the folds of Parnassus, but from that true and unique source which has its origin in heaven and wells up in eternal life. He who has drunk from this source thirsts no more."[50]

The emphasis on the moral dimension of learning which was to make the individual "good rather than knowledgeable," also informed Petrarch's objection to Aristotle, whom he criticized for paying only lip-service to ethical concerns.[51] Aristotle's emphasis had clearly been on logic, he said, and his doctrine was aimed at training the intellect; the truly "useful" teacher, however, made his listeners and readers good men. Petrarch furthermore objected to Aristotle as a pagan philosopher. Speaking as a devout Christian, he contrasted the pseudo-wisdom of his secular philosophy with the wisdom of the apostles and Fathers. The scholastics, he said, had made Aristotle their "god," even though an inept translator had disfigured his works[52] and made them all but incomprehensible. His very name inspired awe in his scholastic followers: "These five syllables, A-RIS-TO-TE-LES, delight many ignorant people."[53] Yet Aristotle was human after all and liable to error, unlike that divine source of inspiration, Christ.[54]

In support of his value judgment Petrarch appealed to Jerome and Augustine, who "did not care what Aristotle said, but what Christ said." Anyone who reversed these priorities and preferred pagan to Christian philosophy was "blind" and would "tumble into the pit of error."[55] Petrarch's own attitude toward Cicero was governed by this principle. He admired Cicero as a stylist and accepted him as a guide to civic virtue, but his pronouncements on divinity were "more inane than fables."[56] Thus Petrarch had no ambition to be called an "Aristotelian" and was prepared to relinquish even the title of "Ciceronian" for the appellation of Christian: "By all means let them be philosophers and Aristotelians, although I doubt that they are either, . . . I do not envy them their noble titles in which they take vain pride, as long as they do not envy me that humble but true title of Christian and Catholic."[57]

Putting his admiration for Cicero in perspective, he likened his own appropriation and adaptation of Ciceronian principles to the biblical "spoiling of the Egyptians"—the metaphor used by Augustine.[58] The process of adaptation must not, however, be carried too far. To find in pagan authors doctrines consonant with Christian morality was not difficult, but it did not follow that they could be put on an equal footing with Christian writers. In considering a writer's moral value, one must not pass judgment on the strength of individual phrases or isolated pronouncements but look for a consistent and methodical approach.[59] No doubt pagan philosophers had written much that was valid and had expressed their views eloquently, but "like poison mixed with honey, they introduced some false, dangerous, and absurd ideas."[60] It was futile therefore to think that pagan philosophy could be completely adapted to the Christian mode of thinking, and ridiculous to speak of Aristotle as a "born-again Christian," as some of his acolytes did.[61]

Rejecting the wisdom of pagan philosophers in favor of a Christian philosophy, Petrarch again waxes mystical. He contrasts the uncertain teachings of pagan philosophers with the infallible teachings of Christ: " I am being savagely attacked . . . because I do not adore Aristotle, but there is another one whom I adore, who promises me not vain and frivolous conjectures about treacherous things which are good for nothing and have no solid foundation, but a knowledge of Himself."[62] Countering claims that Aristotle was a superb source of wisdom, Petrarch firmly stated his own views: God is the sole source of wisdom and virtue.

Philosophy cannot make a person wise, only "divine revelation makes knowledge possible, and to know how to be saved is knowledge enough." The Aristotelians were wrong in their quest "to know rather than love God."[63]

Petrarch's criticism of the dialecticians may be regarded as a prototype humanist argument. While it would be simplistic to say that the humanist-scholastic controversy in the Renaissance began with him, a beginning of sorts was made in the sense that Petrarch was, as he himself put it, "standing on the border between two peoples, looking at once backward and forward."[64] Applying to himself an image that patristic exegetes had used to characterize John the Baptist's position, on the border between the Old and New Testaments, Petrarch portrayed his task as facilitating the transfer of traditional thought or building a bridge between past and present scholarship. For this he seemed to have a unique gift. As Charles Trinkaus put it, Petrarch was able "to discover the cultural and literary modes present within the inherited resources" and apply them to his own time.[65] His criticism accordingly reflects a long literary past—classical, biblical, and patristic; at the same time, however, he clearly stood on the threshold of a new controversy over approaches to learning and was a principal figure in the discussion generated in his own time by the importation of scholasticism into Italy in the face of a concurrent revival of classical learning. Although he was not the original source of the *topoi* that came to dominate the humanist-scholastic debate, he served as a conduit and may have provided the impetus for a sympathetic rereading of the sources on which he himself drew. Many of the complaints he advanced against scholasticism became commonplaces in the fifteenth and sixteenth centuries, but as a prototype his polemic lacks certain features that became inseparable from the humanist argument in its later stages, while it displays others that were untypical. It lacks, for example, any reference to the role of philology in the understanding of the Word of God, an argument that was developed only in the fifteenth century. Indeed, his alternative to dialectic is not philology or rhetoric but a form of mysticism. Nor were Petrarch's professional qualifications or orthodoxy—issues that came to the foreground in later controversies—at the center of the debate.[66]

While Petrarch may be considered the first representative of the humanist position in the Renaissance debate, his younger contemporary Jean Gerson (1363–1429), chancellor of the University of Paris and one of the foremost churchmen of his time, introduces us to some of the key arguments later advanced by the scholastics. In his writings he touched on a number of questions pertinent to the debate, but his position is more equivocal than Petrarch's.[67]

Discussing the relationship between theology and secular learning, and in particular rhetoric, Gerson placed theology at the head of the academic disciplines *(sit omnium scientiarum signum)*[68] and advanced the traditional "handmaid" theory. Queen Theology takes other disciplines "into her service as obedient attendants to wisdom" (9.641) and demands absolute subordination: "Let them yield to Theology and refrain from entering into her schools with importunate questions, for it is proper for servants to come into the presence of the queen prepared and equipped" (3.240). In this context, Gerson criticized theologians who for no cogent reason introduced disciplines foreign to their subject proper. Referring to the familiar simile of the captive woman, he explains that the "paring of nails and shaving of hair . . . signified the removal of superfluous doctrine" (3.240). Sacred must take precedence over secular learning; pagan philosophy can never form the basis of Christian theology but is merely an adjunct.[69] Setting out the relationship between the two spheres of knowledge, Gerson writes:

> Theologians are open to criticism when they put the study of grammarians, secular historians, poets, ancient orators, and mathematicians first and persist in those studies rather than in theological subjects, turning an accessory into a primary matter. If, however, a theologian studies them for pleasure or uses them only in passing, for his own recreation or that of others, it is a praiseworthy pursuit, for it refreshes a mind fatigued by theological studies and adds erudition and elegance. (3. 248)

Insistence on the supremacy of theology—a hierarchy which was occasionally challenged by humanists claiming that poets were the "first theologians"—became an integral part of the scholastic argument. In the later stages of the debate, the question of ranking was often linked to the question of professional credentials and competency and to the notion that biblical humanists were trespassing on a subject loftier than they could encompass.

Another area in which Gerson spoke clearly as a representative of the scholastic camp is the subject of technical terminology. Gerson's position on the question of language can be found in his *De modis significandi*, where he makes a distinction between theological language proper, to be used in doctrinal definitions and disputations at the universities, and classical usage. "A theologian who adheres to the usage of pagan philosophers rather than to that of the holy doctors deserves blame, even if his views are correct" was Gerson's guiding principle (9.630). He further-more distinguished between the technical language and rigorous logic of the professional theologian and the freer, rhetorical usage of the preacher or teacher of the lay community (9.629–630). The preacher was permitted to use rhetoric, indeed he must "descend and be melted by the flame of emotion" (9.641).

There are, Gerson says, following medieval textbooks, two types of "logic" (that is, "science of words"): one to serve speculative theology, and another to serve moral philosophy. The first uses terms in their strictest sense, *strictissima praecisione*, and avoids metaphor or any other embellishments, "so that it may correspond as much as possible to the truth"; the other uses figures and tropes to generate emotion. "It is nec-essary in ethics to generate and rally good emotions and to calm, repress, or eliminate emotions that are evil" (3.58). Failure to respect this distinc-tion courts disaster. "Whoever wants to mix up the two logics and de-mands rhetoric in speculative [theology] or the first type in ethics, will fall utterly into the most absurd and foolish errors" (3.59). One must adapt one's speech to the audience and the purpose at hand. To address a nonprofessional audience expecting an edifying sermon in the terms of pure logic or metaphysic will cause only consternation. It was on account of their disregard for propriety in speech that "theologians nowadays are called sophists and wordspinners, if not madmen (phantastici); they abandon what is useful and intelligible to the audience they address, and launch into pure logic or metaphysic . . . so that they move the listeners to laughter and derision rather than building up in them the true faith" (3.62). Conversely, it is not right to introduce rhetorical terms or new vocabulary into the language of speculative theology. "To take pleasure in devising new terms in matters concerning speculative theology, espe-cially those touching on the mystery of the divine nature, is pernicious and vain curiosity, and must be eradicated . . . and if we find an accepted doctor using terms that are not in general use at the university, we must not introduce them without prefixing an appropriate explanation, such as 'This term is used by so and so in such and such a sense'" (3.244).

Because of his concern for appropriate language, Gerson also ex-pressed reservations about new (and especially vernacular) translations of biblical texts. His stand, based on the traditional tenet that the sense of the Scriptures "is determined by the Church which is inspired and governed by the Holy Spirit and not subject to the judgment or interpre-tation of some individual" (3.335), accords with the position of later polemicists, who insisted that the humanists' philological researches were interfering with the teaching authority of the Church. Gerson's concern for a professional, authorized interpretation of the Bible also extended to the role of the preacher. "It would be better if there were only a select few preaching the Word of God to the people, so long as they did not mangle it by preaching in some faulty manner; for if this most difficult, arduous, and sacred task is committed without distinction to people who are ignorant, undignified, and without order in their life or mind, would it be surprising if they caused scandal among the audience and congregation rather than build up the faith?" (8.249).

Gerson's remarks on theological language and the strictures he places on the exegete are echoed in the writings of later polemicists. What constitutes appropriate language in matters pertaining to religion and theology was a question that became central to the controversy and was vigorously debated in the context of sixteenth-century revisions and translations of the Vulgate.

Although Gerson strongly endorsed the scholastic method, he had harsh words for the style of his colleagues. His own language, free of the barbarisms and solecisms usually associated with the Paris theologians, makes him an exception among the scholastic doctors.

In his account of the Monzon affair, a doctrinal controversy involving a Spanish Dominican on the faculty of theology, Gerson provides a thumbnail sketch of the type of lecturer who gave scholasticism a bad name, revealing in his description a fine satirical vein:

Possessed by some spirit he "pours forth sound without sense" (as Virgil says of the Sybil). So barbarous was his teaching, so confused and inane his speech, that you would hardly credit him with a human intellect . . . Our subtle theologian made the desired impression: with obscure and complex words, intelligible neither to himself nor to others, he filled the ears of the audience and won their admiration. Prick up your ears, students and scholars. Such deep and profound doctrine—unlike any you have ever heard before, I believe! Give this man his due applause—he is a messenger of divine counsel. No, rather hiss him off the stage, especially those of you who do not belong to the crowd that is pleased with the unusual and thinks anything imaginable to be plausible and takes obscurity for subtlety . . . It is out of ignorance that monstrous and chimerical fictions such as these arise; ignorance is the origin of that high-sounding but nonsensical stuff that is noised about. (10.13)

Elsewhere he describes the foolish pride and arrogance of the lecturer:

> There was a fairly large crowd of students. Our doctor did not let
> them wait long. He came with a retinue. He walked with as much
> dignity as his ardent spirit would allow. He stepped up to the po-
> dium (he should never have done so, carrying such "ballast" in his
> head; for what Terence says about flattery can also be applied to
> honor: it makes madmen out of fools) . . . [Gerson here relates the
> content of the lecture] I would have been surprised if our theologian
> at the lectern had not fitted in some boasts about himself. And so
> he did: he rose to his full height, pressed his chest against the lec-
> tern, turned to his audience, and taking a deep breath and emphati-
> cally raising his right arm, he said: "Note, you have heard it here"—
> as if nothing better or more meaningful could be said.   (10.15, 20)

In other tracts, too, especially in his curriculum reform proposal of
1401 addressed to Pierre d'Ailly, and in his *Contra curiositatem studentium*
of 1402, we encounter the type of criticism better suited to the humanist
than the scholastic argument. Gerson deplores the obscurity, inanity,
and uselessness of certain scholastic questions; the intellectual pride and
ambition of the dialecticians; their prolonged and exclusive devotion to
the study of logic. Some scholastics, says Gerson in his condemnation of
curiositas, admire as profound only what they cannot understand.[70] Their
confidence in their intellectual powers and their desire to win an argument rather than inquire honestly into a problem lead them astray:
"Here is contention, dispute, impudence, stubbornness in defense of er-
roneous positions, a preference for one's own views, a reluctance to give
up one's views or those of one's school; finally, a shocking contempt for
the simple-minded and total rejection of humble teaching. What can be
devised that is more inimical to penitence and faith than these?"[71] He
condemns the intellectual pride of those who "know nothing of substance," quoting Paul's warning against "vain questions" and "word
fights" (3.278). These are the studies in which some theologians con-
sume a lifetime, not realizing that "there is a time and a place and a stage
for them, beyond which acolytes are liable to the charge of stupidity,
arrogance, and vain curiosity" (3.239).

In his reform proposal Gerson calls for a more salutary theology. As
it is, the theologians are ridiculed by members of other faculties: "They
are said to know nothing about fundamental truth, moral values, or the
Bible" (2.27). In future, let the members of the faculty "avoid and turn
away from those vain, useless, and sterile teachings; let them neither approve of them nor argue against them in a captious and petty spirit, for

[he says with perhaps unwarranted optimism] God willing, theology is almost rid of those sophisms" (2.27).

Gerson's zeal for reform has its roots in his leanings toward mysticism. He contrasts the "boastful and presumptuous intellect," which foolishly believes that it can understand God and His work, with the humility of the true theologian who, when asked whether the world was eternal, answers: "This question is beyond my ken, because God has and always will do everything according to His will. Ask those about God's will whom He has deigned to enlighten about it" (3.232–233). Gerson repeatedly quotes the dictum: *vitium est velle plus quam oportet sapere et non ad sobriam pietatem*, "it is wrong to desire more knowledge than is our due and which goes beyond modest piety."[72] Theology was not only a matter of book-learning: *sine litteris litteratoria, ut ita dicam, theologia donata est.*[73]

Thus, although Gerson was no doubt a champion of scholasticism, his views are too complex to serve as a paradigm purely for the scholastic argument. He did promote ideas that were adopted by the scholastic protagonists in the debate, in particular the distinction between literary and technical language, the opposition to new translations, and the emphasis on the professional competence of the would-be translator and exegete. On the other hand, he propounded views that were in sympathy with the humanist position, rejecting obscurantism and contentious argumentation. It is not surprising, therefore, to find Gerson quoted on both sides of the debate. A case in point is Erasmus' politic use of his name. Censured by the faculty of theology at Paris for treating scholastic doctors with contempt, he gleefully quoted Gerson's criticism, concluding that the faculty had no reason to take issue with him when similar complaints had been voiced by Gerson, "a writer who enjoys such popularity and prestige with the Paris theologians."[74]

The difficulty of finding a prototype defense of scholasticism in the preliminary stage of the debate has to do with the fact that the scholastic method was too entrenched to need defense in principle, and the prestige of the University of Paris, the citadel of scholasticism, made the *magistri* impervious to attacks. The claim, embedded in its statutes, that it could not err in matters of faith and morals,[75] invested its doctors with a sense of unimpeachable authority. Thus, as Prantl noted in his history of logic, the champions of scholasticism were able "to shut their eyes [to the criticism] and lecture and write unperturbed by it."[76] For a long time it remained inconceivable that theologians should use any other method but dialectic. Indeed, scholasticism was seriously challenged for only a brief period in the early sixteenth century, when humanists and reformers combined forces. The second generation of reformers returned to scholasticism, however, or more precisely, modified the scholastic method for their own purposes. Thus Sebastian Franck called Lutherans "the new scholastics," and Sebastian Castellio accused Calvinists of reviving the "sophistries of the Sorbonne."[79] It has sometimes been asserted that the reason for the survival of scholasticism in the sixteenth century in spite of its generally recognized decline lay in the failure of the humanists to provide an intellectual alternative. It may, however, be more accurate to say that the Reformation scattered the humanist forces, turning their creative efforts into the separate channels of ecclesiastical and pedagogical reform. In both areas their efforts resulted in modification and restructuring rather than complete innovation; and we must not forget that reformation rather than revolution had been their professed aim.

CHAPTER THREE

The Debate as Epideictic Literature

EPIDEIXIS, THE DISPLAY of a writer's rhetorical and literary skills, is characteristic of the controversy in its first stage, though not confined to it. Fifteenth-century polemicists tended to write compositions rather than disquisitions. Wanting to delight as well as instruct their readers, they paid careful attention to language, setting, and characterization. Coluccio Salutati's erudite epistle in praise of classical learning, Leonardo Bruni's urbane *Dialogues*, and the learned exchange between Ermolao Barbaro and Giovanni Pico della Mirandola illustrate the first, more graceful, stage of the debate. As the controversy moved from literary circles to faculty meeting rooms, esthetic concerns drifted into the background. The atmosphere of cultured leisure that characterized the early debate survived in some of the later entries, such as Erasmus' *Antibarbarians*, and left echoes in occasional pieces like Locher's *Dialogue Concerning the Eminence of the Four Doctors of the Church*, Bebel's *Disputation with a Theologian in Orders*, and Mair's *Dialogue Concerning the Subject Matter to Be Treated by the Theologian*. On the whole, however, sixteenth-century protagonists presented themselves more often as aggressive polemicists than as gentlemen scholars. Their exchanges therefore tended to be either deadpan and devoid of artifice or satirical and abusive.

A detailed examination of works representative of the early debate will disclose two characteristics. First, the debate was as yet unfocused. The protagonists seemed at times unsure who the enemy was, striking out in several directions at once. Second—perhaps because the battle lines had not yet been firmly drawn—authors often argued on both sides of the question, though they left prominent clues as to their own preferences.

Before proceeding to illustrate these characteristics, it will be necessary briefly to describe the polemics in question.

The earliest entry, Petrarch's *On His Ignorance*, has already been discussed. His younger contemporary, Giovanni Boccaccio, wrote in defense of poetry and the liberal arts in the *Genealogy of the Gods*, an encyclopedic survey of classical mythology. In this work the scholastic dialecticians make cameo appearances in the company of other enemies of learning: pleasure-seekers, philistines, sanctimonious preachers, and traditionalists. Coluccio Salutati likewise came to the defense of classical learning. In 1405 he wrote a programmatic letter to Giovanni da Samminiato in which he defended poetry and, more generally, secular learning as appropriate to Christians and helpful in understanding Holy Writ.[1] He outlined his plan of defense: "First I shall show how we must understand the term poetry; next I shall make clear that Holy Writ and divine Scripture is related to poetry, . . . thirdly I shall attempt, as far as is pertinent, to show that faithful Christians should not be forbidden to read pagan poets (175:19–24)." Salutati begins by refuting the notion that poetry, being fiction, is deceptive. The Bible, too, makes use of the poetic style and in this guise teaches the truth. "It is the very truth, although told perhaps in complex, metaphorical terms" (199:28–29). It requires a certain effort "to penetrate to the inner core of the prophets' and poets' meaning . . . but shall we not find wonderful hidden truths?" (183:28–30). Secular poetry could be edifying as well. The poet, says Salutati, is a kind of moral philosopher: "He shows what our life should be, designates virtue by praise and vice by blame. For although poets write much that is shameful about men and gods, you will never find them praising these acts" (197:1–3).[2]

In the context of demonstrating the value of secular, pagan learning for the Christian, Salutati uses a number of commonplaces that recur throughout the humanist-scholastic debate on the subject: poetry may contain salacious passages, but so does Scripture—the reader must therefore be judicious; pagan learning, purified to meet Christian standards, may be employed to good effect—here Salutati uses Jerome's image of the captive woman (190:3); indeed, one ought to be familiar with pagan literature to combat pagan philosophy with its own weapons. Salutati also touches on the question of ranking within the disciplines; declaring poetry superior to philosophy: "You seem to think that philosophers are worthier than poets, but how you arrive at this conviction I do not see, since philosophy is necessary for the perfection of poetry. Conversely it is not the case that poetry perfects the philosopher. It follows that poetry is superior to philosophy" (201:20–24). Salutati's addressee, feeling unequal to the challenge of responding on these points, invited Giovanni Dominici, a scholarly Dominican at Santa Maria Novella, to present the counterargument. Dominici did so in a work entitled *Lucula Noctis (Firefly)*, in which he explored the questions raised by Salutati by means of the sic-et-non method.[3] In the course of arguing successively for and against secular learning, Dominici examines some of the commonplaces proffered by Salutati. In the first part of his *Firefly* he treats of the use of secular learning for the purpose of "piercing the enemy with his own sword,"[4] but in his counterargument he restricts this use to professionals: "[pagan authors] need not be read except by a few who are well grounded in the faith and whose task it is to combat infidels and heretics."[5] And he weakens even this concession by claiming that such skills had been more relevant in the past than in his own time: "Perhaps in former times it was necessary to know and be skilled in some sophisms . . . but the sanctity of a simple man was more efficacious in converting the wordy sophist and Arian philosopher than the true eloquence of all the Fathers assembled for this purpose at the Council" (367). Indeed, he concluded that secular learning, those "meretricious arts," as Boethius had termed them, never led anyone to adopt the Catholic faith or love God (368).

Dominici also tackles the notions that poetry is an acceptable genre because Scripture uses poetic language, and that pagan learning can be put to use by Christians on the model of the captive woman.[6] He counters with the Pauline dictum that knowledge puffs up, that truth needs no embellishment (120), and that poets in particular corrupt morals: "They relate crimes, especially carnal vices, devise or recite everything obscene that can arouse libidinous desire . . . and if they add some punishment for the crime related, they pass over it lightly." As a result, "we see the old bacchanals renewed, divine worship removed, piety extinguished, morals corrupted, men turned into beasts, and everything turned upside down" (333–335).

Dominici furthermore takes up the argument that secular learning, though not sufficient in itself, prepares the way toward an understanding of the Word of God, countering that the immoderate pursuit of secular learning has done enormous damage to the Christian religion. Its acolytes are Christians in name only:

> I know what they propose privately, what they say when no outsider is present to judge them. How many there are in whom the Christian religion is strong only in name and in external practice, in whose minds Christ does not dwell through faith, let alone grace!

For a man cannot cultivate friendship in Cicero's style, be moral with Seneca, live in the country with Epicurus, despise the world with Diogenes, reason with Aristotle, be a theologian with Plato, show constancy with Zeno, be undisturbed in adversity with Socrates, look forward to sweet death with Cato, and at the same time reach perfection with Christ. In such a confusion everything returns to the state of ancient chaos. (167)

Significant also is a passage in which Dominici divides "philosophy" (by which he means learning and the learned expression of thought) into "(1) fabulous and theatrical, (2) natural or speculative, reserved for speculative philosophers who debate in their schools, and (3) civil or popular philosophy, which is appropriately used by preachers and during Mass" (337). Dominici approves only of the third kind. He vigorously rejects the first, practiced by poets "who, stroking the ear with their Siren calls, attempt with all their might to destroy the foundations of faith." He has similarly unkind words for the second form, practiced at "those training grounds (or shall I say, brothels of the soul) in which Plato and the Platonists are prattling, as well as the Stoics, the Old and New Academicians, Porphyry, and Cicero writing about the state—none of which can make souls blessed" (343). As for the preachers' "philosophy," it must be informed by Scripture rather than secular learning. Dominici faults his contemporaries on that point: "Scripture is neglected, the holy doctors abandoned, while they give themselves wholeheartedly to those [secular] studies, and in their sermons they stroke the ears of their hearers with words from tragedy, comedy, ethics, physics, astrology, and metaphysics, as if the divine word did not suffice for salvation and those infidels were the underpinning of the Catholic faith" (224). A similar warning is issued to the devotees of rhetoric: "A familiarity with Holy Writ must take precedence over the art of speaking, for without such familiarity no one can be wise; no other philosophy provides a knowledge of the divine, the sole means of becoming wise" (311). Exegetes are cautioned as well not to rely on human faculties: "What madness is this, to write glosses on Holy Writ in the same manner as on secular writings?" (188)

Salutati replied to Dominici's book in an unfinished letter, restating his position. A person's faith was not predicated on his learning, he noted, but secular studies played a useful role in furthering our understanding of Holy Writ: "I confess that sincere faith can be conceived without letters, but divine Scripture and the expositions of the doctors cannot be understood without them."[7]

Leonardo Bruni entered the arena against the scholastic dialecticians with the *Dialogues*,[8] in which he unfolds a discussion concerning the state of learning. He introduces as speakers Salutati, praising the art of disputation, and Niccolò Niccoli lamenting the decline of the art in their time. In this context he inveighs against the modern dialecticians and criticizes even the great literary triumvirate: Dante, Petrarch, and Boccaccio. In a second session he is made to recant, however, and praise those same authors. Significantly, his criticism of the dialecticians is left standing. The modern practitioners of the dialectical method, Niccolò insists, have broken the traditional unity of wisdom and eloquence, which is evident in classical philosophy, and want to "learn philosophy while being ignorant of letters" (67). They restrict themselves to the study of Aristotle's works, which an inept translator has so disfigured that, were Aristotle to come back to life, "he would not recognize them as his own" (69). And this pseudo-Aristotle, speaking "words harsh, awkward, dissonant," they revere like a God. *Ipse dixit* has the force of an oracular pronouncement, "as fixed as those which Pythian Apollo gave forth from his holy sanctuary" (68).

Perhaps the best known entry into the humanist-scholastic debate is the epistolary exchange between Pico della Mirandola and Barbaro.[9] Initiating the polemic in 1485, Barbaro counseled Pico against pursuing scholastic philosophy and sharply criticized its representatives for their barbarous language: "I do not count among the Latin authors those Germans and Teutons who were not really alive in their lifetime, much less will they live now that they are dead; or if they live, they live in torture and reproach; why, it is common to have them called dull, rude, uncultured, barbarians" (13). In his reply, Pico (or rather, the fictitious character suborned by him) defends the thesis that rhetoric and wisdom cannot be combined since their aims are different. Rhetoric deceives, "for what else is the task of the orator than to lie?" (16) Philosophy searches for the truth. Rhetoric is for lawyers, not for philosophers or theologians. For this reason sacred matter is written "rustically rather than elegantly . . . for in every subject concerned with true knowing nothing is more unseemly and detrimental than all that elaborated sort of discourse" (17). The scholastic is not impressed by eloquence, but praises a fecundity of mind that allows him to present a multitude of questions and solutions. The technical language serves as a sort of code to exclude amateurs: "We do not endeavour to entice the multitude but to frighten them off" (20). Pico's scholastic rejects the argument that it is rhetoric that makes a speech persuasive: "What is more moving, more persuasive than reading the holy Scriptures?" (21). Truth needs no embellishment. Indeed, the scholastic rejects even the demand for "correct" speech. What is correct

Latin, after all? Nothing but a convention, a set of rules agreed upon by a number of people. In the same way, the scholastics have agreed on a form of speech, commonly called "Parisian" (22), which is no less respected among them than the Roman usage among the humanists. And if language is not a matter of convention but of nature, who would be in a better position to judge than the philosopher? "Perhaps while the ears reject the names as rough, reason accepts them as more cognate to the things" (23). He concludes by asserting the superiority of philosophy over rhetoric. A person unfamiliar with belles lettres is not humane; a person without philosophy is not human (23). Barbaro, not to be outmaneuvered by Pico's scholastic puppet, brings in a "Paduan" who further muddies the waters by refusing to have scholasticism defended by a humanist masquerading as a scholastic.

Erasmus' *Antibarbarians*, a defense of the *studia humanitatis*, was conceived in the late 1480s as an oration, revised by the author and turned into a dialogue in 1494–95, and finally published, with additions, in 1520.[10] It was the first of a planned four books, a project that remained unfinished, however. The second and third book were to contain an attack and defense of rhetoric respectively, and the fourth a defense of poetry.[11]

Set in a garden, a retreat "even better than the Academy of Plato" (19), the dialogue is said to be the record of a conversation that took place between Erasmus and his friends. The energetic town clerk of Bergen, Jakob Batt, defends the humanities, whereas two other characters, the mayor and the town physician, express their reservations about pagan studies. We encounter the familiar objections born from a fear that Christians might be corrupted and their thought contaminated by pagan ideas. The critic of *studia humanitatis* asks: "Am I to carry books by damned men in my hand and in my bosom, and read them over again and reverence them? Virgil is burning in hell, and is a Christian to sing his poems?" (57). We also encounter the suspicion that human learning is inimical to faith, the view that "secular learning . . . supplies the material for arrogance" (63), and "literature . . . distracts the mind from right living" (75); and we read that polished language, especially poetic language, is incompatible with Christian simplicity. "Beware, they say, he's a poet; he's no Christian," Batt reports. The enemies of learning believe that an elegant tongue is indicative of "disordered morals" (75) and "to speak like Cicero is heresy." In his counterattack Batt contends that the critics of the humanities are "a doltish herd of scorners" whose opposition is rooted in envy and in their own inability to profit from the humanities. He expresses disdain for "the run of present-day theologians who have learned nothing but sophisms" (105) and the dull wits of those "who think themselves particularly sharp—dialecticians in fact" (114). On the problematic relationship between learning and faith, Batt adopts a more accommodating stand. Divine inspiration does indeed furnish a higher order of understanding, but human endeavors also have a role to play in the acquisition of knowledge. He refutes his critics' claim that an understanding of Scripture was reached "not through human study, but by the gift of heaven." In that case, Batt suggests sarcastically, let us abandon ourselves to the mercy of the Holy Spirit. "If a book is to be written, let Him fly to our side and control our pen, with no effort of ours. If a speech is to be given, let Him sit by our ear in the shape of a dove and Himself guide our tongue" (114). Continuing in a serious vein, he offers this considered opinion: "[The Spirit] increases what our industry has produced . . . He does not exclude human work but comes to its aid" (117–118).

The elegant tradition of literary polemics lives on in miniature compositions such as Jacob Locher's *Dialogue* of 1496,[12] which contrasts the liberally educated Fathers with the scholastic theologians, and Heinrich Bebel's *Disputation* of 1506,[13] a literary epistle relating a conversation on the same subject.

In the preface to his work Locher explains that the dialogue he is about to present to the reader—a conversation between himself and the well-known jurist Ulrich Zasius—was written "in the manner of Socrates." It is set in a paradisiacal garden and has the quality of a poetic, dreamlike vision rather than Socratic inquiry. Locher guides his friend through the garden, pointing out the inhabitants of this blessed abode. In the middle of the garden stands a lectern where, Locher says, "the basic principles of our faith" are taught. The four Latin Doctors of the Church, who are "the pillars of the Christian commonwealth . . . and who have rendered the Catholic See unconquerable through the centuries" preside over the lectern (A viii recto). It is their teaching that protects the Church against heretics, not "the tortuous and involved refutations nor the verbose quarrels of the sophists nor their Chrysippean machinations." Unlike the Fathers, these new theologians have produced works "horrid in style and barren in content" and are "slow-witted and involved in the dark snares of arguments." Another characteristic that sets them apart from the Fathers is that the latter, "unlike the majority today who are experts in one subject only, . . . filled the pages of their eloquent books with every kind of secular learning" (A viii recto–verso). Locher concludes with an appeal to the professors of theology to study the writings of the Fathers: "What good is it to spend day and night on scholastic disputations? What good is it every day to weave nets to trap the innocent? What good is your verbose profundity, your inane verbosity? The writings of Holcot, Scotus, Bede, Nicolaus of Lyra, Tinctor, Scriptor, Versor, Ockham, and others whose names I pass over on purpose are widely read and ever present in our schools. O wretched loss of talent! We allow the sacred exegetes of Scripture to lie in darkness . . . for what do our theologians (to whom we defer everywhere in German schools) know that the holy Fathers . . . did not know?" (B iiii recto).

Unlike Locher's dialogue, in which the protagonist preaches to the converted, Bebel's *Disputatio* pits the author against an Augustinian canon who firmly closes his mind against the humanist argument. He expresses severe misgivings about Christians wanting "to speak more daintily after the model of pagan and condemned writers" when they might imitate the style of the theologians and of the Bible, writings that are inspired by the Holy Spirit rather than the "rules of Donatus." Bebel objects to giving theologians permission to speak ungrammatically. It was "a novel and unusual privilege to let theologians speak like barbarians." In his opinion, it was to no purpose to corrupt language and speak unintelligibly, for "no one can understand a person who fails to observe idiom" (L ii verso). He concedes that in the early days of Christianity the Fathers were forced to introduce new terms to express new religious concepts, but on the whole their style "was golden, so to speak, and most elegant by comparison with those who now call themselves theologians. Their speech was grave . . . [whereas] that of recent theologians is rustic and barbarous, or rather, as Pico della Mirandola says, 'Gallic and Parisian'." Theology is mixed up with "the most knotty and thorny discipline of the philosophers and dialecticians." As a result, theological questions are "so entangled and so puzzling that one would need a sphinx to interpret them or a Delian God to expound them" (L iii verso). In another reference to the exchange between Pico and Barbaro, Bebel indicates that he would not go as far as demanding rhetorical embellishment and poetic imagery from theologians, but he expects a certain gravity and decorum. He counsels modern theologians to imitate the Fathers and refrain from "obscuring the theological truth with their minute, morose, and inextricably knotty questions." He singles out for criticism "Albert, Thomas, Scotus, Ockham, Aegidius, Alexander of Hales, and Holcot," none of whom offer "even the shadow of ancient eloquence" (L iii verso).

His interlocutor, Bebel reports, defended scholastic philosophy as necessary in the battle to overthrow heretics, whereas he himself saw philosophy as a seedbed of heresy. No one had ever heard of "a poet or an orator or anyone other than a philosopher exciting heresy" (ibidem). He noted that Jerome had not used the scholastic method and in fact criticized such quibbling (L iiii recto). These arguments greatly incensed the canon. "As you know," Bebel tells his correspondent, "that kind of man is difficult and cannot bear to be put right." He therefore withdraws gracefully: "Take it in good part, dear Father. I did not mean this to be an assertion but merely put it forth for discussion. I did not mean to insult theology or philosophy, for we use these disciplines, as we do other things, either to our benefit or our detriment" (ibidem).

In the other camp, John Mair, the Scottish theologian, who had a distinguished career at Paris, presented a defense of the scholastics. Entitled *Dialogus de materia theologo tractanda* (A Dialogue Concerning the Subject Matter to Be Treated by the Theologian),[14] it records the conversation between Gawain Douglas, prefect of St. Aegidius in Edinburgh, and Mair's pupil David Cranston.[15] Douglas complains that modern theology is contaminated with Aristotelianism. In theological writings, "Aristotle is cited more often . . . than the Doctors of the Church." Cranston defends scholasticism.

> CRANSTON: In their writings the [scholastic theologians] introduce sometimes the philosopher, at other times the Doctors of the Church, depending on the subject under discussion. In doing one thing, they do not pass over the other, showing that theology, the goddess of sciences, does not differ from true philosophy and advancing the young in their faith by leading them by the hand.
>
> DOUGLAS: With due respect, your answer does not satisfy me, for I cannot see how the great number of frivolous scholastic positions . . . benefits theology. Indeed, they do not help to open up theology, they obfuscate and obscure it . . .
>
> CRANSTON: This is how authors have written on the Sentences for the past three hundred years, and if you think that it was done without good reason, remember that a common error becomes law (as they say). Some prefer the Bible and the easier parts of theology, others recondite and intricate reasoning . . . and what some consider futile questions often provide stepping stones to our understanding of Holy Writ . . .
>
> DOUGLAS: If this is done in a compendious manner, I don't object . . . but the *sententiarii* spend most of their time on Aristotelian philosophy, and they use not only his writings but also his style of writing . . . [here Douglas quotes at length Valla's criticism of the scholastic method and style, claiming that this furnished an

explanation why students were turning away from theology]. It is easy to see that large numbers come to study the *Summulae* [that is, there is a large enrollment in the preliminary courses] in the Colleges of Navarre or Bourgogne, but at the end of the course of studies there is a dearth of candidates for the licentiate and the regents go away with an empty purse. The reason why things go wrong is that the wheat is left behind for the chaff.

Cranston suggests that students do not go on to theological studies because they desire more lucrative careers.

> CRANSTON: For there are not many Parisians from wealthy houses who graduate in arts or theology. Rather, they turn quickly to law so that they can become courtiers. And no matter how you teach theology, the situation will remain the same. As for Valla, it is not relevant to reply to his arguments. That man did not spare anyone, as you know, and he introduced more errors into his dialectic (or rather mad philosophy) than a leopard has spots, because he did not want to adopt the theological manner of speaking.

The dispute between the two men remains unresolved when Douglas changes the topic, wanting to know Mair's opinion on the matter. Here Mair, who has been hiding behind Cranston's persona throughout the dialogue, is teasing his readers and ultimately giving them the slip by allowing Cranston to answer evasively: "Mair could maintain either position if he so desired, as you know." The conversation ends with trite civilities.

Carefully crafted compositions like Locher's, Bebel's, and Mair's were outnumbered in the sixteenth century by unvarnished academic controversies and caustic satires. Interestingly, Erasmus and Locher compressed and repeated in their personal literary careers the stages through which the humanist-scholastic debate went as a whole. Disguising their early attacks on the scholastic theologians as literary compositions, they later dispensed with niceties and adopted the confrontational style that typifies the sixteenth century.

The polemics of Petrarch and his fifteenth-century successors, representing the first phase of the debate, are characterized by two elements, as noted above: a vagueness in pinpointing the enemy and a latitudinarianism which allowed the polemicists to argue on both sides of the question. The first characteristic is evident in the prevalent method of group-targeting. We have seen that Petrarch refrains from naming his opponents or singling out a school of thought. This is the dominant approach in the Quattrocento as well. There is a pronounced "them-

and-us" attitude, but "they" (that is, the enemies of the *studia humanitatis*) have a group personality and speak in unison. There appears to be
one script for all. They are contentious, have a penchant for quibbling,
and are slavishly devoted to Aristotle. They hate poets and speak barbarous Latin. Their professional identity is not always clear. Erasmus'
"barbarians," like Petrarch's and Boccaccio's adversaries, come from all
walks of life; Bruni's dialecticians and Pico's scholastic are philosophers,
but in medieval and Renaissance usage this designation often included
theologians. Indeed, theologians are usually among the targets. The critics Petrarch answers in *On His Own Ignorance* are dilettantes, but he was
deeply concerned about the use of the scholastic method in theology.
Theologians also have a prominent spot in Boccaccio's *Genealogy of the
Gods*. They "raise question after question about the highest truths: for
example, whether one Deity can consist of three persons; whether God
can create anything in His own image; why He did not create the world
a million years sooner; and the like."[16] Similarly we find among Bruni's
dialecticians theologians "confounded by British sophisms," followers of
"Ferabrich (Ferrybridge), Buser, Ockham" (69). Locher and Bebel, finally, addressed themselves exclusively to the subject of scholastic theology, and Mair speaks through the persona of a theologian, the profession
on which the debate came to focus in the next stage. Thus the defenders
of scholasticism in the early phases of the debate are a mixed group of
dilettantes and professionals; the defenders of humanistic studies, or
rather the humanist characters in the pieces mentioned, are a similarly
disparate group. Some are professional teachers, others gentlemen
scholars or civic leaders. Some defend poetry, others concentrate on
rhetoric, a third group is concerned with biblical exegesis.

In the later stages of the debate, protagonists tend to circumscribe
their own intellectual affiliations more clearly and to narrow the scope
of their subject accordingly. Almost without exception, the polemicists
of the sixteenth century are professionals—teachers of the humanities
or theologians—and they take aim at other professionals. They tend to
target specific incidents or passages in specific works. Rather than attacking or defending secular learning in general, they might focus on
one aspect such as the respective merits of the dialectical and philological methods, the value of textual criticism and the use of Greek manuscripts, the desirability of vernacular translations of the Bible, or others.
Later polemicists were more specific not only in targeting the subject
matter but also in targeting individuals. Even when the anonymity of
the person attacked was preserved formally, transparent pseudonyms or
references to the nationality, personal attributes, or stylistic idiosyncra-

sies of the enemy provide enough clues to allow the reader to identify the target. In the first phase of the debate, by contrast, arguments are multifaceted and the enemy of a generic kind.

This brings us to the second characteristic of the early debate: its latitudinarianism. The genres and rhetorical devices chosen by the polemicists lent themselves to presenting a number of viewpoints. The literary epistle allowed the writer to stay away from offering formal proof and even to defer politely to the opponent. Salutati avoided formal reasoning, noting that he was observing the requirements of the genre. *Non probationibus docui*, he declared: "I have not used proofs to make my point" (203:1). Syllogisms would have been out of place in a literary epistle. When he briefly lapsed into a more technical argument, perhaps to show that it was not ignorance of dialectic that prevented him from using the scholastic method, he recalled himself: "I don't know how I wandered from my purpose" (180:4–5). Dominici answered Salutati with a treatise in the scholastic tradition. Yet he gave himself room to argue on both sides by adopting the sic-et-non method, listing first the arguments that might be presented by the opponent and then refuting them. While Salutati's literary epistle evinces the author's familiarity with classical models of style, Dominici's usage betrays a more traditional medieval schooling. He employs the terminology of scholastic handbooks on logic.[17] The use of technical terminology is deliberate, we are told, for "there is nothing more inimical to the search for truth than using vague terms" (p. 126).

The sic-et-non method is the scholastic equivalent of the classical (and humanistic) dialogue. It allows arguing *in utramque partem*, but unlike the classical method, with which it shares the feature of exploring both sides of a question, it does not end in suspended judgment. The ancient method, introduced by the sophists, served partly to display the speaker's virtuosity, partly to indicate his skepticism. The function of the scholastic method appears to be the documentation of a thought process. The writer demonstrates that he has done his homework, so to speak, has explored the pros and cons of a question, and arrived at his verdict in a rational manner. Both the classical and the medieval method, then, have an epideictic element, showing the speaker's skill of invention. The object of the scholastic speaker, however, is to instruct his audience by giving a step-by-step explication of the process that led to the verdict, a process which, like a scientific experiment, can be verified and repeated.

In Dominici's case the sic-et-non method is somewhat modified or diluted by the insertion of homiletic asides. Whether this shift in style from logical argumentation to rhetoric occurs consciously or unconsciously, it betrays Dominici's real sympathies and anticipates his verdict. Thus he introduces an argument which has his true support in this manner: "Now we must marshal our forces . . . so that the fifth argument [that Scripture cannot be understood without secular learning] may lose its apparent force" (p. 232). After making his case, he concludes with considerable warmth:

> Indeed if the whole world fully believed in Christ, I think that all of philosophy, with the exception of a small portion of the liberal arts, ought to be abolished because it is superfluous, because it is misleading, because it is inimical to faith, because it is a blasphemy of God, because it is false, . . . because it is honey smeared with poison, full of snares, an invention of the demons. For, as I said before, all wisdom is from our Lord God. (421)

Rather transparently, the first part of Dominici's treatise, which defends secular learning, is argued dispassionately; the second, containing the views he endorsed, shows greater vigor and involvement. For example, he makes an emotional plea for a curriculum based on Christian sources:

> Sacred writings are neglected, Christian books lie in squalor, while those of the pagans are covered in silk and studded with gold and silver and treated like treasures; and all Christian schools are filled, day and night, even during breaks, with the sound of pagan rhetoric; Christ is preached only on some feast days to simple women, for an hour at best . . . Let all men and women everywhere attend the schools of the philosophers, if they really produce such champions of faith as, they say, one may expect in the future . . . but those schools are brothels that nurse long-haired young men who turn into followers of Venus . . . and zealots of Jove. (122, 145)

Occasionally, Dominici interrupts his argumentation for the sake of an anecdote, the staple of pulpit oratory. He tells the story of two men, one "who attempted to prove that the language of Scripture was wrong in many places; and another, a layman . . . [who] said that it should be read after dinner by the fireside instead of fables." Dominici reproved both men and warned them of God's wrath. "They went away laughing and scorning God's revenge, but a little while later the layman died . . . no one was present at the time, and he died in his bed without benefit of confession. The other one was for some reason or other incarcerated and deprived of food, drink, and company, dying of starvation, also unconfessed" (243–244). A shaggy-dog story is used to illustrate the point that philosophers steeped in secular learning are bound to lose faith: "In the city of Padua the ghost of a dead man rose from his grave at twilight time. Many attested to it. Yet the professor who held the chair of [natural] philosophy at the university, being unable to deny the fact, immediately called together his students, and attempted to discredit the miracle and explain it by natural causes" (261). The evil consequences of the man's acquaintance with secular studies were evident, Dominici indicated: he no longer believed in miracles and was trying to destroy the faith of others as well.

There are enough emotionally charged passages in the *Firefly* to signal Dominici's preferences to the reader. The sic-et-non method camouflages his position to a certain extent, as does his conventional courtesy and perfunctory deference to his opponent. Yet even though he assures Salutati that he "will attempt to think whatever you think" (4) and goes as far as citing his opponent's arguments with tentative approval (70), we know that his ultimate purpose is to refute Salutati. Nor can frequent quotations from the classics persuade the reader that Dominici is a friend of the *studia humanitatis*—rather, we have here another instance of an author proving to his adversary that he does not militate against his methods merely because he is incapable of using them himself.

The dialogue, a favourite genre of the humanists, afforded them ample opportunity to examine both sides of a question by introducing appropriate characters. It also allowed the writer to remain formally uncommitted by refraining from comment in his own person.[18] In Bruni's *Dialogues* the signs of literary conceit are present everywhere. We encounter artful tergiversation designed to obscure the author's intentions and let the reader discover the mental landscape for himself. The epideictic character of Niccolò's speech on the decline of the art of disputation is revealed when Salutati points out that the eloquence of the speaker belies the subject. "His complaint was in truth confuted by his speech . . . he bewailed the decadence of the times and said that all capability of disputation had been taken away, but in proving this he himself disputed very finely" (71). Salutati furthermore notes that Niccolò's criticism of Dante, Petrarch, and Boccaccio was a "stratagem," and Niccolò happily confirms: "My only reason for attacking yesterday was to stimulate Coluccio to praise them" (78). The reader, then, has been forewarned. What we have here is a variation on the sic-et-non game.

The dialogues of Erasmus, Bebel, and Mair constitute similar efforts to soften the polemic by literary devices. Although both Erasmus and Bebel are committed to the humanist point of view, they allow the other side in the dispute a voice. A certain balance is preserved in Erasmus' *Antibarbarians* in his portraying the champion of humanism, who is

given the attractive lines, as a hot-head, whereas his opponents, who defend the reactionary position, are depicted as level-headed and concerned citizens. Nor are all the good arguments reserved for the humanist. Others, too, present their views with flair and finesse, so that a
certain suspense is maintained and the outcome of the discussion is not
a foregone conclusion. In Mair's dialogue the disputants are also closely
matched. Both argue vigorously, with the critic of scholasticism at an
advantage, at least quantitatively. In all three cases, however, judgment
is suspended. The dialogues of Mair and Erasmus end amiably, in the
latter case with the participants retiring to the mayor's house for dinner.
In Bebel's dialogue the reactionary canon is certainly fed inferior lines,
but the exchange ends in the accommodating manner characteristic of
the first phase of the debate, with Bebel softening the polemic by dis-
claiming any intention to dispute seriously and stressing the academic
character of his speech. Locher's use of the dialogue is the least skillful.
Although the elaborate scenario he creates gives his work a Quattrocento air, his "dialogue" is little more than a speech addressed to a yes-
man.

The exchange of opinion between Pico and Barbaro was carried on in
a series of letters, but they succeeded in introducing dissenting voices in
the shape of fictitious speakers. By giving third-person rather than first-
person accounts, they avoided presenting their own views unvarnished
and unadorned—a literary mannerism of the time. The correspondents
used another device as well to stay at arm's length from the dispute. They
declared their compositions rhetorical exercises. Pico, the creator of the
scholastic champion, humorously acknowledged that his champion was
perhaps "slightly more eloquent" than his scholastic brethren and
"championed his barbarism as little like a barbarian as possible" (16).
Barbaro was of course fully aware of the conceit: "Under the guise of
defending [the scholastics] you utterly kill those you defend . . . in our
circles, with which you quarrel in word but agree in thought, what you
did is most gratifying to everybody . . . we should call you a deserter if
your writings expressed your true sentiments" (27). In both Pico's and
Bruni's cases, the polemic is carried on with persuasive arguments, but a
certain implausibility or absurdity warns the reader of the epideictic nature of their exposition. The eloquence of the characters introduced by
the author—Niccolò in the *Dialogues,* the scholastic in Pico's letter—
belies their respective purposes. Form contradicts contents. The "barbarian" and the representative of a "decadent" age argue eloquently and
speak in impeccable humanistic Latin. In each case, the writer chose a
form or literary technique that allowed his opinions to be expressed in

the voices of others. This permitted a certain latitude of opinion and, consequently, a more balanced presentation of the subject matter than we encounter in the polemics of a later age, which required the author to maintain and defend one point of view.

In the controversies discussed so far, the authors kept at a distance from their subject by fictionalizing it. In a number of cases, however, their bluff was called by real-life adversaries challenging them directly. Bruni, Pico, Locher, and Erasmus presented their views in third-person accounts in a literary setting, but they were forced by circumstances to give a straightforward account of their position on the issues under debate, thus providing us with a "control-group" of writings. Bruni, who had related a polemical exchange in his *Dialogues*, became involved in an actual controversy with Alonso of Cartagena. In Pico's case, too, there was a real-life sequence to his literary exercise. On publishing the *Nine Hundred Conclusions or Theses* in 1486,[19] he was called upon to justify his views before a papal commission. The scholastic champion in his letter had defended the use of technical terminology against the stylistic criticism of the humanists; ironically, the verdict of the papal commissioners sounded much the same note as the fictitious scholastic. Erasmus' career provides another example of life imitating fiction. He was obliged to defend his interest in secular studies in circumstances less charming than the garden scene in his *Antibarbarians*. Locher found himself under attack as well. These last two cases belong to a later period, however, in which the debate was carried on in the academic milieu, a subject that will be examined in more detail in the next chapter. At this point the focus will be on the responses of Bruni and Pico to their factual contemporary accusers.

In 1416 Bruni published a new translation of Aristotle's *Ethics*. In his preface he described the current version as puerile and boorish. The translator (Grosseteste), unable to cope with the difficulties confronting him, had left a number of Greek words untranslated, "a beggar in the midst of the wealth" offered by the Latin language. He spoke "half Greek, half Latin, deficient in both languages, competent in neither."[20] Bruni's sharp criticism of the traditional version provoked a reply from Alonso of Cartagena, Bishop of Burgos.[21] The ensuing exchange between the two men, called by Giovanni Gentile "a typical controversy between a scholastic theologian and a humanist translator," serves as a foil and commentary on Bruni's *Dialogues*.[22]

Alonso studied at Paris and Salamanca, which is to say that he was trained in the scholastic tradition. His attitude toward the classics was ambivalent. Early in his career he translated Cicero's *De inventione* into

Spanish, and in his preface criticized contemporaries for "citing texts and determinations" rather than using "good reasoning" as taught by Cicero.[23] Nor, apparently, did he have objections at that time to theologians using Aristotle's *Rhetoric*.[24] In a later work, *Oracional* (1454), however, he commented adversely on the humanists' interest in classical style, reproaching them for showing a preference for pagan over Christian rhetoric. The Fathers, he noted, combined wisdom with eloquence, but their eloquence was rooted in Scripture: "They adapted [rhetoric] to the standards of Holy Writ . . . and wrote in a Catholic manner, with wisdom and piety, fusing it into one; and although they displayed much eloquence in their books and in some places drew on the natural sciences, they always returned to Scripture and made it the foundation of their words."[25] These were the models to follow. "It displeases me," Alonso wrote, "that people aim for that ancient pagan style . . . employed by the Greeks and Romans before they received the holy faith, and turn away from the sweet and salutary eloquence of the holy doctors."[26]

There is an undercurrent of nationalism in Alonso's polemic against Bruni and the latter's reply. The bishop portrays his countrymen as scholastics, the Italians as humanists. The Spaniards' strength, he says, lies *in scholasticis actibus ac in disceptationibus causarum* (163), whereas the Italians excel in literature. Indeed Bruni himself might be called a "new Cicero" (164).

Alonso's critique of Bruni's translation of Aristotle's *Ethics* is strangely abstract since, as he freely admits, he knows no Greek. While modern readers might be struck by the absurdity of his enterprise, it fits into the tradition of medieval scholasticism, which put a higher value on logic than on experience. Thus Alonso was not deterred from the task at hand by his lack of Greek. He was not examining "what was written in Greek," he explained, "but rather whether it could be written thus" (166). In other words, he was arguing about principles, not about the specifics of a particular language. In principle, then, there was nothing wrong with leaving Greek words in the text when Latin lacked an equivalent expression. "Was it not better to leave them as they were, that we might have them in our Latin vocabulary, declined according to our rules, their meaning made clear by the context and what follows, rather than to disturb the whole order of the text with circumlocutions?" (169) In another, typically scholastic argument Alonso attempted to restrict usage. Since Aristotle's *Ethics* were a philosophical treatise, the rules of rhetoric did not apply, he contended: "In philosophy words are not to be used without restriction, for the improper use of words leads by degrees to an error about things" (169). Alonso advocates a strict delineation of disciplines and of professional competence, an argument that was to become increasingly more prominent in humanist-scholastic confrontations:

> Anyone who has a right to claim for himself the art of rhetoric, declares that he has left philosophy to others. Believe me: anyone who wants to subject rigorous, scientific conclusions to the rules of rhetoric is foolish, for to add or subtract words belongs to the area of sweet persuasion and is abhorred by rigorous science. In my opinion this is what is appropriate to the wise man: to use in disputation words in their strictest and most proper sense, that is, scientific language ... for elegant diction, if it is not guided by strict judgment, confuses the simplicity of things, which in turn disturbs the correct understanding of scientific truths. (176)

The argument that eloquence gets in the way of truth, that eloquent words are too vague to use in a rigorous examination of the truth and indeed confound the truth, became one of the staples of scholastic apologiae.

Bruni answered his critic, but addressed himself to Francesco Piccolpasso, Archbishop of Milan, rather than to Alonso himself. His reply is disappointing as a reasoned defense of his position. To put the best possible construction on his motives, one might say that he did not take his critic seriously. Instead of coming to grips with Alonso's arguments, he belittled him as a reactionary: "Some people defend obstinately what they have learned in their youth" (186). Naturally, he seized on the fact that Alonso knew no Greek. "What method of discussion is left to him other than guesswork, since he is dealing with a subject totally unknown to him?" he asked pointedly (189). Their discussion was about translating from Greek into Latin and to dispute with Alonso about this was "like arguing with a fortune teller or a dreamer" (201). He scoffed at Alonso's view that scholars should stay within their area of specialization. Alonso himself was, after all, a dabbler in several disciplines: a jurist turned theologian. And one might with justification apply to him the reproach that "those who pursue everything, have nothing in their grasp" (188).

Up to this point Bruni is merely unkind. Elsewhere he manifests a degree of malice. Alonso had noted the grave responsibility of the translator. If the readers had no Greek and could not refer to the original text, they depended on the integrity of the translator. He could lead them by the nose, "which of course we must not think in Leonardo's case, but which it was in his power to do, if he had wanted it" (166). Bruni elevates this comment to a personal attack: "He has childish suspicions about me, for he says I could pretend that something is written in the Greek which is not . . .; if Alonso were a good man he would not suspect such things of others" (187). Similarly, Bruni translates an innocuous comment about the natural talent of Italians for literature into a slight. Alonso had written: "As soon as they [the Italians] begin to think, they take up the pen"; Bruni paraphrased this remark: "He says that the Italians reach for the pen because they have time on their hands" (187).

Although the controversy between Bruni and Alonso de Cartagena arose from a specific occasion—Bruni's translation of Aristotle—and re-volves around issues pertinent to it, the polemic nevertheless contains elements characteristic of the larger humanist-scholastic controversy. Typical of the scholastic argument is Alonso's unwillingness to apply general literary criteria to a technical text; typical of the humanistic ar-gument is Bruni's refusal to accept the idea of narrow specialization which would restrict the application of language skills to nontechnical literature.

In Pico's case, the papal investigators of his *Conclusions* not only had reservations about the orthodoxy of his views but also registered com-plaints about his style: "Some [of the conclusions] would seem to deviate from the straight path of orthodox faith partly on account of their usage, partly because they are doubtful and ambiguous. Furthermore, they are couched and even buried in the obscurity of new and unusual terms."[27] One of the examiners, Pedro García, who continued the debate with Pico in *Determinationes magistrales* (Rome, 1489), pointedly contrasted his own style with that of Pico, saying in the dedicatory letter: "Against the apologia of the conclusions of the said Giovanni Pico I have written a book in humble style and in the scholastic manner of the Paris theolo-gians."[28]

In his *Apologia*, Pico speaks rather than exercises his mind. He uses the scholastic method not because he considers it necessary and appro-priate to the subject, but because he needs to communicate with his crit-ics. "I must now change my style," he explains in the concluding passage of his preface to the *Apologia*, "since I am addressing myself to barbarians and (as the proverb says charmingly) stammerers understand only stam-merers."[29] He reveals another significant difference between his ap-proach and that of the scholastics. Unlike them, he does not belong to a philosophical school and will not allow his range of inquiry to be circum-scribed by loyalties to one school of thought:

I have sworn allegiance to no one. I have gone through all teachers of philosophy, examined all manuscripts, studied all schools . . . I let myself be driven wherever the winds carried me. For this was the custom observed by all the ancients: to examine every kind of writing, to pass over no commentary unread or unexamined; this was moreover taught especially by Aristotle, who was for this reason called "The Reader" by Plato. Indeed it demonstrates a narrow mind to keep within the confines of one school or academy. Nor can anyone choose from all the sources what is right and proper for his own purpose, unless he has familiarized himself with all of them. In each school, furthermore, there is something noteworthy, not shared with any other. To begin with our time and the most recent heirs to philosophy: Duns Scotus has something vigorous and minutely accurate, Thomas is solid and fair, Aegidius terse and exact, Franciscus sharp and acute, Albert broad in the old tradition and grand, Henricus, in my opinion, sublime and venerable . . . [he goes on to discuss classical philosophy] . . . Thus I wanted to proffer not merely the opinion of one philosopher (as some are pleased to do) but a multifarious doctrine, so that by gathering these several schools of thought, by means of a multifaceted examination of philosophy, the splendor of truth (as Plato says in his letters) might shine forth in our minds like the sun rising above the ocean.[30]

The views formulated by Pico were reaffirmed by his nephew, Gianfrancesco, whose tract *De studio humanae et divinae philosophiae libri duo* (Bologna, 1497) illuminates several aspects of the humanist-scholastic controversy.[31] Gianfrancesco's feelings about the merits of scholastic theology, Parisian style, were mixed. He noted that the *modus Parisiensis* neglected all esthetic considerations and traded in "petty questions and titillating subtleties." Gianfrancesco disapproved of the contentious nature and staged character of scholastic disputations, their "histrionic maneuvers and novel techniques of disparaging the adversary," but he balanced this criticism with praise for the "powers of judgment and subtlety of thought" these disputations promoted. Of particular interest in the context of the humanist-scholastic controversy is Gianfrancesco's division of theologians into four categories: the theologians of old who combined wisdom with eloquence; those "who write in the Parisian style"; experts in canon law; and finally those who combine all three areas, a task that takes "Herculean bravery." His uncle, Gianfrancesco said, belonged to this last category: "If Giovanni Pico had lived, he would have fulfilled all the requirements." In his driving intellectual curiosity that could not be confined to the limits of one discipline and would not be compelled by tradition, Pico was the consummate scholar.

This chapter has examined the largely epideictic nature of the early debate. It is clear that any published work serves an epideictic function in the most elementary sense of the word. It "displays" the views and skills of the author. I am using "epideictic" in a more specific sense, however, referring to a method of format that allows authors to distance themselves from the subject at hand or even deny personal involvement. This does not mean that they did not have an opinion, only that civility or skepticism prompted them to make room for alternatives. It is significant in this context that even in the polemic between Bruni and Alonso of Cartagena, which strikes a personal note, epideixis is the *professed* ideal. In spite of the animosity Bruni displays in the exchange, he wants it to be seen as a contest of wits: *certamen litterarum, in quibus non serio sed ingenio decertatur* (210). His remark, even if only perfunctory, represents an ideal. The preference for this type of exchange over a serious engagement is also expressed in Poggio Bracciolini's comment on the case. He refrained from criticizing Bruni's attitude but pointedly praised his adversary's detachment: "In my opinion at least, the Spaniard expresses himself with moderation . . . This kind of disputation, *undertaken as an intellectual exercise*, is praiseworthy if it is free of abuse."[32] It was obviously easier to praise this attitude than to maintain it, for Poggio himself was criticized by Salutati for lack of courtesy and scholarly detachment. "You delight too much in open disapproval," Salutati wrote. There was nothing more foolish than to be provocative when one could speak in veiled terms and use "concealed jibes."[33] In later stages of the humanist-scholastic debate, such literary conventions tended to be viewed in negative terms and considered a mark of indecisiveness or hypocrisy. The conflict between Luther and Erasmus in the mid-1520s is telltale. Although their dispute over free will does not belong to the humanist-scholastic debate as such, it illustrates the decline of latitudinarianism in the sixteenth century under the impact of the Reformation. Erasmus called his work a *diatribe*, that is, a "comparison" of Scriptural passages for and against the existence of free will. His de facto suspension of judgment—he accepted free will not as a result of the comparison but on the authority of the Church—was a decidedly humanist maneuver. Moreover, as Marjorie Boyle in her analysis of the Erasmus-Luther conflict notes, "the scholastic resort to metaphysical analogy was here displaced by a humanist perspective which was innately historical," in the sense that right and wrong are revealed only through perspective and time.[34] Erasmus, the humanist, was presenting his arguments in the urbane manner that had now become an anachronism.

The crisis of the Reformation increased the tendency to dogmatize, and the general trend was to move from discussion to assertion. Characteristically, Luther rejected Erasmus' academic treatment of the question and demanded a clear-cut statement of position and personal commitment. He was ready, he said, to defend his position to the death "even if the whole world should tumble down all together into chaos, and recede to nothingness."[35] Luther's violent response to Erasmus' cordial gesture indicates a general trend and the direction that the humanist-scholastic debate took in the sixteenth century, when it was riding on the coattails of the Reformation.

CHAPTER FOUR

The Debate
at the Universities

B Y T H E E N D of the fifteenth century the humanist-scholastic debate, which was conducted in its earliest phase on the Italian literary scene, spread to universities in Northern Europe and thus to a new setting that pitted "poets" (that is, professional teachers of the *studia humanitatis*) against theologians. Some of the themes addressed by the Italian polemicists of the fifteenth century recur in these later controversies. The scholastic style and method continue to be a matter of contention; the place of pagan literature in Christian education likewise remains a disputed subject. Other questions, so far only touched upon, move to center stage. They concern the qualifications and competence of humanists to engage in biblical studies and the primacy and regulatory power of theology over other disciplines. There are also first indications of a shift in the charges brought against the humanists, from frivolity and lack of respect for the Christian tradition to heterodoxy, a charge that eventually came to dominate the debate in the Reformation. As the tone of the debate changed, so did its form. Literary epistles and dialogues, once the preferred medium of the protagonists, were now outnumbered by designated polemics and satires. As the debate moved into the faculty meeting rooms, moreover, it left its mark on the administrative records of universities in the shape of reform proposals.[1] Structural and curricular reforms were introduced at most Northern universities during the first half of the sixteenth century. Their implementation was uneven, however, which makes it difficult to make general pronouncements on the practical impact of humanist criticism.[2] The following examples, illustrating developments at individual universities, capture the prevailing mood.

Conditions at the University of Leipzig in 1502 are described in an interesting collection of documents submitted by members of the university to their patron, Duke George of Saxony, who was assessing the need for a reform.[3] What emerges from the submissions is a picture of corruption and incompetence, along with resentment and serious differences between younger and older masters as well as between the lower and higher faculties. The main complaints were directed against the theologians, who lectured only desultorily. A typical grievance stated that biblical studies, "on which Christian faith and the business of the Christian Church are based," were being neglected. Lectures were cancelled, and students who had incurred the expense of moving to Leipzig did not get their money's worth. "We cannot go on as before, when one lecturer covered eight chapters in Jeremiah in 24 years," one complainant wrote. "And there are several doctors and holders of chairs who have given less than fifty lectures on Scripture in ten years or more" (115). Another remarked sarcastically: "Even if someone reached Methuselah's age, he would not get through Isaiah, the way lectures go nowadays" (130). A third confirmed the negative verdict: "Many doctors of theology are not in residence and do not concern themselves with education; even if they were recalled they would bring little glory to the faculty of theology" (106). There was no system to the instruction received by students: "Our theologians grow like grass in winter."[4] Not only were students neglected and consequently left the university, but the negligent theologians continued to collect pay. This generated resentment among "the others, who put in much effort and time and are no further ahead" (104).

The complaints also indicate a generation gap in the faculty of arts. Older professors, who sat on the faculty council and wielded considerable power, insisted on the importance of seniority and complained that "the young *magistri* treated them with contempt and irreverence" (143). Others noted that the faculty of arts "had always been governed by the counsel of the older doctors," but now the younger ones exhibited a rebellious spirit and treated their seniors "with contempt and ridicule."[5] Heinrich Stromer of Auerbach, by contrast, alleged that the university's troubles stemmed "from the tyranny of the old *magistri*, who seek only their own advantage and obstruct and drive away the young and industrious lecturers. The remedy is to dismiss the authoritarian and grim old *magistri*, who do no good … because they are more concerned about money than about the general welfare" (109). In the same vein, others complained of the "arrogant attitude of the ruling doctors" (101) and that "the burden of lecturing and examining falls … on the young *magistri*" (104).

Competition for students and positions of authority was brisk. Several of the respondents commented on the existence of a well organized clique, called Schwäbischer Bund, which rigged elections;[6] others noted that careers came at a price. No matter how learned a man was, he could advance "only with the help of St. Denarius."[7] Others again complained that their students were being lured away. One respondent, who wished to remain nameless, reported that students "were drawn away from me by a magister by name of Konigeshoff [Nicolaus Appel], who acted with cunning and enlisted the help of his cronies, Magisters Wimpina and Stolberg." A formal complaint to the dean and the rector had no effect. "No one helped me," the writer lamented (135). Similarly, Leonardus Mertz, who had no qualms signing his name to the complaint, noted that he was forced to surrender students he had taught for some years to the older professors, or else they would obstruct their students' graduation (102). Another submission also documents the dirty war: "They draw away students, detach and lure them away by cunning" (138). A mean spirit of competition prevailed. Martin Meyendorn summed up the complaints of many, when he said that the university could only prosper if the squabbles between the faculties were stopped. There would be trouble as long as "one faculty wants to patronize, harm, or annoy another," and as long as the faculty members were motivated by "selfishness, arrogance, and ambition" (100).

The humanist-scholastic debate formed a subtext in the grievances and surfaced in the demands for curriculum reform. In the submissions we find complaints of too much emphasis being placed on logic and not enough on literature, even though the latter was a popular subject and "students were willing to attend lectures."[8] Some of the grievances were redressed by Duke George, who reacted to them promptly by opening up the faculty council and providing a stipend for a lecturer in poetry. Tensions continued, however, and both Hermann Buschius—who was appointed to the lectureship—and his successor were engulfed in controversy and left the university under disagreeable circumstances. It did not help that the lectureship funded by the duke did not make the holder a member of the faculty. This lack of integration into existing university structures was not an uncommon situation for individual humanists, and indeed, for institutions with a humanistic mandate. The organization of the College de France in Paris, the Collegium Trilingue at Louvain, and the short-lived Collegium Poetarum in Vienna are cases in point.

An atmosphere of contention and dissatisfaction similar to that at Leipzig also prevailed at the University of Cologne, one of the most conservative institutions, about which the poet Conrad Celtis wrote:

This is the city where I learned
to proffer fraud and sophistry
with syllogistic knots, as taught
by dialectic with contentious tongue.
. . . . .
No teacher here of Latin style,
no student of smooth rhetoric
. . . . .
They laugh at learned poetry;
the books of Vergil and of Cicero
are feared by them more than the
    meat
of swine is by the stomach of a Jew.[9]

The dogged traditionalism of members of the university made them the butt of humanistic satire. A sharp decline of students in the 1520s, brought on by a combination of circumstances, notably the uncertainty of the times which discouraged travel and made financial commitments difficult, and an unattractive curriculum which no longer satisfied students or guaranteed employment, led to reform proposals but had few tangible results. In 1525 students addressed a petition to both the faculty and the city (since the university was a municipal foundation), complaining that the courses offered were outdated and all areas neglected, except dialectic "of the most barbarous sort."[10] The resistance to the introduction of humanistic textbooks and courses by the established professors allowed only modest reforms in that area. In Cologne, as in Leipzig, there was an obvious generation gap between the older salaried and beneficed professors, who were generally conservative in their outlook, and the younger generation with tenuous positions on the fringes of the power structure, who were more inclined toward humanism. The submissions by faculty members indicate that the university suffered some of the same problems as Leipzig: an unfairly distributed work load, suspended lectures, negligence and mismanagement.[11] Nor were the problems cleared up by 1533, when Agrippa of Nettesheim appealed to the Cologne city council, noting the poor public image of the university: "It has become a by-word [for incompetence]. When anyone wants to designate a plan as exceptionally ill conceived, he calls it a 'Cologne decision'. Your University is now universally known as a destructive persecutor of the best disciplines and a champion of futile writings."[12]

A decline in student numbers also prompted the University of Heidelberg to re-examine its policies in 1521. The records of the faculty of arts reflect a desire to update the curriculum in order to remain competitive. Tübingen had recently hired Johann Reuchlin to teach Greek and Hebrew. "One can easily guess that this will be to the detriment of our institution," an entry in the records reads.[13] It was necessary to take steps to safeguard the interests of the faculty. "With one voice it was therefore decreed to submit a request to the university that, being our mother, it consider the common welfare and come to the aid of literature and the progress of studies." A letter was accordingly sent, describing the loss of reputation suffered by the faculty of arts: "It is being treated with disdain and contempt by many people; having once been the most flourishing of all German academies, it is now in decline and shrinking and we hear predictions of its demise (if only they were false!)." The reason for the decline in student numbers was a lack of prominent humanist teachers: "Granted, our university is not without men known for their learning, but they are not of a stature to command the same admiration as those who have many publications to their name and have become famous—Dr. Johann Reuchlin, to name one of many, who has been hired as professor of Greek and Hebrew at Tübingen and receives a public stipend." The faculty wanted to attract an equally famous humanist to Heidelberg and asked that Erasmus be approached, "that his talent may restore liberal studies to their former glory." A crisis was at hand. Students were tired of the lectures offered, "especially those on Aristotle," and many had departed for Tübingen or Wittenberg. The rest only remained because their professors begged and pleaded with them. "The number of students is very small now, everyone despises the manner and method by which subjects are taught and dealt with at our academy." Johann Sturm, who was subsequently invited to submit proposals for a reform, suggested that Aristotelian texts be studied henceforth in new translations, that "that barbarian" Petrus Hispanus be replaced, and that logic be taught not "from the dregs of sophistry" but from humanistic texts such as Rudolf Agricola's *De inventione dialectica*. Sturm also proposed that more attention be paid to good authors and that daily lectures in Greek be introduced. That there was considerable opposition to curriculum reforms along humanistic lines can be seen from the remarks of Jacob Wimpheling and Jacob Spiegel, who had also been asked for an opinion: "The reform must start with the theologians, but they will put up the greatest resistance of all."[14] Subsequently, lecturers in Hebrew, Greek, and ancient literature were appointed, but the fact that all three left in the mid-1520s shows that the climate for teaching the humanities remained unsettled.

At Erfurt the champions of the humanities had confronted similar resistance at the beginning of the century and saw the hard-won gains in a reform implemented in 1518/9 endangered once more in the turmoil of the Reformation.[15] The old guard had been ousted and the humanities had triumphed briefly, only to be met by a new foe: radical preachers. The situation is vividly described in Eobanus Hessus' dialogue *The Runaways* (1524). In the opening scene three friends lament the decline of the university, described as "deserted" and "desolate."[16]

> PHILOTIMUS: After the noblest subjects were introduced—Greek, Latin, and also Hebrew—and the three languages vied with one another, as it were, in one gymnasium, . . . how suddenly did our hopes fade . . . and the victory almost gained was wrenched from our hands.
>
> POMPONIUS: Who deprived you of it? Who wrenched it away?
>
> PHILOTIMUS: Boors without learning, blathering demagogues crawling out of their dens of ignorance everywhere, a plague besetting studies, unbelievably ignorant runaways . . .
>
> POMPONIUS: What runaways?
>
> PHILOTIMUS: . . . I mean those who, though they are totally ignorant of all literature, launch fatal missiles under the pretext of sanctity and evangelical piety, hiding under these sacred names as if under a shadow (C iv verso-D i recto).

In another dialogue, *Misologus*, Eobanus Hessus returns to the subject of the university's decline. One of the speakers, Stromegerus, lays the blame for it at the feet of the evangelical preachers. Confronting one of them, Misologus, he argues: "The humanities are taught to adolescents in the universities so that when they ascend to what is truer and better, they will be prepared and able to use the humanities as tools to attain these noble goals. For who does not realize that the theologian needs a knowledge of languages and, more importantly, eloquence. For the more sublime goals cannot be attained in any other way than by going through the studies I have mentioned." Misologus answers him with an emotional outburst:

> I detest universities and execrate them, for from them fatal poisons arise and spread over the whole world, a doctrine that teaches nothing but human conventions.
>
> STROMEGERUS: This is the fault of the times rather than the universities. For we disdained the noblest ancient disciplines, or rather neglected them, and therefore fell into that pit of barbarity from which we have just emerged with the greatest difficulty. And I am all the more indignant because now that good literature has be-

gun to raise its head a little, it is so harshly repressed everywhere
that there is little hope for it to prevail.

MISOLOGUS: But there is poison in those studies which you call
'humane' . . . like the companions of Ulysses among the lotus-
eaters, youth no longer thinks about their home, that is, true and
Christian philosophy.

STROMEGERUS: But can't you see, Misologus, that it is not our purpose to prefer the orator or the poet or the pagan philosopher to
the Christian theologian? Rather, we wish the theologian to be
trained in pagan disciplines that he may use them as ancillary sciences (as has been explained) to reach the summit (B iv recto to
C i verso).

These examples illustrate the discontent at Northern universities at
the beginning of the sixteenth century that was partly informed by the
humanist-scholastic debate. At most institutions where reform proposals
were discussed, we find evidence also of feuding between individuals,
often with a ripple effect. The original pair of contestants attracts partisans who write on their behalf, resulting in a spate of apologiae and anta-
pologiae. The confrontations range from spats to lengthy scholarly polemics. At one end of the scale we have, for example, a graffiti contest
between two students at a local inn—a story related by Mutianus Rufus.[17] The student of the humanities treats the assembled crowd to proverbs in Greek script; the other produces bits of logical propositions in
Latin. The patrons favor the student of Greek, rewarding him with a
free dinner. The scholastic earns only derision and contempt, at least
according to our source, who is of course a champion of humanism. At
the other end of the scale is the complex and drawn-out Reuchlin affair,
which gave the theologians of Cologne a reputation for obscurantism
and spawned doctrinal controversies, law suits, scurrilous satires, and a
flurry of correspondence among the partisans of the two factions. The
central question in the Reuchlin case—the value and place of Hebrew
literature in Christian scholarship—was debated in the shadow of antisemitism and institutional power struggles, but was also contested in the
name of humanism and scholasticism.

At the University of Leipzig, the battle was fought on a smaller scale,
but with no less vigor. The central issue here was the place of pagan
literature in the curriculum and the primacy of theology. The controversy, prompted by the claim of the poet Sigismund Buchwald of Vratis-
lava that poetry was the source and origin of theology, quickly mush-
roomed. The matter was first taken up by Martin Polich of Mellerstadt

and Conrad Wimpina, then by their "seconds" Johann Seitz and Hermann Buschius.[18]

A controversy at the University of Ingolstadt had a similar multiplier effect. Here Jacob Locher infringed on theological territory by praising poetry at the expense of theology and recommending a return to the Fathers, the "classics" of the Church. His provocative writings prompted an indignant reply from an elderly theologian, Georg Zingel, who had the support of the rector as well as of the well-known scholar Jacob Wimpheling. The controversy issued in a variety of publications: scurrilous invective by Locher, articles in the scholastic fashion by Zingel, an institutional response by the rector, and a double-barrelled entry by Wimpheling—a learned apology of scholastic theology and a personal attack on Locher in the form of a mock-confession.[19]

Mutianus Rufus' correspondence mentions a similar disturbance at the University of Erfurt in 1513, involving the poet Tilman Conradi. The "sophists," he reported, suborned another humanist, Euricius Cordus, to represent their side. Mutianus pleaded with the two humanists to close ranks against the common enemy, or else "the victory will belong to those who fear for their *Parva logicalia*, who are gnawed by the worm of envy, who cannot joyfully embrace the eloquence of others, who are still eating acorns after agriculture has been invented, and blink at the light of a more polished learning with blinded eyes. They are people of the sort that are commonly considered saintly and who have for many years imposed on good minds their flawed precepts and lies, not to say nonsense." He advised Conradi and Cordus to join hands and say to each other: "This is patent madness. Let us follow the Muses. Let us be good friends and not place too much trust in the theologians. They don't like either of us." In another letter, Mutianus described the indignation of the established professors at being criticized by "poetasters" and their resentment at the new emphasis on literature and language studies. He felt overwhelmed by their numbers: "How can you [Urbanus Rhegius] and I reform so many *magistri?*" he asks in desperation.[20]

The conflict was not confined to German universities. A letter written in 1518 by Thomas More to the senate of the University of Oxford offers evidence of similar tensions and divisions there.[21] A group of theologians called themselves Trojans, to mark their opposition to Greek language studies. According to More, they had first "made fun of the students of Greek learning" (133) and soon began to revile not only Greek studies but also "stylistic refinement in Latin" and, more generally, "all liberal arts" (135). More vividly describes the machinations of the ringleader of the Trojans: "Climbing into the pulpit clad in an academic gown, with a furred hood on his shoulders," he denounces the champions of classical Latin, "of which he understands only a little," and, more generally, "liberal studies, of which he understands even less, and specifically the Greek language, of which he understands not one iota" (137). More ends his letter with a plea that the senate "suppress such unsavory factions" and restore peace, for a university "racked by contention" will go to ruin.[22]

As More was addressing his concerns to the University of Oxford, Erasmus became the focus of the humanist-scholastic debate at Louvain. Considerable resentment against the Collegium Trilingue, in whose organization Erasmus had taken an active interest, played a role, but his philological work on the New Testament and his emphasis on language studies in theology had also made him unpopular with the faculty of theology at Louvain. The merry-go-round of polemics began in 1514, with an exchange between Erasmus and Maarten van Dorp, and continued over the next two decades with attacks by Jan Briart of Ath, Edward Lee, Jacques Masson, Vincentius Theoderici, and Frans Titelmans, all members or associates of the faculty of theology.[23] Erasmus in turn was supported by an international coterie of humanists who obliged him by denigrating the Louvain theologians in letters and lampoons. The confrontations between Erasmus and the Louvain theologians at first centered on style and on the role of philology and language studies in theology but, in a characteristic development, progressed to doctrinal quarrels.

A similar combination of traditionalism and fear of heterodoxy had made Elio Nebrija's position at the University of Salamanca difficult. The application of philological skills to biblical studies made him persona non grata, and the Inquisitor Diego de Deza confiscated his manuscripts. Even the more enlightened team of scholars working on the Polyglot edition at Alcala had difficulties with the uncompromising humanist's stand on textual criticism.[24]

Paris was more successful than other universities in Northern Europe in holding the humanists at bay, but there too we find cracks in the institutional solidarity. Noël Béda, syndic of the faculty of theology and the most zealous persecutor of humanism, which he equated with heterodoxy, occasionally found it difficult to rally the support of his colleagues. Contemporaries alleged that pressure tactics were used to bring dissidents in line. Erasmus—admittedly not a neutral source—described the procedure: "Matters are decided in private at first. The better sort of men are excluded, suitable men taken into confidence; then the matter is introduced with a recommendation to maintain solidarity. Threats are added." Some people kept silent because they were intimidated, he said; others suppressed their opinion to further their careers; still others did not understand the implication of their vote. And this is how decrees were made at Paris.[25] An anonymous pamphlet which appeared in 1547 repeats some of the same accusations. There are a great number of yes-men on the faculty, we read. Speaking one's mind is discouraged. "If anyone dared as much as open his mouth to say what he thinks and to ask questions, his eyes would be torn out of his head."[26]

The Paris theologians, moreover, had the authority to define ortho-doxy and were prepared to enforce their point of view with inquisitorial proceedings. Although the implementation of verdicts did not come within the scope of their responsibilities, their recommendations could lead to embarrassment, financial loss, exile, and even death. The human-ists Lefèvre, Erasmus, and Berquin were among their prominent victims. The hostility of the Paris theologians toward the *studia humanitatis* is expressed in Dullard's pronouncement "The better the grammarian, the worse the theologian and dialectician," which is echoed in Erasmus' sar-castic comment on the progress of his studies at Paris: "I am trying with might and main to say nothing in good Latin, or elegantly, or wittily, and I seem to be making progress; so there is some hope that, eventually, they will acknowledge me."[27] Efforts to reform the faculty of theology in 1533 accordingly met with stiff resistance. The theologians were con-vinced that "reform in the Faculty . . . would, in turn, promote reform in the Church."[28]

The situation at Italian universities was rather different. The earliest humanists disdained university appointments, preferring chancellor-ships and posts as ducal or apostolic secretaries to academic careers. This changed in the second half of the fifteenth century, when professorships in the humanities became prestigious and well paid. Rivalry between hu-manists and theologians did not arise, however, because the scholastics' presence at the universities was negligible, theology being taught mainly at religious houses.[29] Even in Italy, however, the progress of the *studia humanitatis* was not unimpeded, especially at smaller institutions. Ac-cording to Aonio Paleario (1503–1570), the studio of Lucca (admittedly a cultural backwater) put up considerable resistance: "There was incredi-ble plotting against *bonae literae* by those who practised a sordid and flawed style . . .; the barbarians defiled not only philosophy and civil law, but even poetry and rhetoric; and if the most eloquent and learned men had not objected, *bonae literae* would have been cast into eternal night."[30]

By citing the controversies at universities as examples of the humanist-scholastic debate I do not mean to exclude other designations. The conflicts mentioned were no doubt informed by a variety of motives: personal animosity, professional envy and career ambitions, confessional divisions, traditionalism and resistance to change. It is common practice for polemicists (past and present) to camouflage the pettiness or lack of respectability of their own cause by attaching it to a larger, more respectable and rationally defensible issue. It is not surprising therefore to find sixteenth-century controversialists pinning their personal peeves to prominent movements. They could thus claim that theirs was not a personal attack on X but an attack on a "champion of pagan humanism" or, conversely, one of the "scholastic barbarians." The very fact that the writers in question used slogans associated with the movements of humanism or scholasticism is significant, however. It means that they considered them readily identifiable and expected them to appeal to contemporary readers. The presence of catchphrases and characteristic arguments does not automatically designate a polemic as an example of the humanist-scholastic debate, but it shows that those arguments were regarded as effective and that the controversy was a live issue. To further document the existence, intensity, and scope of the conflict, and to pinpoint recurrent themes, a thematic approach will be adopted in the following. Within the ongoing conflict, two issues are holdovers, so to speak, from the previous century: misgivings about (or, on the humanistic side, defense of) classical literature and arguments for and against the scholastic style and method.

The first issue is tackled, for example, by Johannes Landsberger, a student of the Leipzig humanist Jacobus Barinus. His *Praise and Blame of Poetry* (1494)[31] is cast in dialogue form and introduces two characters, Emulus ("Envious") and Fautor ("Champion"). Emulus expresses misgivings about the popularity of poetry, an impious subject in his opinion. He proposes a more suitable curriculum for students, recommending speculative (rather than positive) grammar as a stepping stone to logic. Logic, he says, sharpens the mind; poetry and *studia humanitatis*, by contrast, corrupt morals. Fautor, in turn, defends the merits of literary studies. As the dialogues unfolds, each speaker cites authorities in support of his position. Fautor refers Emulus to Jerome's criticism of dialectic and Augustine's praise of Virgil; Emulus parries by noting that Plato drove the poets out of the ideal state. Fautor then argues that classical authors offer a storehouse of knowledge.[32] He concedes, however, that not all pagan literature is suitable for Christians and therefore proffers the familiar advice: readers must be judicious and, like bees, collect from all sources what is appropriate. What appears to be objectionable at first glance may have its uses: the poets' description of vices will repel readers, their paganism warn them to adopt the Christian way of life. After all, even the Bible, the most salutary book, related salacious stories, and Christ himself [sic] recommended the spoiling of the Egyptians. Emulus remains unconvinced by these argument. *Studere poetis est errare,* he concludes, "to study poetry is to fall into error." Fautor, however, has the last word, accusing his adversary of criticizing what he is unable to achieve himself. Characteristic of the second, more earnest phase, the dialogue does not end in polite accommodation. The author does not attempt to camouflage his sympathies and, except for the metaphorical naming of the protagonists, makes no effort to create a literary setting for this purely didactic dialogue.

The points made in Landsberger's dialogue are repeated in a quodlibetical disputation held at the University of Leipzig on the *quaestio* "Whether the poets, called divine seers, . . . ought to be driven out of the state, as some say, quoting the godly Plato."[33] The respondent, one Matthaeus Lupinus, argued in this manner: If Leipzig drove out all poets, no faculty would remain intact. There would be no hymns to God and no poetry to arouse the virtuous emotions of youth. Those who cited Plato were misrepresenting the philosopher. He had not wished to drive out all poets, but only those who aroused excessive and undesirable emotions. If Plato were alive today, Lupinus said, he would no doubt object to the fire-and-brimstone sermons of certain preachers. He put the question into its historical context, quoting Plato's acknowledgment that "there was an old disagreement between poetry and philosophy." Modern theologians, continuing this debate, claimed that poetry was contrary to the teachings of Scripture, but they were in fact ignorant of the poet's task and unable to distinguish between good and bad poets. He concludes with quotations from the Old Testament to show that poetry was an accepted part of Church tradition.

We find the same motifs in the controversy between Wimpina, Polich, and their respective followers, also at Leipzig. Wimpina, speaking in defense of theology, published a tract under the lengthy title *Apologia in defense of sacred theology against those who have tried to set up poetry as its source, head, and mistress, thus failing to acknowledge and respect the sacred science of God, which is truly the ruler of our religion and architect of all sciences* (Leipzig, ca. 1500). The title serves as a summary of the contents. The author explained that he could not accept "a poet putting himself ahead of a theologian and, so to speak, pushing the theologians off the citadel, wanting them to yield to the poets" (A v recto). Although he points out that he is directing his words not against all poets but only against those who made excessive claims for themselves, Wimpina shows considerable hostility against poetry as a subject, repeating the old clichés about the poet's frivolity and "deceptive froth" (*fucata spumositas*, A ii verso). "Giving their lives completely over to poetic fiction, they are swollen with ambrosia and soaked in nectar from Pegasus' source" (B i recto). No wonder they disdain Aristotle, from whom scholastic doctors like Thomas Aquinas and Albertus Magnus drew their wisdom, and look down on the Bible "besmeared as they are with poetic make-up and Apollo's rhetoric" (ibidem). Their minds corrupted by these studies, they "turn to the soft delicacies of the Muses and are sickened by the writings that give true satisfaction and pleasure" (B vii recto).

A contemporary polemic between Locher and Zingel at Ingolstadt attracted the attention of Jacob Wimpheling and prompted him to write in defense of theology. Wimpheling was an unlikely protagonist in the polemic. He had, after all, written an *Oration in Support of Harmony between Dialecticians and Orators* (1499), in which he praised poetry and preached the compatibility of literature and logic.[34] Moreover, during his long career at the University of Freiburg, he had published poems, a play in the classical manner, and manuals on grammar and style in which he promoted classical learning and supported the study of poetry, drawing the line only at "lewd and obscene" poets like Juvenal and Catullus, who were obviously unsuitable for use in school. Indeed he complained in his *Castigationes* (Strasbourg, 1513) that students did not study "any poets and were quite ignorant of the difference between verse and prose."[35] Nor had Wimpheling always been on bad terms with Locher. In 1505 the latter had praised Wimpheling's *De integritate*, and Wimpheling was sufficiently flattered to add Locher's endorsement to the text. "The chapters are pertinent," Locher had written to Wimpheling, "and your style is conversational, almost stoic but not crawling on the ground, and well suited to this kind of instruction. What you teach is pious and worthy of a theologian and of benefit to chaste persons."[36]

It seems, however, that Wimpheling was exercised by the general lack of respect shown to theologians in his time. In his *Apologia pro republica Christiana* (Pforzheim, 1506) he protested: "The error and blindness of certain scholars of our time is such that they disdain the Bible and biblical studies, that they call a man a theologian to deride him or show their contempt. 'He is a theologian,' they say, jeering and laughing, caring nothing for him, thinking him worth nothing, as if he were a man of no merit, good for nothing, worthy of no honor. I have heard it quite often."[37] He therefore decided to become involved in the Ingolstadt controversy, contributing a curious piece, *Confessionale*, a model "confession" written for Locher's use. It reinforced the negative image

promoted by the opponents of the *studia humanitatis* of the poet/human-
ist as corruptor of youth. Wimpheling suggested that Locher confess his
sins and address himself to God as follows:[38]

> Forgive me for scandalizing young students with filthy words,
> speaking of the sex act and in this manner inciting or inflaming their
> libido; for expressly naming that act in the most boorish manner
> and saying that you "couldn't sweat it out," indicating that conti-
> nence was impossible. Forgive me for writing and posting poems
> against certain people, whom I called "pseudotheologians"; . . . for
> inveighing against Georg Zingel, with whom I once shared a table;
> . . . for inciting, during a public lecture in 1505, my audience (about
> a hundred students) against good Christians and saying that they
> should attack and mug them; . . . for wearing the most outrageous
> clothes, split and particoloured, which is inappropriate attire for a
> scholar, and for inciting young students to do likewise, acting as
> their head and leader. Forgive me for threatening, when I did not
> get my wish in everything, to leave and take a great part of the stu-
> dents with me . . . forgive me . . . for praising Ovid and criticizing
> . . . Christians for the sake of a lightweight pagan . . . Forgive me
> for wanting people to defer to me in the school and in processions
> . . . although I am nothing but a poet laureate, that is, have only a
> degree of sorts in poetry or the art of versifying, telling pagan sto-
> ries, and explaining certain poets, which any insignificant school-
> teacher can do for boys in private school every day and everywhere
> . . . forgive me, dear God, for being so vindictive that I carped more
> about Georg Zingel than any historian ever did about Nero or He-
> liogabalus . . . I would rather suffer the deserved penalty and dis-
> honour than be cast into the eternal fire by you, the most equitable
> of judges.

In his second contribution to the dispute, *Against Locher's Shameful Pamphlet . . .*, Wimpheling also showed considerable hostility toward poetry.
It offered "poison covered with honey," he said, "so that if I had children
or nephews I would not want them to attend lectures in poetry."[39] This
partisan piece shows Wimpheling in the persona of the polemicist, a role
that obliged him to take a more radical stand than he could consistently
maintain. For this reason we find him, a year later, offering this clarification of his stand in an open letter "to all poets and champions of
poetry":

> Do not suspect, I beg you, on the basis of my defense of scholastic
> theology . . . that I disdain all poets and all poetry, as [Locher] dis-

dains all sacred questions . . . Even as an old man I still take pleasure in Prudentius and Baptista Mantuanus, so that you can clearly see that I am no hater or enemy of the poets . . . [I advocate] using studies not for flattery, not for pleasure, not for vanity, but for understanding more sublime writings, for praising God, and bringing advantage to the state, realizing that one kind of study is appropriate to youth, another to the mature adult or the old man.[40]

The texts quoted so far show that the controversies originating at universities in Northern Europe perpetuated some of the views expressed by Italian polemicists concerning the place of pagan learning in Christian education. A second theme that is taken over into the sixteenth century is the discussion concerning style and method. Once again we find humanists painting scholastics as barbarians and sophists, but whereas the scholastics left few marks on the literary landscape of fifteenth-century Italy, they found their voice in the academic feuds of the sixteenth century. Thus scholasticism had vocal defenders in Wimpina, Wimpheling, and Masson, whom we have already mentioned as protagonists in the debate, as well as the Spanish theologian Melchior Cano, who was active a generation later.

In his *Apologia on Behalf of Sacred Theology*[41] Wimpina demanded that a debate which concerned theology be carried on in a scholastic or, as he puts it, "Aristotelian" manner (A iii recto). On second thought he decided that this method was wasted on an irrational poet "who is wrapped up in his verses and frenzied by his Muses." He must be treated "not with arguments and syllogisms, but with fists and sticks" (A iv recto). In spite of these threats, however, he kept to the academic arena.

Martin Polich of Mellerstadt, who answered Wimpina in a tract entitled *Brief Statement . . . in Defense of Poetry* (1500), challenged the importance of using the scholastic method in theology and contrasted it with revealed truth. A theologian held that title "not by virtue of disputing in the circle of scholastics or standing at the lectern, but by being anointed by the Holy Spirit and illuminated by God . . . This is the theology of all the saints and even the angels. Yet they did not learn it from a lecturer."[42] This divinely inspired theology is superior to its human counterpart since all human effort is futile, and the Church admonishes us "not to be carried away by windy science and not to waste a Christian life on disputations and questions, but to walk in humility, modesty, and charity." Polich adds to this criticism of scholastic theologians the usual *loci communes:* their speech is barbarous; they have an inflated opinion of themselves and their titles; they treat of inane matters, "old wives' tales and sodden dreams," and vain questions, "for example, how Adam would have fathered children if he had not sinned, and numerous other such questions which even a madman like Orestes would call mad."[43]

Polich's apologia prompted an antapologia from Wimpina, *Response and Apologia . . . against the Brief Statement . . .* (1502),[44] in which he tries to overwhelm his adversary with a flood of quotations from patristic and scholastic authors. His defense of scholastic theology furthermore stresses its rational and orderly character. The scholastic "makes use in the first instance of rational argumentation and strives to defend faith against garrulous challengers who show more bluster than ability. Should the certainty of rational arguments fail us, we do not take refuge in poetry . . . but in Holy Scripture, which is our basic authority and from which we draw certainty in argumentation" (B iii verso). Scholastic theology is organized according to rational principles. "Our sacred theology is not disorganized but tightly structured, covering a multitude of interconnected questions." This structure is "derived from authority, reason, and definition, on the basis of which theology determines, examines, and explains what is knowable" (D v recto). Poetry, by contrast, cannot determine anything with certainty but merely "provides an impression of things through figurative representation and produces belief [rather than knowledge]" (D iii verso). Wimpina challenged his adversary to face him in a public disputation before members of the university, adding ominously, "or before an examiner of heretical depravity" (F v recto).

The value of the scholastic method was also discussed in the dispute between Locher and Zingel at Ingolstadt. In 1496 Locher published an oration *On Humanistic Studies and in Praise of Poetry,*[45] in which he praised classical philosophy, the theology of the Fathers, and finally "the admirable and useful discipline of the poets and orators . . . Here is where we learn to soften barbarous words, to express concepts elegantly, to speak always with beauty, fluency, and order" (b ii verso). In *Theologica Emphasis,* published the same year, he again praised the Fathers at the expense of modern theologians.[46] His effusions did not endear Locher to the theologians, nor did his next publication, a collection of "elegant phrases" from the Psalms, which were meant as a challenge to present-day theologians wasting their lives on "obscure, garrulous, and mouldy matters of slight service to the Church."[47] The resulting tensions led to his resignation in 1503 and prompted him to publish the extravagant *Comparison between the Mule and the Muse.*[48]

Poetry, he claimed in this piece, was the forerunner of theology: *ex poetis facti professores theosophiae* (C ii recto). As for the accusation that the poets were frivolous and obscene, in Locher's opinion there were "more poets than theologians in heaven" (A v verso). His criticism of scholastic theologians rested on the usual commonplaces. They were "arrogant boasters relying on barbarous words and gross solecisms"; they liked to create "Gordian knots," spread their "logical nets," and treat of inane questions.[49] Putting his feelings into verse, he proclaimed:

> No theologian he, who's born of strife, a son
> of Buridan and Ockham or of Scotus' blood,
> Marsilius' scion, or Maufelt's, or else
> Burleus' or Brulifer's or Holcot's son. (B ii verso)

The illustrations accompanying his text graphically depict Locher's preferences. In one woodcut, the triumphal float of Theology is moved along by the Fathers. In another, straw is threshed by five scholastics, named "Sophister," "Must-eater," "Phoebus-hater," "Petty," and "Logi-grackle." The meaning of the illustration is explained in a remarkable collection of mixed metaphors:

> Competing on the threshing floor, they flail the empty straw, going after chaff; they draw doctrine from the murky raintrough; they search for wisdom in a multifarious griffin of complex questions and in inextricable knots; they card the useless and gross goatswool; in enigmatic coils and entangled refutations, in the wordy labyrinth of error, they look for the clear and true theological tradition. They make plain matters difficult, seek for a knot in the bulrush, want to please God with loquaciousness, whereas he cares for neither logic nor sophistic garrulity . . . and so the days pass and they make no progress. (D i verso)

Zingel answered Locher's attack in typically scholastic fashion, by excerpting twenty-four articles from Locher's tract and submitting them to the rector, alleging that they were heretical or at any rate scandalous and "offensive to pious ears."[50] Thus a second round of polemics began, which included Wimpheling's defense of scholastic theology.[51] In it he argued that the method of posing questions, condemned by Locher, had been used by the prophets, evangelists, and Christ himself. Indeed, Augustine wrote that "the truth cannot be investigated by any better method than question and answer." Scholastic disputations were necessary and useful in the pursuit of truth, Wimpheling said, and the method was validated by the practice of "numerous and great men . . . in Paris, in many German universities, and in the sacred houses of the mendicant orders, who read these questions avidly, elucidate them, excerpt them, seek the truth in them, and on their basis teach the people ... What difference does it make whether they are written in a humble or proud style, as long as the truth is clearly found in them?" Scholastic questions were necessary "to overcome heretics"; and dialectic was one of "the principal pillars of the Catholic Church."

Wimpina and Wimpheling proffer a number of arguments that were to become standard elements of defenses of scholastic theology: it presents an orderly approach; it rests on tradition; it offers certainty; it equips the theologian with effective weapons against heretics. These arguments recur in the controversy between Erasmus and the Louvain theologians Maarten van Dorp and Jacques Masson.

Attacking scholastic theology, Erasmus had caricatured the traditional curriculum in a letter to Dorp. He provided this thumbnail sketch of the type of theologian that aroused the humanists' contempt:

They get by heart a few rules from [the grammar of] Alexander Gallus, and strike up an acquaintance with a little idiotic formal logic, and then get hold of ten propositions out of Aristotle, and even those they do not understand; after that they learn the same number of *quaestiones* from Scotus or Ockham, intending to resort for anything else to the *Catholicon*, the *Mammotrectus* and similar wordbooks, as though they were a horn of plenty. Whereupon it is astonishing the airs they give themselves, for nothing is so arrogant as ignorance ... Nothing is so brazen, so pig-headed, as ignorance. These are the men who conspire with such zeal against the humanities.   (CWE Ep 337:325–41)

In his reply Dorp defended scholasticism and its representatives. He noted that the Pope had canonized Thomas Aquinas, "accepting as miracles the *quaestiones* he left behind." He furthermore cited Jerome, who had stated that heresies were "undermined by the art of dialectic," and Augustine, who taught that our understanding of Holy Writ was aided by "the discipline of logical argument, of syllogism and definition and analysis."[52] Language studies alone could not prepare the theologian for his task. It was essential that he be versed in scholastic writings as well. "Otherwise how shall we know how the sacraments ought to be administered, what their proper forms are, when absolution should be given to a sinner ... and countless points of the same kind? Unless I am much mistaken, it would need far less work to learn a large part of the Bible by heart, before you had learned to solve one of these knotty problems.

Yet many questions of this sort occur every day." These could not be solved without recourse to scholastic writers.[53]

When Dorp, who had written partly under pressure and partly for the sake of advancing his career, let himself be persuaded by Erasmus' arguments in favor of language studies, the Louvain theologians found a new champion in Jacques Masson. Masson accordingly published a dialogue *On the Three Tongues*,[54] in which he rejected the notion that language studies were essential to an understanding of Holy Writ. His dedicatory letter is testimony to the ongoing war between humanists and theologians. The humanists, he complains, "criticize scholastic exercises and reject scholastic doctors for their dry and humble style." He lamented that they "drew away students from Thomas, Bonaventure, Alexander of Hales, and other scholastic authors, calling it a waste of time to spend any time of one's life on them" (43–44). In the dialogue itself he praised scholasticism. There were five reasons "why the writings of scholastic doctors should be read" and must form an integral part of theological studies: (1) "The scholastics proceed in order . . . and treat everything distinctly and in its place"; (2) "you will find the entire material in scholastic writers . . . whereas in the old writers you find only certain aspects; thus you find in the scholastics in one place what you have to gather from ten or more places"; (3) "the scholastics teach according to the established rules of faith and sound doctrine . . . using plain and unequivocal words"; (4) "in the old times many matters were uncertain and unresolved, which were later determined by the Church . . . the old theologians speak of these matters in a rather careless and simplistic fashion"; (5) scholastics supply arguments against pagan philosophers who are "fierce enemies of faith" (72–73). After listing the advantages of the scholastic method, Masson answers two common objections: scholastic theologians deal with "curious and superfluous questions" and "contaminate theology, mixing in the leaven of Aristotelian philosophy" (74). His defense of scholastic quibbling is lame: "This is true of any profession: scholars do not work in isolation or on specific subjects but deal with everything in their subject area and for everyone's good, and in all of this there may be something which at some time or in some context or for some people is of no use" (74). His reply to the second objection is more elaborate. "If someone is dissatisfied with Thomas or Scotus because they seem too Aristotelian," there are alternatives: Bonaventure, for example, or William of Auxerre. In an interesting twist Masson cites Pico della Mirandola in defense of scholasticism. "He attests to having studied Thomas, Scotus, and Albert for more than six years. That divinely gifted man would never have done so unless he considered them good authors, in whom he found the truth. He was not offended by their humble scholastic style, for he sought not after deceptive words but after the truth" (74–5).

Similar arguments in defense of scholasticism appear in Melchior Cano's *De locis theologicis* (Salamanca, 1563). The Spanish Dominican had enjoyed a distinguished academic career teaching first at Valladolid, then being appointed to the first theological professorship at Alcala, and finally succeeding his mentor Francisco Vitoria at Salamanca.[55] In *De locis theologicis* he first announced that he was adhering to the scholastic terminology: "Let no candidate of polite literature demand polished speech from me in a scholastic disputation." He furthermore defended the scholastic style: "If the theologian does not bring eloquence to his task, I am far from despising him. Indeed, I demand that [he abstain from eloquence]." Praising scholastic theology, Cano offers the familiar arguments. The neglect of scholastic theology left the church exposed to heresy: "No one can despise scholasticism without danger to the faith. Ever since the rise of scholasticism, there has always been (and there is now) a connection between disrespect for the school and pestilential heresy." Granted that there are contentious and quibbling scholastics, the vices of individuals should not obscure the usefulness of the discipline. The scholastic method "clarifies and brings out of the darkness into the light what is hidden in Holy Writ and in the apostolic traditions." It provides a rational framework for faith; it defends the Church against heretics, "keeping the wolves from the flock." Scholastic theology is the "true theology, which combines all goals: a knowledge of God, an understanding of celestial things, and prudent application in human affairs . . . if we want to achieve these goals we must apply ourselves to scholastic theology, without which we cannot attain perfect Church doctrine."[56]

By the time Cano published his *Loci*, humanists had been attacking the scholastic edifice for a century, but formal replies from the scholastic camp were slow in forthcoming, perhaps, as suggested earlier, because scholasticism was so entrenched at Northern universities that its representatives could afford to ignore the voices of protest. The first and best-known defense of scholasticism therefore came, paradoxically, from Pico, who played devil's advocate. As the debate moved to universities north of the Alps and the scholastics encountered critics in their own backyard, it became impossible to keep a disdainful silence. The scholastics began to develop a canon of arguments in response to the humanistic attacks, as the above examples demonstrate. They defended their method as a useful and effective tool in training the mind and defending the orthodox faith. Ignoring internal divisions, they represented scholastic theology as a comprehensive, well-structured, monolithic body of doctrine capable of answering questions of orthodoxy with authority. They furthermore defended the "Parisian style" as the technical language needed to discuss theological matters with precision, and they rejected grammatical and rhetorical considerations as not applicable to their subject.

The examples cited so far also document the continuity of the discussion concerning the value of pagan literature and the debate over the merits of the scholastic style and method. But new issues came to the foreground in the second phase of the debate. They concern professional qualifications and ranking of academic disciplines.

The question whether humanists were competent and qualified to treat theological subjects is related to the larger question of whether or not a union of rhetoric and philosophy is possible. The separation of the two spheres was approved by some, lamented by others. Humanists generally deplored the dichotomy and advocated a return to the golden age of the Fathers, who had combined the qualities of wisdom and eloquence. Urbanus Rhegius' observations in the *Opusculum de dignitate sacerdotum* (Augsburg, 1519) are representative of the humanist point of view. Some people consider "the combination of eloquence and wisdom a chimaera or a centaur, whereas . . . they cannot and should not be separated." The Fathers had combined eloquence with wisdom. Jerome was knowledgeable in both dialectic and philology—"if he had not been equipped with these arts, how could he have become the hammer of heretics?" Yet some scholastics wanted to "restrict the scope of intellectual inquiry, even though the intellect is capable of many disciplines . . . Where there is eloquence, they say, there cannot possibly be erudition."[57] This was indeed the opinion of some scholastic theologians; others, however, did not fail to appreciate the power of rhetoric, the esthetic appeal of poetic language, and the satisfaction derived from a well-turned phrase, but wanted metaphor, simile, and other embellishments restricted to pastoral theology. Speculative theology, they said, should observe more stringent rules and employ the proper technical terminology.

A significant factor in the debate was the attitude the protagonists displayed toward the adversary's discipline. While both sides were critical of each other, the humanists invited the scholastics to enter into their realm and become humanistic theologians. The scholastics extended no such invitation; on the contrary, they expressly rejected the notion of "theologizing humanists," as Béda termed them. Hermann Buschius is representative of the humanistic position when he praises all-round learning, *kyklopaideia*, and notes that the scholastics reject this ideal, concentrating on one discipline—dialectic—to the exclusion of all others.[58] When humanists went beyond talk and actively interfered with theological prooftexts by extending their publishing activities from secular to sacred writings, the debate issued into a turf war.

In the debate involving the qualifications of the biblical scholar the scholastics took, as expected, a restrictive attitude. Their position (generally accepted in the Middle Ages) was that not every Christian was entitled to discuss, interpret, translate, or paraphrase Scripture; only those who were inspired by God, authorized by the Church, or academically qualified by a degree in theology could engage in such pursuits. The humanists, by contrast, argued that the tasks involved were a matter of human skill rather than divine inspiration, of ability and learning rather than authorization or academic standing. Underlying the debate was the fundamental distinction between laity and clergy, a distinction challenged during the Reformation and contrasted with the concept of a "priesthood of all believers." It is in these more fundamental questions that academic turf wars were anchored.

Lorenzo Valla was an early victim of efforts by theologians to circumscribe their sphere of operation and to exclude nonprofessionals from their territory. The Italian humanist undertook a study of the New Testament, collating the Vulgate with a number of Greek manuscripts and writing notes (first version dated 1443) concerning the accuracy of the Latin translation with respect to syntax and meaning. The work aroused considerable opposition, as did other of his writings which were seen to infringe on the subject of theology. In his *Antidotum*, Valla tells of an encounter with an indignant critic: "He immediately began to admonish and reprove me, telling me not to put my sickle into a crop that was not mine, to be content with my own field of learning, and to refrain from treating divine law with unwashed hands."[59]

The phrase "to put one's sickle into another man's crop," used in the Decretals in the context of delineating secular and ecclesiastical spheres of influence,[60] became the catchphrase of theologians protecting their academic turf. Thus when Sebastian Brant entered in a dispute concerning the Immaculate Conception of Mary, he was accused of trespassing on theological territory and reproved in a poem composed by the Dominican Wigandus Wirt:[61]

> With unwashed feet and words you touch what is divine,
> and with your oxen plough another's fields;

> unwilling to content yourself with your own lot,
> you put your unjust sickle to another's crop.

We encounter the phrase again in a letter addressed by Johann Seitz to Wimpina, in which he complimented him on his response to Polich, that "garrulous physician" who had dared to initiate a "grammatical dispute with theologians." Polich, his critic charges, had gone beyond his territory and "put his bold sickle into the theologians' crop."[62]

A few years later Crotus Rubeanus quoted the phrase in a letter to Reuchlin, relating that he had an argument with a monk "because he spluttered something about you, a lawyer, having put your sickle into the theologians' crop."[63] The phrase appeared again in Dorp's protest against Erasmus' efforts to correct the Vulgate. It was not for grammarians, Dorp said, "to put their sickles into other men's grain."[64] Similarly, Jacques Hasard, in a letter to Erasmus on the subject of his corrections to the Vulgate, insisted that philologists and theologians must keep to their respective disciplines: "Let each put his sickle into his own crop."[65]

The catchphrase pinpoints a problem that arose from the humanists' interest in textual criticism. The invention of printing had turned textual criticism from a scholar's pastime into a professional pursuit (or, as some put it, a trade for university dropouts). Printers needed an archetype to set their forms. If a text existed in more than one version, as was often the case with classical texts, one manuscript had to be chosen over another or a new text had to be established by collating manuscripts. Both processes, and in particular the latter, involved passing judgment on the text. Publishers naturally turned to humanists for this task, since it involved a knowledge of the classical languages, their special area of competence. As long as secular texts were involved, complaints arose only concerning the quality of the editor's scholarship, but when scriptural, patristic, or other theological texts were under consideration, further complications arose. The content was obviously within the competence of theologians, but in the fifteenth century few of them had the requisite language skills to supervise a critical edition. The printers' needs and the humanists' interests led to a disregard of traditional professional boundaries.

Erasmus, who published Valla's annotations on the Vulgate in 1505, defended the Italian humanist's work against charges of professional trespassing: "Will they maintain that Valla, the philologist, does not have the same right [to treat of Holy Writ] as Nicolaus [Lyra], the theologian? . . . When Lyra treats of words, does he do so in his capacity as theologian? Does he not rather act as a philologist? Indeed this whole business of translating Scripture is the business of a philologist." Elsewhere he made a point of complimenting Valla, the humanist, on his contribution to biblical studies: "Personally I think that Valla deserves much praise for applying himself so diligently to Holy Writ, considering that he was a man of letters *(homo rhetoricus)* rather than a theologian."[66]

A generation after Valla, Aurelio Brandolini, a versatile Neapolitan humanist attached to the papal court, wrote an "Epitome on the Sacred History of the Jews" based on the Bible and Josephus' history. He, too, faced questions concerning his professional qualifications. In his preface to the *Epitome*, addressed to Cardinal Francesco Piccolomini of Siena, he noted that his critics, "the class of men that boasts of their knowledge of sacred matters and abhor our writings," had used these arguments:

> A person who had not obtained the glory and distinction of a doctorate in theology was not permitted to write anything about sacred matters . . . that people like myself who are not doctors of theology (as they call themselves) had no right to deal with sacred matters. This was their task proper and only they were entitled to write about it; others were not. Secondly, even if others were entitled to write something on the subject, they were certainly not permitted to put the Bible, which contained all the mysteries of our religion, into different words or a different style or to change anything at all.

Brandolini scoffed at this insistence on academic qualifications: "Nowadays academic honors are conferred on anyone on account of power, wealth, or patronage, so that I cannot see how they can be proof of learning. For what men who are made doctors in this fashion either teach or write?"[67] "How much is their teaching worth? How much value should we put on their writings? On the other hand, there are many great scholars who do not have academic titles . . . it is not right that doctors rather than scholars *(magis doctoris esse quam docti)* should be entitled to write; nor is the man who lacks academic honors less competent to take this field than the man who walks around puffed up by such honors and the title of doctor."[68] Brandolini makes two other points in refuting his critics: every Christian is entitled to study the Bible; and a strict separation of biblical studies from other disciplines is not possible. Anticipating Erasmus' dictum that "every Christian can be a theologian," he asks: "Why do you suspect that I am not a theologian, when you know that I am a Christian?" Concerning the relationship between theology and philology he says: "What prevents me from being both a philologist and a theologian? for all disciplines are so related and interconnected that anyone who strives for perfection in one must touch on and acquire the others as well."[69]

At the end of the century the great Spanish philologist, Elio Antonio Nebrija, encountered similar difficulties. In an apologia addressed to Cardinal Ximenes, he noted that he was obliged to defend his biblical studies against those "who said a man trained only in grammar was not permitted to touch Holy Writ."[70] He mused that he could have avoided trouble had he busied himself with frivolous stuff: "If I had spent my time on fables and the figments of poets, had I wasted good time on writing stories, everything would have been wonderful . . . and everyone would have loved and praised me and congratulated me on such nonsense." He accepted the restrictions that prohibited the laity from pronouncing on theological questions, but pointed out that textual criticism fell within the philologist's domain: "What? Will Antonio Nebrija be refused permission to discuss orthography, when a scribe is permitted to corrupt every third word?"[71] Nebrija's contemporary and colleague at the University of Salamanca, Arias Barbosa, had a similar complaint. He deplored the segregation of academic disciplines favored by the theologians, noting in the apologetic preface to his commentary on Arator: "They are convinced that one person cannot possess a variety of skills. Therefore they cannot understand that I, a poor grammarian, should dare to interpret the verses of a poet-theologian like Arator. They say that this is the business of theology professors."[72]

In the conflict between Wimpina and Polich at the beginning of the sixteenth century, Polich noted how jealously the theologians guarded their title and position. This was the case not only at Leipzig, but at universities in Germany, France, and Italy as well, he said.[73] A few years later, humanists in Germany were galvanized by the Reuchlin affair, which was to some extent regarded as a showdown between philologists and theologians. Reuchlin himself noted the monopolizing tendencies of the theologians: "They consider no one else learned and set themselves up as the pillars of the Church . . . they have harassed a number of jurists and all the poets," he wrote. At first he showed a willingness to defer to the theologians. It was difficult "for a layman and one, moreover, who has been married twice, to explain the subtle points of theology," he wrote to the theologians of Cologne. "I do not claim such competence . . . I leave this to your excellent faculty." His attitude changed, however, as the controversy dragged on. "When I saw the immense stupidity of those great men, whom the common people regard as wise, and the injustice of those hypocrites and their intolerable malice, I found my strength again, took heart and became eager to defy them."[74] Hoogstraten had called him a grammarian out of his depth when it came to theological questions.[75] Reuchlin turned the question of competency against his critics. "Who set them up as judges over me and the counsel I gave?" He had been asked by the Emperor for a legal opinion, and even if it was a matter for theologians to decide, the qualifications of his adversaries were questionable.[76] Pfefferkorn was a recent convert. Arnold of Tongeren was "no Doctor of theology, except perhaps one who had been given a doctorate on the basis of nothing, for that is done sometimes."[77]

The dispute over academic qualifications is also reflected in contemporary satire. The *Letters of Obscure Men* lampoon the caginess of professional theologians. One of the fictitious writers reports the following dinner-table conversation between an unnamed guest and Petrus Meyer, city priest of Frankfurt and a supporter of Hoogstraten:

> [The unnamed guest] said: "Listen, Dr. Johann Reuchlin is more learned than you." And he snapped his fingers at him. Then Prof. Petrus said: "I'll be hanged if that's true. Holy Mary! Dr. Reuchlin is a schoolboy as far as theology is concerned. A schoolboy knows more of theology than Dr. Reuchlin. Holy Mary, believe me, I know what I'm talking about. He knows nothing as far as the Book of Sentences is concerned. Holy Mary, now that's subtle stuff! Men can't understand it like they do grammar or poetry. I could be a poet if I would know how to put verses together 'cause I've taken a course in Leipzig in Sulpitius on the quantities of syllables. But listen, let him come and ask me a question about theology and argue the pros and cons!" And he proved with many arguments that no one is a perfect theologian unless by the grace of the Holy Spirit: "It is the Holy Spirit that instils this art. And poetry is the work of the devil, as Jerome said in his epistolary." Then that buffoon [the unnamed guest] said that it wasn't so, that Dr. Reuchlin also had the Holy Spirit and that he knew theology quite well and had written a very theological book, the title of which escapes me, and he called Prof. Petrus a beast. And he said that Prof. Hoogstraten is a cheese-paring monk. And everybody around the table laughed. And I said that it was a scandal that a Professor got no respect from a simple fellow.[78]

In another letter, the writer is doubtful about accepting advice without being assured of the adviser's qualifications: "He calls himself a theologian, but he appears to be more of a poet."[79] The contempt of the theologians for anyone who was not a professional is noted by Pirckheimer, who writes with rhetorical exaggeration: "They turn their noses up on St. Jerome, calling him a 'grammarian' and they consider Augustine ignorant. He would—so they blather—not understand their language."[80] Hermann Buschius reports how contemptuous the Cologne theologians were of the verdict rendered in favor of Reuchlin by the Bishop of Spires. He was no Doctor of theology, after all. Observing a man reading the verdict, which was posted on the church doors, Hoogstraten told him to read the verdict of the Paris theologians instead, "'Hey, you!' he hollered, 'why are you looking at that stuff? Why don't you instead read this here?' . . . [when the man continued reading, he added] 'What? You dare to put the verdict of that boy-bishop of Spires ahead of the verdict rendered by eighty doctors of theology from Paris?'"[81] The closed mind of some theologians and their misgivings against meddling humanists and other nonprofessionals can also be seen from an anecdote related by the English diplomat and scholar Richard Pace, in *The Benefit of Liberal Education* (1518). A "Scotist" whom Pace tried to engage in a discussion about Erasmus' alleged heresies demurred, noting: "Your Lordship is no theologian. I am a scholar, I would have you know, I have read at Pisa."[82] The prize for arrogance goes to Cousturier, however, who discounted Pope Leo X's endorsement of Erasmus' New Testament with the words: "Leo was no theologian and had no experience in these matters; he was therefore not capable of rendering a valid judgment."[83]

That the hostility of theologians against trespassing humanists was not merely a matter of clerics trying to keep out laymen but also a dispute about academic qualifications is clear from Erasmus' own case. Erasmus was a member of the Augustinian Canons, but his status as a religious made no difference to his critics at Louvain. The only thing that counted in their eyes was an academic degree. The statutes of the University of Louvain (1485) declared that no one was to be admitted to the faculty unless his doctorate or license was from "a reputable university known for its rigorous examination." A regulation was passed to exclude those who had bought their degrees (*bullati*) or received them under extraordinary circumstances (*per saltum*) or were moving from one university to the next (*discurrentes*) so that their qualifications were difficult to assess.[84] Accordingly, Erasmus, who had obtained his doctorate at Turin *per saltum*, was not admitted to the *collegium strictum* of the faculty of theology, but after some negotiations he was given adjunct status—"coopted into the faculty," as he put it.[85] He found to his chagrin that this did not carry weight with Paris theologians. Noël Béda, who as syndic of the faculty wielded considerable power, failed to recognize him as a "fellow-theologian" (*syntheologus*).[86] In fact, he was incensed that

Erasmus—in his opinion nothing but a philologist—would meddle in matters outside his expertise. "There are people," he said, "who, being competent only in the humanities and in language studies, have undertaken to discuss all sacred matters." These "theologizing humanists" looked down on the scholastics, saying that they were "not competent in their own field, grew old in a jungle of arguments and sophisms, and had barely reached the threshold of the divine Word." They boasted of their own achievements at the expense of the theologians, "making derogatory remarks about the scholastic doctors, calling them 'rabbis', thickheaded barbarians, ignorant of polite literature and for that reason opposed to the humanists."[87]

Lopis Stunica, a graduate of the University of Salamanca living in Rome, shared Béda's views. Both Erasmus and Lefèvre had overreached themselves. They had exceeded the boundaries of their professional competence : "Erasmus has won considerable fame among the champions of the humanities . . . but, not content with his portion, . . . he undertook to translate the New Testament from Greek into Latin and added annotations . . . Up to this point he had experience only with secular authors and learned secular eloquence from them; proud of his pure style he thought he had leave to do anything and everything."[88]

The Paris theologian Pierre Cousturier likewise snubbed Erasmus. In his *Antapologia* (Paris, 1526) he voiced suspicions about his academic qualifications and expressed contempt for this "new type of professor" and his alma mater—"a hapless university for granting a degree to such an antitheologian." In his opinion, he was merely "a grammarian who knows nothing about dialectic philosophy and theology, yet presumes to tackle everything." In an earlier work against new translations of the Bible, *De tralatione Bibliae* (Paris, 1525), he lashed out against meddling humanists in general. They were "vain and presumptuous men who treat Holy Writ arrogantly and without respect, who interpret it perversely and teach and boast of what they have never learned, . . . who do not realize that there is a difference between faith and theology and that if someone is a believer it does not immediately follow that he is a theologian."[89]

When the faculty of theology at Paris publicly censured Erasmus' works in 1531, the examiners issued an official warning to biblical humanists: "Those who think that a knowledge of Greek and Hebrew is the equivalent of consummate theology should take note that those who know languages but have not received instruction in the discipline of theology are to be considered philologists (*grammatici*), not theologians."[90]

The battle over academic qualifications is also documented in a complaint filed by Béda in 1534 against the lecturers of the Collège de France. In a document entitled "Requête contre les lecteurs royaux," which he presented to the Parlement, he asked that "they be prevented from interpreting any part of Holy Scripture in Hebrew of Greek." He expressed indignation that "simple grammarians or rhetoricians who had not studied in the faculty of theology, had the gall to give public lectures on Holy Scripture and to interpret it . . . an action that might lead to serious consequences with respect to the faith and the Christian commonwealth." He pointed out that the lecturers had not been certified by the faculty of theology which had sole jurisdiction over religious instruction. He feared that these dilettantes "who perhaps have no understanding of theology" might criticize the Vulgate and apply human skills to an inspired text, "presuming to correct the said translation, as did Erasmus, Lefèvre, and others, to the great detriment of Christendom."[91]

Closely linked to the debate over professional qualifications is the dispute over ranking—the implication being that humanists were seeking to improve their standing by breaking into a more exalted discipline. At Wittenberg the statutes gave poets a place beside the *magistri artium*, "for the laurel and the magisterium are comparable,"[92] but some scholars would have denied all academic standing to them, let alone allowed a comparison between poets and theologians. Wimpheling, for example, protested that Locher's claims for the importance of poetry were preposterous, for the poet "has no academic standing whatsoever except for being called 'poet,' if one can rightly speak of a degree in poetry, which is only a very small part of one subject, grammar, which in itself is the lowest step in the liberal arts. Poetry barely deserves the name of a science or liberal art, for it is not based on any principles and can produce neither proof nor conclusions."[93] In a similar vein Johann Eck intoned that "no one could doubt that the most sacred discipline of theology, which has been devised by God, was more excellent than the other disciplines, devised by the human mind."[94] Such claims to superior rank were at the root of the interfaculty disputes at Leipzig and Ingolstadt. In his *Apologeticus* Wimpina had reproached his opponent's audacity in praising poetry at the expense of theology. "Prudent men," he said, assigned first rank to theology. "Anyone suggesting that poetry was preferable to theology was demented or showed complete ignorance of the subtle nature of theology." He repeatedly stated that his quarrel was not with all poets but merely with those that attacked the primacy of theology. He "wished poetry safe and sound everywhere, as long as it is not preferred to theology"; and he respected poets "as long as they do not think of themselves as theologians and the champions, leaders, and fountainheads of theologians."[95]

This is in fact what Locher claimed, thus arousing indignation among the theologians of Ingolstadt. In the poem preceding the text of his *Comparison between the Muse and Mule*, he insisted that divine inspiration played a role in both poetry and theology. Poets were the "first theologians," "divine seers spring from our stock." He therefore protested against Zingel, "that ignorant theologian who compares the poets with mules, as if they were infertile." In fact, the mule image was more suitable for theology. "Does the mule give birth? Yes, to stinking dung, from which rises the boorish and wordy theologian who bursts with jealousy and all the time sows the seeds of dissent and is driven by black furies."[96]

Wimpheling, who defended the primacy of theology against the claims of Locher, had affirmed his creed first in *De ortu progressu et fructu theologiae*, where he noted that "theology, . . . born from a higher order, surpassed all sciences."[97] In his reply to Locher, Wimpheling again addressed himself to those "who pay too much tribute to the Muses and poets." He conceded to the "versifier" a knowledge of mythology, metric, and the art of declaiming "like an actor with fake tears," but would not concede to him the higher skills needed to interpret Holy Writ.[98]

The primacy of theology was challenged also by Lucio Flaminio Sicculo in an oration delivered at Salamanca in 1504. He assigned first place to rhetoric. The other arts, he said, "were handmaids of eloquence and serve her; without her splendor and ornament they would be mean and . . . and there would be uncertainty in the minds about everything, and matters would remain unknown." Rhetoric, he continued, was a discipline "more suited to discover the truth than that which they call by a Greek loanword 'dialectic,' which—if it can be called an art of speaking at all—is more concerned with judgment than with invention."[99]

A similar challenge was issued by Petrus Mosellanus in an inaugural address he delivered in 1518 at the University of Leipzig. He depicted language studies as fundamental to other disciplines,[100] asserting that "on [the knowledge of languages] depends the integrity of all divine as well as human disciplines." Conceptualization and rational thought are impossible without language, so that "if we are deprived of the support of languages we must necessarily err in our judgment." A ranking of academic disciplines with language studies as the preeminent and principal subject is also implied in his statement that language studies "can illumine every kind of discipline, but if they are lacking, everything remains obscure. They are in every respect beneficial to theologians, useful to jurists, even pleasant for students of medicine, fruitful for philosophers, in short, there is no discipline in which language studies are not absolutely necessary."

Mosellanus' oration sparked protests in the theological camp. In a reply, Masson reasserted the primacy of theology: "Theology . . . uses all disciplines as servants and instruments. They are not as essential to her as she is to them . . . thus one must think more highly of the most sacred discipline of theology. She does not depend on other arts; rather every art and science bows to Her Highness . . . Theology is the apex of all arts, its head and summit."[101]

A practical example of the competition for rank is recorded in the *Acta* of the University of Louvain. On several occasions, during graduation ceremonies, "a great difference and dispute arose about the order in the procession of the professors." At a meeting in August 1520, the "rector reported that he had received complaints from several members of the university, especially members of the theological faculty, because on the occasion of granting a doctorate to a jurist, the doctors of the college of both laws were given precedence over the professors of the faculty of theology, which seems to be and obviously is an absurdity." The rector appealed to those present to put away all partisan thought and show regard for the honor and welfare of the university. He appointed a committee with representatives from each faculty "to resolve the matter in an amicable manner" and report back within eight days. The fact that the matter was raised again at other meetings shows, however, that no speedy solution had been found.[102]

The theologians' insistence on first place in the academic hierarchy is lampooned in the *Letters of Obscure Men*. One of the writers reports indignantly that a lecturer at the University of Leipzig said "one poet was worth ten magisters; that in [academic] processions the poets ought to take precedence over the magisters and licentiates."[103] Interestingly, disgruntled theologians at Ingolstadt had in effect proclaimed that a poet was *not* worth two magisters. When Celtis was hired in 1492 at twice the usual rate of pay, they suggested "he should be let go and two [magistri] hired for the stipend he receives."[104]

In assigning poetry a higher rank than theology, Locher, Flaminio Sicculo, and Mosellanus are, however, in the minority. Although there was competition for rank, most humanists were prepared to pay homage to Queen Theology. Polich, setting his own record straight, wrote that Wimpina was fretting unnecessarily. "No one in his right mind would attack theology." Buschius, writing on Polich's behalf, likewise called the suggestion that "some poet preferred his subject to theology" a calumny. Similarly, Johannes Murmellius, who was instrumental in introducing humanistic curriculum at the cathredral school in Münster in the early 1500s, praised language studies yet asserted that theology "is of all sciences the mistress and queen." Disclaimers can also be found in More's letter to the University of Oxford. The liberal arts, he said, played an ancillary function. It was a case of "despoiling the women of Egypt to grace Queen Theology."[105] Although Dorp suggested that Erasmus introduced a preposterous order, "letting the grammarians sit on the throne and act as censors of all the other disciplines," the latter denied that he had meant to challenge the primacy of theology. Indeed, the metaphors he uses clearly reflect the traditional hierarchy of disciplines. In ranking them, he speaks of Queen Theology and her humble attendant, grammar. He compares theologians and philologists to Moses and Jethro respectively, and likens the services of grammarians to sweepers and cooks in a king's palace. In the conflict between humanists and theologians, both parties had shown a regrettable lack of moderation, he said. "One party [the theologians] clings with tooth and claw to things as they are, the other [the humanists] break in with undue violence, more like an enemy than a guest. Both sides are wrong."[106] He reassured theologians that the study of languages and literature would complement rather than threaten theology:

> The humanities are not brought in to do away with subjects which are taught, to the great benefit of the human race, in all our universities, but to purify them and make them more reasonable than they have been hitherto in some men's hands. Let theology by all means be the queen of sciences: no queen is so effective that she can dispense with the services of her handmaidens . . . if only those who are keen to enliven traditional learning with all that the humanities can offer would contribute their services courteously and peaceably, and those who have grown grey in the ancient subjects would not be so grudging towards themselves and their juniors but would welcome the new arrivals to share the rights of citizens in a generous spirit, we should see each group bring ornament and profit to the other.[107]

A conciliatory tone was also adopted by Matthaeus Adrianus, who taught Hebrew at the *Collegium Trilingue* in Louvain. Addressing a speech in praise of language studies to Masson and his colleagues on the faculty of theology, Adrianus suggested that praise of one's own discipline should not come at the expense of other faculties. If professors of dialectic wanted to eliminate rhetoricians, and if theologians were critical of students of literature, each discipline would be shortchanged.

Acknowledging the preeminent position of theology, he pleaded for tolerance: "Even if theology is the 'eye', must the 'tongue' be cut out as a useless member? Even if dialectic is the 'ear', must we cut off the 'feet'?"[108]

The disputes discussed so far show humanists up against the university establishment. A special case are the controversies surrounding the work of biblical humanists, which deserve to be discussed in more detail in the next chapter. In their instance the establishment that presents the challenge is the Church, but the protagonists are often the same we have encountered in the academic environment. As is to be expected, the spokesmen of the church are almost always scholastic theologians; their adversaries are professional teachers of languages and literature.

CHAPTER FIVE

Biblical Scholarship: Humanistic Innovators and Scholastic Defenders of Tradition

IN THE SIXTEENTH CENTURY the humanist-scholastic debate came to share the stage with two movements: the Reformation and the Catholic reaction. As Charles Gordon observed, "the essential ingredient of any successful movement [is] a sense of outrage."[1] The defenders of the old Church were indeed outraged. Not only had the humanists trespassed on territory subject to the jurisdiction of the Church, they were also promulgating scandalous and unheard-of views. They criticized the received text of the Bible, subjecting the Word of God to the rules of grammar and rhetoric, challenging the principle of inspiration, and undermining the traditions of the Church.

The charge of undermining custom and tradition, regularly incurred by the biblical humanists, was a grave one in the eyes of their contemporaries. Jacob Wimpheling noted the traditionalism of his age:[2]

> They will go on in the corrupt old way. Tradition is their only argument, the only defense of their folly. 'It is now fifty years (or: two, three, four centuries),' they cry out, 'that the text has been read this way; this is how our forefathers recited it.' My reply is that the same argument was used by Symmachus ... to draw Theodosius away from the Christian religion: 'The ancients worshipped idols. Our forefathers and the old ceremonies must be respected. Saturn, Jupiter, and Mars must be our gods. We are not the betters of our forefathers, nor do we wish to appear wiser than they. The old customs are tried and true.' The authority of tradition is so imprinted on their minds that they think it must be a crime to examine tradition.

There was no need for Wimpheling to invoke Theodosius when Jerome offered a more pertinent example. The Church Father encountered much the same criticism in his own day as the biblical humanists met in the Renaissance. In his prefaces to various books of the Bible, Jerome defended his enterprise against the traditionalists. "People are absurd," he observed. "They are always after new pleasures. Our seas cannot satisfy their appetite. How is it that in the case of Scripture alone they are content with the old taste?" His new translation was unpopular because it was like "an attempt to change an old man's speech and to recall an aging world to its youthful beginnings. For who among learned or unlearned people will not cry out on taking up the book and finding that the reading differs from that which he drank in with his nurse's milk? Who will not immediately call me a falsifier, a sacrilegious man who dares to make additions, changes, and corrections in old books?" The judgment of these people was faulty: they "evaluated intellectual gifts by the same standards as wine"—that is, the older the better.[3]

The Italian humanists of the Quattrocento were reliving Jerome's experience. Valla noted that people "value antiquity so highly . . . that they claim it possesses all excellence." He argued in vain that "in matters that are subject to reason later ages may surpass antiquity."[4] Valla's contemporary, Gianozzo Manetti, also faced the charge of innovation when he undertook a new translation of the Psalter. In an apologia he reminded his critics of Jerome's experience and answered them in Jerome's words. It was wrong to "evaluate intellectual gifts like wine."[5] Brandolini likewise reported that he had been criticized for breaking with tradition. "A new Bible is being made," critics said of his Epitome, "the old one is going to be abandoned." Like Manetti, he invoked Jerome's example and noted that it was unreasonable that his enterprise should come under fire: "I, who expound the sacred histories in polished and lucid language, am said to 'make a new Bible,' you, who corrupt it with barbaric commentaries, 'preserve it intact and inviolate'"![6]

The humanists of the sixteenth century fared no better than their Italian forerunners. A decree issued at the University of Tübingen in 1505 stated: "We desire that teachers refrain from . . . pursuing novelties, scandalously finding fault with the text of the Bible."[7] The Carmelite Nicolaus Baechem, a member of the theological faculty at Louvain, was one of the most outspoken defenders of tradition. His philistine attitude and strident manner of advertising his reactionary views soon made him the butt of humanist jokes and puns on the Carmelite order. "At Louvain I heard a '*Camel*ite' preaching that anything new was to be shunned," a character in Erasmus' *Apotheosis of Reuchlin* reports. "A saying fit for a *camel*," is the reply. "The man—if that's what he is—deserves never to change his socks and dirty underwear, forever to eat rotten eggs and to drink nothing but soured wine."[8] The poet Riccardo Sbruglio composed a mock biography of Baechem, entitled *The Life of St[upid] Nicolaus*, in which he traced the Carmelite's rise from "collector of cheeses and women's wills" to theology professor and reported that "he condemned what is new and praised what is old in all his sermons." Sbruglio appended a poem in atrocious Latin supposedly composed by Baechem in an effort to provide an alternative model of style for students corrupted by the New Learning and to prevent them from reading "Jerome and Augustine and the other poets."[9] The same campy humor characterizes the anonymous *Council of Theologists* (ca. 1520), which purports to record the proceedings of a faculty meeting called by Jacob Hoogstraten to deal with Luther and the New Learning. The traditionalists are well represented on this faculty, which includes fictitious along with historical figures. Several representatives, when asked to give their opinion, express concern about "innovations." Eduardus [Lee] disapproves of "that new fashion and those new doctors, Jerome, Augustine, and Athanasius"; Petrus [Meyer] sadly notes that the biblical humanists "now drag into the light Jerome and Chrysostom and those other poets." "Men are always looking for something new," another says, warning the innovators: "'Do not transgress the limits set by your fathers', says the Wise Man. We have received these teachings from our teachers before us. Why would we want to abandon their heavenly doctrine?"[10]

The lampoons offer a comically exaggerated version of points made by the protagonists in earnest. In the polemical literature of the time, biblical humanists were frequently accused of being "lovers of innovation," a charge that carried historical ballast and put them in a class with plotting revolutionaries and political assassins. Conversely, Agrippa of Nettesheim claims that "a certain theologian was not ashamed to preach that custom rather than Scripture must be observed."[11] Similarly, Pierre Cousturier wrote a fiery book against new translations of the Bible in which he insisted that "one must not lightly reject what has been sanctioned by long tradition" and fought against those "who were drawn on by a desire for new things."[12] This view was supported by the Carthusian John Batmanson, whose motto, as Thomas More put it, was *vetus melius est*, "older is better."[13] Similarly, the Louvain theologian Frans Titelmans lumped together Valla, Lefèvre, and Erasmus as "partial to novelties," "after new things," and meddlers promoting instability. "And so I am totally against those arrogant men eager to promote their own interests, who seek to suppress the old and replace it with something new. This may be acceptable in secular disciplines, but in matters of the faith it cannot or ought not to happen without the consent and judgment of the Church."[14] *Novitatis amator,* "lover of novelty," threatened to become Erasmus' sobriquet. At a conference called by the Spanish Orders to examine the orthodoxy of his works, the label appears no fewer than five times in the verdicts.[15]

While the faculties of Paris, Louvain, and Salamanca were known for their traditionalism, Lopis Stunica, a collaborator on the Complutensian Polyglot, could be expected to take a more sympathetic view of biblical humanism. Yet he too insisted: *vetera non immutanda,* "what is old must not be changed." It seems that Stunica completely divorced investigative scholarship from the process of evaluating the findings. One was the task of the philologist; the other that of the theologian. Philology was merely a shadow power; the real power of rendering judgment was vested in the theologian who held the magisterium. Stunica therefore disapproved of the format of Erasmus' edition of the New Testament, in which a revised text was presented and the changes explained in the annotations. The correct approach, in his opinion, was to reproduce the Vulgate text and confine variant readings or alternative translations to the notes to indicate the tentative nature of the philologist's findings.[16] This was the rationale behind the format adopted in the Polyglot edition, which printed the Vulgate side by side with other texts, thus avoiding any decision about variants and at the same time protecting the editors from the accusation of innovation. For the same reason Josse Clichtove prefaced his *Epitome historiae sacrae* (1521) with a disclaimer stressing that the author was by no means foisting a new version of the Bible on the reader; rather, Clichtove cautioned him not to put his trust into the epitomized text but, when in doubt, to "have recourse to the primary sources."[17]

Several biblical humanists anticipated the opposition of the traditionalists. Lefèvre addressed the issue in his preface to the *Quintuplex Psalterium:* "And lest this appear too innovative and unusual, remember that Origen made a five-fold version of the Psalms, . . . and far from anyone reproaching him for this work, the praises he earned for it have come down to our own time."[18] Erasmus was fatalistic about the critical reception of his New Testament. "I knew that it is human nature to object to novelty in everything, but especially in the field of learning, and that most people expect to find the old familiar taste and what they call the traditional flavor."[19]

The epithets "bold" and "presumptuous" feature prominently in the traditionalists' descriptions of efforts to correct Scripture. Cardinal Bessarion, whose work preceded Valla's and inspired the Italian humanist to undertake his collation of manuscripts, faced criticism from defenders of the Vulgate, who indignantly declared that "nothing must be changed in

Scripture." He noted the objections made to his correction of the Vulgate text of John 21:22: "They conclude that it was an offense against the Gospel to change this passage. They would sooner die than make such a bold move; no one could be considered a Catholic who was of the opinion that the authoritative text of the Gospel ought to be changed; anyone who was bold enough must be censured."[20] Valla was similarly obliged to defend his corrections of the Vulgate against accusations of boldness and presumption. "They object: 'One must not discuss such matters, pious ears may be offended.' Really? . . . Pious ears must not be offended? And who are these people with pious ears? People who cannot bear the truth? Who refuse to be instructed?"[21] Manetti, too, reported that he was accused of "arrogance" for attempting a new translation; and in Spain Nebrija had to defend his textual criticism against charges of scandalizing people and giving offense. He did so in terms reminiscent of Valla: "I would like to know from them, first of all: Who are these people to whom I give offense? Are they the learned or unlearned? Or rather, are they people who think they are learned when they are not? . . . who 'love the uppermost seats in the synagogue' and 'the first seats at table' . . . I have no objection to giving offense to them, since even our Savior gave offense to the Pharisees."[22]

In Northern Europe humanist ventures into scriptural studies were criticized in similar terms. Men who wanted to change the Vulgate were "driven by a great madness," Cousturier wrote. They deserved to be scourged for their presumption. They did not deserve the name of "translators." "I know of certain new and bold translations . . . published in my time with sacrilegious presumption by certain exceptionally arrogant 'translationists'—for so I shall call them. When I read some passages and considered how boldly they had acted, I was deeply disturbed. I cannot describe the great consternation I felt, the great indignation and sadness that overcame me."[23] Béda had the same emotional reaction. "I was stunned," he wrote after examining Lefèvre's work, "for who could say anything more preposterous than that the text of the Bible . . . is full of errors." Stunica expressed similar indignation on reading Erasmus' New Testament edition: "I was greatly taken aback by the man's audacity."[24]

The accusation of presumption was invariably linked to views on the authorship of the Vulgate and the principle of inspiration. In the eyes of the traditionalists, the hubris of the new translators consisted in criticizing or correcting a great luminary of the Church, Jerome, thought to be the inspired author of the Vulgate. It is of course ironical that Jerome, who in his own time was considered a bold innovator and, as we have seen, faced many of the same accusations as the humanists in the Renaissance, had been transformed by the passage of time into the voice of tradition.[25]

In defending themselves, the humanists once again followed Jerome's example. The Church Father had countered accusations that he was displaying an unduly critical spirit and, more significantly, challenging the principle of inspiration, with four arguments. Firstly he denied that his undertaking to revise the biblical text implied disrespect: "Let it be known that in fashioning a new text, I am not reproaching the old translators, . . . especially since there are as many versions as there are copies." "I beg you, dear reader, do not consider my work a reproach to the old translators."[26]

Secondly, he reassured the traditionalists that he was not trying to foist his translation on them as an official version: "Let those who want to do so keep their old books, written on parchment in purple, gold, and silver, written in uncials, as they say, fancy works of art rather than books, but allow me and my friends to have our plain sheets, a correct rather than beautiful text." "Let those who wish read my work, those who are unwilling cast it aside."[27]

Thirdly, he insisted on the legitimacy of the editor's task. He explained that the Scriptural text was not carved in stone. There was no archetype but rather a multitude of different texts, and a choice needed to be made among the variants. He explained his editorial function: "Since today various copies are in circulation in various regions and that genuine translation of old is corrupt and vitiated, you [Chromatius] think it is up to my judgment to decide which among the many variants is the true one, and to make old into new . . . I say this with due respect for the old translators, merely to answer my critics who snap at me like dogs and slander me in public." He explained the process by which he sought to arrive at the correct text. Collating the available texts, he noted the variants. "If the genuine text must be sought among the many variants, why should we not turn to the Greek original and correct what was incorrectly rendered by translators who made mistakes, or wrongly changed by inexperienced and presumptuous men, or added or changed by nodding scribes?" If there were variants in the Latin text, "running in diverse channels and rivulets, they must be pursued to the one and only source."[28]

A fourth argument Jerome used in placating his critics was to note that he did not mean to challenge the principle of inspiration. He was collating and, in the process, revising and correcting the texts circulating, but he did not ascribe the errors he found in the Septuagint "to the seventy translators who, filled with the Holy Spirit, gave a correct version; rather, I blame the scribes who changed what was correct into something incorrect." Even if he had wanted to correct the authors of the Septuagint, it was no sacrilege, he declared more boldly, for the principle of inspiration did not necessarily extend to the translator: "It is one thing to be a prophet, another to be a translator. In the prophet's case the Spirit predicts the future, in the translator's case, his learning and verbal dexterity produce a translation according to his understanding."[29]

The same arguments and counterarguments recur in the humanist-scholastic debate. Some examples will demonstrate how they were woven into the controversy. Bessarion noted that Jerome's revision had been criticized, yet had become the standard translation. He had thus set a precedent for the philologists of his own day and validated their efforts. The biblical text had once more been corrupted and stood in need of another revision. It had been vitiated by omissions, additions, and changes. This situation had to be redressed: "We must cut out what was added, add once again [what was omitted], and correct the errors." For this purpose the original text must be consulted, as Jerome and Augustine recommended. "Are we not told by the most holy doctors that much has been corrupted and is still in a state of corruption on account of the variety of translators, the lack of experience of editors, and the carelessness of scribes who were asleep?" In this process one must of course "take recourse to the original language and to older manuscripts; and the variants in the Latin text must yield to the Greek." In view of Jerome's and Augustine's recommendations, Bessarion had no qualms about his undertaking and proceeded "without fear or risk of unjust calumny . . . and with complete disregard for the feeble threats and reproaches of insignificant men."[30]

Valla found himself in much the same situation as Bessarion. His critic Poggio noted indignantly that " Valla has such contempt for Holy Writ that he claims there are many faulty passages in it . . . and reproaches Jerome in many places, as if Holy Scripture had been misinterpreted by him."[31] The accusation of disrespect was rejected by Valla, using Jerome's own arguments and indeed invoking his example: "What is Holy Writ? Does every translation of the Old or New Testament qualify? But there is a multitude and variety of conflicting translations! . . . Where among them would you say is 'Holy Writ'?" To establish the definitive version was difficult, he explained,

at least as far as the New Testament is concerned, for it had many translators, as can be discovered in writers of old. But you will object: later on Jerome translated both the Old and the New Testament. I only wish we had both texts in their uncorrupted form . . . in my opinion, if Jerome came back to life he would correct what has been corrupted and vitiated in some passages, as has been shown by me in my Collation of the New Testament, which you call an odious work. In short, if I emend anything, I do not emend Holy Writ, but the translations; nor am I acting out of contempt but in a pious spirit; and I merely offer a version that is better than the previous translator's. Thus my version, provided it is faithful, might be called 'Holy Writ' rather than his, even if, strictly speaking, only what the saints themselves wrote in Hebrew or Greek is Holy Writ; for there is nothing in Latin.[32]

Like Bessarion and Valla, Brandolini, too, noted that the accusations brought against him could and had been brought against Jerome and admitted of the same excuses that were extended to the Church Father; and Manetti similarly fended off critics claiming that after Jerome had revised the translation, any further efforts were "superfluous, more than inane, and presumptuous."[33]

The controversy was carried over into the sixteenth century, with Lefèvre and Erasmus becoming the main targets of the traditionalists. Lefèvre defended his new translation in his preface to the Epistles of St Paul: "Some think my endeavor insolent and accuse me of temerity and audacity, indeed condemn me for it." They would have a point if Jerome's translation were extant. "But we shall stand excused, once they realize fully that we have made no daring move against St. Jerome's translation, but are dealing with the Vulgate, which existed long before Jerome, that blessed and glorious luminary of the Church, and which he himself criticizes, adding his voice to mine."[34] Similarly, Erasmus defended his task using Jerome's arguments. He was not setting himself up as a critic of the Church Father but rather following in his footsteps and emulating his work. If Jerome's translation were extant, "there would perhaps have been no need for my collation," he wrote.[35] Unfortunately, the biblical text, revised by Jerome, had once more been corrupted. How else could one explain the discrepancies between the manuscripts in circulation and the biblical quotations in the Fathers? The mistakes and variants were a consequence of "a translator's clumsiness or inattention" or had been introduced in transcription. "The true and genuine reading has been corrupted by ignorant scribes, which we see happen every day, or altered by scribes who are half-taught and half-asleep." Erasmus hastened to add that "no one asserts that there is any falsehood in Holy

Scripture itself." He reminded his critics that Jerome had made a distinction between the inspired author and the translator who relied on human skills and was therefore subject to error. He quoted the Church Father's words in this context: "It is one thing to be a prophet; another to be a translator."[36] It was wrong to think of the current, faulty version in terms of a *textus receptus*. It did not have the formal approval of the Church, as the traditionalists implied. Could anyone name the synod that had approved it? What sort of decree could the fathers of the council have drawn up? he asked ironically.

> Perhaps on terms like these: "This version is of unknown authorship, but nonetheless we approve of it, nor do we wish it to be an objection that the Greek copies have something different, or [the text differs from patristic texts] . . . Moreover, whatsoever in future may in any way, whether by men with little education or rather more self-confidence or by scribes unskilled, drunken, or half-asleep, be corrupted, distorted, added, or omitted, we in virtue of the same decree approve, nor are we willing that any man should have licence to correct what has once been written." A very comical decree, you say. But it must have been something like this, if you are to frighten me from this kind of work with the authority of a synod.

Erasmus furthermore rejected his critics' concerns that the authority of the Bible would suffer if mistakes were discovered. His critics, he said, were concerned not about the authority of the Bible but about their own authority,

> for it may look as though there were some things they did not know. It is they who try to stop me with the authority of imaginary synods; they who build up this great threat to the Christian faith; they who cry 'the Church is in danger' (and no doubt support her with their own shoulders, which would be better employed in propping up a dung-cart) . . . There can be no danger that everybody will forthwith abandon Christ, if the news happens to get out that some passage has been found in Scripture which an ignorant or sleepy scribe has miscopied or some unknown translator has rendered inadequately.[37]

In any case he had no ambitions to make his new translation the official version of the Church, Erasmus said, echoing Jerome's disclaimer: "Let those read it who will, let those who are unwilling put it aside."[38]

The traditionalists staunchly refused to accept these explanations and justifications. The text circulating in their time was Jerome's translation, they insisted. It was a flawless text and could be nothing but flawless, for the Church Father had been guided by the Holy Spirit. "Listen, you egregious fool, . . . thickheaded fellow and captious critic more wicked than a sophist," Cousturier fulminated, addressing himself to Erasmus and Lefèvre,

> the Vulgate text has been revised so thoroughly that no flaw can be found in it. Anyone who thinks differently is, like you, out of his mind. And it is such a fair version of the Greek original that there is nothing left to be desired, for it is beyond doubt that Jerome himself undertook the emendation not only taking prudent counsel but also being guided in a mysterious way by the Holy Spirit . . . consider furthermore that any error in the translation of Holy Writ which constitutes the basis of the Catholic faith would have been quite fatal.

Criticizing the Vulgate, which had been used by the Church for centuries, was "tantamount to saying that the Church, that the sacred general councils erred or were negligent."[39]

Cousturier frequently returned to the subject of inspiration. The Septuagint translation was "produced under inspiration," he said; Jerome's translation, too, was inspired. According to Cousturier, "no one could ever produce a faithful and appropriate translation of Holy Writ unless he was specifically inspired (*peculiariter afflatus*) by the Holy Spirit." If Jerome had made no such claims for himself, it is because he thought humbly of his gift.

> Nevertheless he calls his work of translation somewhere 'sacred' . . . In many places in his commentaries he says likewise that one always needs the succor of the Holy Spirit in expounding Holy Writ. If he thought that in expounding Holy Writ one needs the blessing of the Holy Spirit, must we not believe that he thought it was even more necessary in the task of translation? Of course we must. Therefore, if he spoke of his translation in humble terms, it was partly due to his modesty, partly to avoid giving his rivals an occasion to ridicule him.[40]

Cousturier put stringent demands on the biblical translator. He must of course be a man of the highest moral integrity and of consummate learning. Furthermore, he must be motivated by piety rather than ambition and undertake the task because of necessity rather than inclination. Finally, he must have God's blessing and work under divine inspiration:

First of all he must lead a most sacred life, for this task does not suit those who lead a profane life. Furthermore, great learning is required, for it is not enough to have a knowledge of languages. One must also have a more than average understanding of the letter and spirit of Scripture. In addition, sincere intentions are required. For anyone who undertakes the task thirsting for vain glory or wanting to criticize or being impelled by some other evil intention is not suitable for the task. Moreover, the translator must have a pious and cogent reason for his enterprise. For those, who embark on a superfluous task are generally not supported by divine power. Yet divine aid is absolutely necessary in the task of translating Holy Writ. And finally, the translator must enjoy heaven's grace and a very special grace at that, which will choose and direct the translator. For he must not approach the task unless he is divinely chosen and aided. Or else he would produce not a divine version divinely inspired, but a profane work guided by human intelligence.[41]

None of the modern translators qualified for the task, none had the requisite qualities or disposition.

Cousturier's contemporary and fellow Paris doctor Noël Béda likewise took aim at Erasmus and Lefèvre. In reply to the latter's contention that Jerome was not responsible for the current Vulgate version, he replied:

[You say:] All scholars and all men of sound judgment know that the edition of the Pauline Epistles used by the church is not Jerome's translation; for he argues against it, proves it wrong, and condemns it . . . I dare say, Lefèvre, your statement is neither pleasing to God nor to the late holy doctor . . . And who are those "scholars" who deny Jerome's authorship? You mean perhaps to say "We who speak Greek, who add the charm of human wisdom to God's Word, are the only scholars, the only men of sound judgment."[42]

Yet Béda's views on the principle of inspiration were somewhat more qualified than those of his more radical contemporaries. He claimed for Jerome the respect due to a luminary of the church and an authorized translator, but applied the principle of inspiration only to the original biblical authors. "For only those writers can be said to have been divinely inspired who put on paper not what they had learned through human efforts (though with the help of God, without whom nothing can go right), but what they knew because the Spirit of God had poured it into them in a supernatural manner—only the writings included by the

Church in the sacred canon of the Bible are writings of this kind. All the other writers who came later wrote as human beings."[43]

So far we have been dealing with principal objections to textual criticism. In defending the Vulgate, the scholastic doctors of Paris and Louvain saw themselves in the role of guardians of doctrine. They resisted changes to the textus receptus because it could be construed as a challenge to the principle of inspiration or at any rate a challenge to the hallowed traditions of the Church. There was also fear that a change in the wording might give rise to doctrinal disputes. A case in point was Erasmus' change of *poenitentiam agite*, do penance, at Matthew 3:1, to *resipiscite*, repent. The Erasmian translation was seen to impugn the concept of external penance imposed by the Church (or volunteered by the penitent) in the form of prayers, donations, or pilgrimages. Similarly, his drawing attention to the uncertainty concerning the exact words used by Jesus to consecrate the bread and wine at the Last Supper cast doubt on the efficacy of the words used by the priest during Mass.[44]

A more practical reason for the objections of the scholastic doctors was that the Vulgate was used as a prooftext in disputations. Beatus Rhenanus, in the preface of his edition of Tertullian (1521), specifically noted the concern of scholastic doctors for standard vocabulary: "They ratified that those discussing divine matters not only should follow the accepted statements of the school but should use the vocabulary and formulas of speech developed in that school . . . This was done not without reason, namely for preserving the unity of teaching."[45] The same concern presumably applied to the language of the Vulgate. A standard version was needed to avoid confusion in disputations. When humanists emphasized that they were not trying to replace the official text used in the liturgy at Mass and in disputations at the universities, they were addressing such concerns.

Another group of scholastics fought against the humanists not because they rejected all changes to the Vulgate, but because they questioned the premises underlying the corrections. They did not deny that the Vulgate was flawed and might benefit from a revision, but they either denied that this required consultation of the text in the original language or restricted corrections to scribal errors and rejected the idea of revising language and style. In the first case, they argued that textual problems could be solved by reference to patristic exegesis and scholastic commentaries written or translated into Latin. Their objections to consulting the text in the original were informed either by suspicions against Jews and Greeks as heterodox or misgivings about curriculum changes, for if theologians were required to consult the original texts, language studies would have to become part of their training. In the second case—objections to literary criticism—the argument was that the Bible, being a revealed text, was in a category of its own. The divine truth had no need for embellishment and was not subject to the rules of grammar and rhetoric.

Let us examine these arguments separately, first the resistance to textual criticism based on Hebrew and Greek manuscripts. In 1311 the Council of Vienne, motivated by missionary concerns, recommended the study of Hebrew, Arabic, Syriac, and Greek, but although the decree was reissued by the Council of Basel (1434), no concerted official effort was made to meet this goal. A marked distrust prevailed against Jews and Greeks, whose texts were thought to have been falsified to deceive and mislead Christians.[46] To express an interest in Hebrew studies without asserting a missionary or polemical purpose remained risky for some time. The first study aids, for example Petrus Nigri's *Stella Meschiah* (1477), were written with the evangelization of the Jews in mind. When Steuco published a commentary on the Pentateuch based on his study of the Hebrew text in 1529, he still found it politic to assert an apologetic purpose.[47] Research motivated by a humanistic interest in languages, by contrast, was suspect. Manetti, one of the first humanists to study Hebrew in the fifteenth century, was criticized for producing a new translation of the Psalter from the original. Pico, another student of Hebrew, came under attack when he attempted to reconcile Jewish and Christian thought in his *Nine Hundred Theses*. In the sixteenth century Reuchlin, who contributed significantly to the study of Hebrew with his *Rudiments of the Hebrew Language* (1506), also fell victim to the prevailing paranoia. His defense of Hebrew literature made him the butt of antisemitic sentiments.[48] Even progressive humanists found it difficult to keep their interest in language studies untainted by racism. As a result we find some surprising inconsistencies in their remarks. Wessel Gansfort, for example, relied on the *Hebraica veritas*, the original Hebrew text, for some of his criticism of the Vulgate, yet designated the Jews as *hostes veritatis*, "enemies of the truth."[49] And Erasmus, who was instrumental in the organization of the Collegium Trilingue at Louvain, nevertheless expressed fear that Hebrew studies "may give that pestilence [the Jews] that was long ago suppressed a chance to rear its ugly head," and exclaims: "If only the Church of Christians did not attach so much importance to the Old Testament!"[50]

As for Greek, resistance to it in reactionary circles began to mount in Northern Europe at the beginning of the sixteenth century. Before then

Greek scholarship had been too rare to be considered a threat. Opportunities to study Greek had been limited. Erasmus and Budé tell us that they were largely self-taught because there was a scarcity of books and teachers in their youth. There were technical obstacles to the dissemination of Greek: few printers in the West had Greek type before 1500. The work of biblical humanists came to fruition only in the sixteenth century. Among the prominent examples of works based on collating original texts are Valla's notes on the Vulgate, first printed in 1505 under Erasmus' aegis; Lefèvre's *Quintuplex Psalterium*, which appeared in 1509; the Complutensian Polyglot printed 1514–1517; Nebrija's *Tertia Quinquagena*, the fruit of many years of scholarship, finally published in 1516; Erasmus' bilingual edition of the New Testament, which appeared in 1516; Sanctes Pagninus' *Veteris et Novi Testamenti nova translatio* of 1528; and Robert Estienne's critical *Biblia Latina* of 1527–1529. In the prefaces to these editions we find defenses of textual criticism and the need to consult scriptural texts in the original.

Lefèvre refers to his researches in the preface to the *Quintuplex Psalterium*, addressed to Guillaume Briçonnet. He states that he placed variant texts side by side to allow readers beset by scruples concerning the text and its interpretation, "to compare and collate the texts." Obviously wanting to avoid controversy, he refrains from discussing the reasons for, or implications of, the existence of variants in the text or his own purpose in bringing them to the reader's attention. A verse prefixed to the Caen edition of 1515 by Pierre Des Prés simply notes that Lefèvre shows up textual corruptions by comparing the Greek text with the Hebrew: "Graeca sub Hebraeo libans primordia fonte / Tersa locis reparat plurima menda suis."[51] In his commentary on the Catholic Epistles Lefèvre acknowledged his role as textual critic succinctly: "We find [in the Epistle of John] a great deal of divergence from the genuine text, the work of unfaithful translators."[52]

In the prologue to the Complutensian Polyglot, addressed to Pope Leo X, Cardinal Ximenes showed similar discretion. He explained that he made an effort to collate and "use as prooftexts the oldest and most authentic copies everywhere," among which was a Greek codex from the Vatican library. His grateful acknowledgment of the loan was not only polite but also politic. Ximenes intended to disarm would-be critics by advertising the fact that the Pope approved and supported his undertaking. Indeed, the edition was not published until a papal imprimatur was obtained in 1520. It was necessary to resort to the original text, said Ximenes, not only for the sake of establishing the correct text but also for a better understanding of its meaning, for "words have their own unique character, and no translation of them, however complete, can entirely express their full meaning."[53]

Nebrija commented on his research in the *Apologia* prefixed to the *Tertia Quinquagena*, explaining that his method was "to compare more recent Latin manuscripts with those of venerable age" and these in turn with Greek and Hebrew texts to decide on the correct reading. For it was not good enough to adopt the wording of the majority of Latin manuscripts simply because a greater number of texts shared it, especially since some people were naive enough to count individual copies of printed editions. They were obviously unaware that "all copies which come from one printing must be counted as one." Nor should numbers alone determine a reading, for "in every matter subject to judgment the witnesses should be weighed, not counted." Nebrija's enterprise had been criticized by the scholastics, but "Is this not a better occupation," he asked, "than disputing the ridiculous question whether the quiddities of Scotus, passing through the side of a point, can fill the stomach of the chimera?" He discounted the argument that Hebrew and Greek manuscripts were suspect because they may have been willfully corrupted by heterodox parties, challenging his critics to point out specific passages. He was not aware of any doctrinal dispute based on variants. Rather, he said, "the text was the same, and the controversy was all about the meaning."[54]

Erasmus also defended his enterprise at length in the prolegomena to the New Testament edition. Like Ximenes, he had dedicated it to Pope Leo X to give it authority and to protect himself against criticism. In his dedicatory letter he listed the manuscripts he had collated and emphasized the importance of checking the Latin against the Greek, "the fountainhead, as it were." Like Ximenes, he noted that the Greek text helped not only in establishing the correct reading but also in understanding the full meaning of the text. It was difficult to render idiomatic expressions, "the figures and full meaning of a Greek phrase," into Latin. He used arguments similar to Nebrija's in allaying his critics' suspicion of Greek manuscripts. They alleged that they had been willfully corrupted after the schism, but Erasmus pointed out that the Greeks and the Catholics disagreed on the interpretation rather than the reading of the doctrinally problematic passages. In later editions of his New Testament he legitimized the use of Greek texts by linking his own cause with that of Ximenes, and pointing out that the Complutensian Polyglot was based on Greek manuscripts from the Vatican Library—proof positive that the Pope endorsed such collations.[55]

Like Erasmus, Sanctes Pagninus sought the protection of the Pope for his new translation of the Bible, dedicating it to Clement VII. In his prologue to the reader he spoke disparagingly of the scholastics, who "boast of being Averroists, Thomists, or Scotists. They are intimately acquainted with their teaching and know it by heart, disputing about instances, relations, quiddities, and formalities. These are the only pursuits they consider erudite, subtle, and seraphic." How useful, by contrast, was his own philological work on the Bible![56]

Robert Estienne likewise explains and defends his method in the preface to the reader accompanying his *Biblia Sacra:* "We thought it worthwhile, before tackling the printing, to consult old texts and extract from them the authentic reading; it was our purpose, in reliance on their authority, to correct what was corrupted and thus satisfy scrupulous readers who are offended by the alteration of even a single word."[57] He listed the manuscripts consulted and noted historical precedents of textual criticism to justify his own undertaking.

The prefatory remarks of the biblical humanists attest to the hostile climate in which they were publishing. Several scholastic doctors on the faculties of theology at Louvain and Paris voiced the traditionalist argument. At Louvain, Dorp objected to Erasmus' planned revision of the Vulgate, declaring categorically that the textus receptus "contained no error and no falsehood." He questioned Erasmus' method of collating manuscripts: "To correct the Latin copies by means of the Greek requires careful thought," he wrote. "Now that so many heresies have arisen in Greece, and that long schism, how can we be certain that their copies have not been corrupted?" Dorp's colleague on the faculty of theology, the Carmelite Nicolaus Baechem, whose traditionalism has already been mentioned, rejected Greek texts wholesale, pronouncing Greek the "source of all evils."[58] Another Louvain theologian, Frans Titelmans, shared the suspicions. He was not against the philological approach as such, he said, but caution was advised. "I am far from asserting that a knowledge of Greek contributes nothing to the understanding of Scripture or that collating Greek manuscripts is useless . . . I am merely saying that the Greek codices we have now are, I fear, more corrupt and less trustworthy than our Latin ones."[59] In Paris resistance to the biblical humanists was even fiercer. Cousturier was outspoken on this point: "Greek books are not to be trusted at all," he declared, and "to bring out a Greek manuscript for the purpose of emending the Latin Bible" was unacceptable. "To use such prooftexts is insane and I completely reject and refute the practice." "The New Testament cannot be restored on the basis of Greek codices; they vary among each other, they are suspect, and they offer no security or authority." The study of glosses was enough.[60] The German Franciscan Ferber of Herborn agreed with Cousturier: "Who in his right mind . . . would safely entrust himself to Greek and Hebrew manuscripts?"[61]

The resentment against the biblical humanists rose dramatically when they went beyond defending their own practice to suggest that the philological method be adopted by all theologians. For this purpose language studies must form a part of the theologian's training. Nebrija noted that ignorance of Greek (and, for that matter, classical Latin) prevented theologians from reading the Fathers, "those holy men who are the founders of our religion," and caused them to turn to inferior (scholastic) authors because "they wrote in a language they could understand."[62] Reuchlin maintained that "not one of the Latins can explain the Old Testament unless he first becomes proficient in the language in which it was written."[63] Willibald Pirckheimer elaborated on this statement in his defense of Reuchlin, outlining a curriculum for students of theology that included language studies and generally reflected humanistic preferences. The candidate's training should include the following subjects: instruction in the three biblical languages; dialectic (but the "genuine" kind); rhetoric, "to teach and motivate the Christian people through the Word of Truth"; philosophy, including not only Aristotelian doctrine but "that divine Platonic philosophy"; and history, because the Bible was replete with historical narrative.[64] Erasmus was one of the most insistent champions of language studies. His *Methodus*, a tract included among the prolegomena to his New Testament, was essentially a proposal for curriculum reform. It appeared as a separate, revised and enlarged, publication in 1518 under the title *Ratio verae theologiae*, and came under immediate and vigorous attack by conservative theologians.[65] In Erasmus' view, language studies were fundamental to the theologian's training.

> Our first care must be to learn the three languages, Latin, Greek, and Hebrew, for it is plain that the mystery of all Scripture is revealed in them. Do not immediately shy away because of the difficulty of the task, dear reader, as if you had been pricked with a nail. If you do not lack a teacher, if you do not lack the will, it is almost less trouble to learn these three languages than it is to learn to stutter one wretched half-language in the manner current today (the reason being the ignorance of the teachers). We do not demand that you advance to a miraculous level of eloquence. It is sufficient that you progress to the point of speaking neatly and elegantly, that is, obtain a modicum of knowledge enabling you to pass judgment. For

it is quite impossible to understand what is written, if you are ignorant of the language in which it is written—to say nothing of the role played by other human disciplines. In my opinion, we must not listen to those who grow old and stale involved in sophistical nonsense, saying: "Jerome's version suffices." For those who give this answer are most likely people who make no effort even to learn Latin, so that Jerome's version is wasted on them. As for the rest, I would say it matters a great deal whether you take something from the sources or from some puddle.[66]

Cousturier reacted with anger to Erasmus' proposal that language studies should form an integral and even central part of a theologian's training:

We do not need a knowledge of foreign languages for an understanding of Holy Writ and for this reason it is vain and frivolous to spend time on learning them. Nor is it necessary to learn them for the purpose of producing a new translation of Scripture, for the Vulgate translation is quite sufficient. . . . It is completely insane and smacks of heresy for anyone to affirm that one should sweat over foreign languages for this purpose. Anyone who holds this opinion has the wrong view of the Latin Bible, thinking that we must take recourse to other languages because the Latin translation is supposedly not faithful or not appropriate. That smacks of perverted heresy. And anyone who is liable to such madness is a perverted heretic.

In a calmer mood he added: "If anyone wants to study Greek and Hebrew for other purposes [than correcting the Vulgate], that is his business."[67]

The negative attitude of the scholastic doctors toward language studies was lampooned in contemporary satire. The writers suggested that the motives of the critics were not as respectable as they gave out. Their concerns were less for the protection of doctrine than for covering up their own ignorance. They feared for their reputation and authority, yet were too lazy to learn now what they had neglected in their youth. In the *Council of Theologists* a recalcitrant Dr. Duplicius declares: "And even if they recommend it a hundred times, I won't learn Greek and Hebrew. I can hardly read the Psalter—and now they want me to read that fantastic stuff."[68] Another anonymous German skit offers this dialogue between Ortvinus Gratius, Lupold, and Gingolph, whose pidgin Latin had already been lampooned in the *Letters of Obscure Men:*

ORTVINUS: Professor Lupold, do you think that God cares much for that Greek stuff?

LUPOLDUS: For sure not, Professor Ortvin. . . .

GINGOLPHUS: They want us to believe that they are something wonderful, just because no one understands them.

ORTVINUS: Strictly between us, let me tell you: the most illustrious doctors of Paris will send an embassy to the Pope to have them [the humanists] excommunicated, because they make heretics of everyone.[69]

We have seen that the humanist editors attempted to legitimize their enterprise by obtaining papal endorsement through the official imprimatur or dedications. Elsewhere, we find them validating textual criticism and language studies by reference to the Fathers of the Council of Vienne. Nebrija, Erasmus, Pagninus, and Estienne all specifically cited the conciliar decree. Erasmus likewise defended his enterprise with the argument: "I am supported by the holy authority of the pontifical council, whose decree is still extant in the decretal letters, to the effect that the leading universities, as they were at that period, should engage persons capable of giving complete instruction in the Hebrew, Greek, and Latin tongues, for as much as they claimed that Scripture could not be understood, much less discussed, without them."[70] Similar arguments can be found in Petrus Mosellanus' inaugural lecture given at the University of Leipzig, in which he explored the usefulness of language studies in various academic disciplines. A new age had dawned, he declared, "and the study of the three tongues, Hebrew, Greek, and Latin, is becoming popular."[71] He cited the decrees of the Council of Vienne promoting language studies and found encouragement for such studies also in the Fathers. If Jerome came alive, he said, he would support the cause in words like these: "In learning languages I followed the Spirit of Christ and especially Paul, who lists the study of tongues among the blessings of the Holy Spirit . . . without it the Christian religion, which depends on the correct understanding of Scripture, cannot survive . . . Therefore, if you want to hear my advice . . . embrace the study of the three languages, which Christ on the cross consecrated with his blood."[72]

The same triad of witnesses—Paul, Augustine, the Council of Vienne—is also invoked by Robert Wakefield, England's first salaried teacher of Hebrew. Shortly after being appointed to his post at Cambridge, he wrote an *Oratio de laudibus et utilitate trium linguarum Arabicae, Chaldaicae et Hebraicae* (London, 1524) in which he argued: "Pontifical legislation [that is, the decree of the Council of Vienne] shows how valuable, how necessary, for understanding sacred Scripture is a knowledge of the languages listed above." Wakefield then invokes the authority of "our teacher and mentor, the multi-lingual apostle Paul ... who frequently condemns the stupid philosophy of the sophists and reckons the gift of tongues to be one of the endowments and gifts of the Holy Spirit." Finally, he quotes at length from Augustine's *De doctrina Christiana*, affirming that he was inspired by this work to devote himself to the study of languages.[73]

The same combination of arguments is advanced by Matthias Flaccius Illyricus in the preface of his *Clavis Scripturae* (Basel 1580). The theologians, he says, have been "corrupted" by Aristotelian logic and are no longer able to comprehend the language of the Bible. "They disapprove of examining the Hebrew and Greek sources, contending that they give rise to heresies." This was contrary to the practice of the Fathers —Jerome, who "excelled in languages," and Augustine, who recommended language studies in *De doctrina Christiana*. It was furthermore contrary to the decrees of the Council of Vienne, which encouraged the pursuit of language studies.[74]

The humanistic defense of language studies is summed up by Philipp Melanchthon in his famous inaugural speech at the University of Wittenberg (1518).[75] He notes the objection of critics "that Greek is espoused by certain people who have too much leisure and for the purpose of showing off; Hebrew is dubious as far as faith is concerned," but these critics, Melanchthon said, were merely rejecting the unfamiliar. He congratulated the students of Wittenberg on having made progress in language studies and "taking in the very sources of the disciplines from the best authors." "Since theological writings are partly in Hebrew, partly in Greek—for we Latins drink from these streams—we must learn foreign languages lest we go into our encounters with the theologians blindfolded. It is language studies that bring out the splendor of words and the meaning of idioms and ... as we turn our mind to the sources, we begin to savor Christ."[76]

Generally speaking, the merit of language studies was readily acknowledged by the reformers. Luther, not always kind to humanists, nevertheless shared their appreciation for a knowledge of the biblical languages. He recommended that a good library contain "Holy Scripture in Latin, Greek, Hebrew, German, and in whatever other languages it may be available. Then there should be the best and oldest commentaries, if I could find them, in Greek, Hebrew and Latin. Then books that aid us in acquiring the languages."[77]

The scholastic doctors soon developed a set of counterarguments.

Jacques Masson rightly pointed out that the conciliar decree cited by the proponents of language studies recommended such studies only for missionary purposes and did not justify textual criticism. Frans Titelmans made the same point.[78] This objection was acknowledged by Matthaeus Adrianus, who taught Hebrew at the Collegium Trilingue in Louvain. He contended, however, that Masson's (and Titelmans') objections did not invalidate the humanist argument. Even if the decree did not specifically refer to Hebrew and Greek in the context of textual criticism, it was still a recommendation of language studies in general. They were indeed necessary for an understanding of Scripture, he insisted: "How will you read, if you do not know letters? How will you understand what you read, if you do not know languages? Who will listen to those who stupidly argue that a knowledge of languages was once necessary, but that times have changed?" It was not enough to read translations, because translators made mistakes. The divine mystery, moreover, was hidden in "the very idioms of a language. What will a theologian do here, if he is ignorant of languages? He must either trust in guesses or allow himself to be led by another's intelligence." Adrianus, too, spoke of the three languages as having been sanctified by the inscription on the cross.[79]

St. Augustine was invoked as a patron by both parties in the debate. This was possible because the Church Father's remarks on the subject were even-handed and explored both sides of the question. By quoting his views selectively, both humanists and scholastics could lay claim to his support. Mosellanus' inaugural lecture held at Leipzig and Jacques Masson's response may serve as examples of this process. Mosellanus noted that critics of language studies often claimed that the apostles were given a knowledge of the tongues by the Holy Spirit, rather than learning them through human endeavor. The implication was that God would provide the necessary skills to those who had a need for them. Human interference was not needed. Mosellanus answered this argument:

Augustine in his book *On Christian Doctrine* replies: . . . If anyone obtains an understanding of Scripture without human effort, he must truly be congratulated for having received such a great gift from God, but no one should derive from this an excuse for his own laziness . . . This is Augustine's argument, and it is a weighty one. Moreover, what can be more foolish than to expect from the greater power of the divine what we human beings can learn in sufficient measure from other human beings? What can be more impious than making God the champion of our laziness . . . and waiting for Him to send down from heaven such a treasure and bestow it on people unexpectedly while they are sleeping on both ears, as the saying goes? Especially when God himself, who is most industrious and most averse to idleness, commanded us to live by the labor of our own hands and wanted our life to be nothing but a perpetual struggle? The advice contained in the proverb circulating among the Greeks for many centuries is very true: in vain you ask for God's help, if you don't put your own shoulder to the wheel.

A little later in the same oration Mosellanus puts these words into Jerome's mouth: "I see it was in vain that I and Augustine advised that the books of the Old Testament be checked against the Hebrew and those of the New Testament against the Greek. . . . Christianity cannot survive without language studies, for it is totally dependent on a correct understanding of Scripture . . . and Augustine taught in his *Christian Doctrine* to what extent pagan learning is to be applied to sacred matters."[80]

In Masson's reply to the oration, *Dialogus de tribus linguis,* two characters named "Petrus" and "Joannes" represent the views of Petrus Mosellanus and Jacques Masson respectively. Petrus challenges Joannes, "the student of scholastic theology": "Do you then reject what Jerome and Augustine say, that the text of the New Testament must be corrected against the Greek?" Joannes does not reject their advice, but qualifies his approval: "I accept Jerome's and Augustine's advice on this matter, but as human and fallible, because it rests on conjecture. Let no one think of it as a certain and infallible rule or definitive solution." Later Joannes analyzes Augustine's words more closely. Asked why "Augustine says in book II of his *Christian Doctrine* that we need Latin and two other languages, Greek and Hebrew, to understand sacred matters," he replies, introducing a fine distinction: "Examine Augustine's words and consider the rationale behind them. First of all, he does not say that we need those languages to understand sacred matters, but to understand Scripture." As to the rationale, Augustine advised his readers to have recourse to the texts in their original language because there was a great variety of translations in his time.

You see that this rationale is no longer valid because we do not have a multitude of Latin translations. If there is any need [to consider the original text] because our one translation is corrupt or found to contain some errors—assuming that the Greek and Hebrew texts are without corruptions—. . . the process of inspecting the original text does not immediately remove all doubt about the Latin or all error, for there are ambiguities and equivocations in the originals and other problems they have in common with the Latin texts.

Furthermore, Augustine's advice was not categorical: "He gives us a choice, saying that we should *either* consult the original *or* enlist the help of those who know Greek and Hebrew." Indeed, Augustine himself was a case in point. He undertook to expound Genesis without having a knowledge of Hebrew. Yet "he was a better exegete and had more profound insights than many polyglot authors."[81]

In making these arguments for and against language studies and textual criticism based on Greek and Hebrew manuscripts, humanists cited the example and advice of the Church Fathers and the decrees of the Council of Vienne; scholastics put a different construction on those recommendations, insisting that the theologian could dispense with language studies and was well served by the Latin Vulgate. Objections to literary criticism were formulated on similar grounds. Critics of humanist endeavors to revise the language of the Vulgate gave at least two distinct reasons for their resistance. The first objection was based on the principle of inspiration. It was the logical extension of the arguments advanced against textual criticism. The defenders of the Vulgate claimed that not only the contents but also the form was sacred. "I cannot allow anything in God's work to be called flawed," Edward Lee wrote, "and the word of the apostle is the work of God."[82] Béda likewise insisted that the original author (though not the translator) was guided by God in his thoughts and in his style. He therefore called literary criticism of the original text blasphemous, because it "suggested that God did not know how to write."[83]

A second objection was based on the familiar saw that truth needs no embellishment. This argument comes in three variants: anyone criticizing the style of the Vulgate was frivolous and betrayed a lack of moral earnestness; the desire to impose a pagan style on the quintessential Christian book was blasphemous; rhetorical pomp did not become a simple Christian mind.

Familiarity with classical literature had made humanists sensitive to and critical of the pedestrian Latin of the Vulgate. Their criticism was received with indignation by traditionalists, although it was by no means unprecedented and merely echoed the verdict of the Fathers. Jerome had found the biblical idiom barbarous. "The unpolished speech was horrible," he said, but its salutary contents compensated the reader for its stylistic shortcomings. Origen likewise acknowledged that the Bible was full of solecisms and therefore "despised by non-Christians."[84] Renaissance humanists aligned themselves with this judgment. Boccaccio described the Bible as "obscure and ambiguous." Petrarch, too, confessed that he had been repelled in his youth by the unpolished language of the Bible, although he was willing to concede that wisdom could exist independently of eloquence: *doctrina sine eloquentia esse potest.*[85] Among the biblical humanists, Brandolini referred to the "plebeian simplicity" and "inelegant style" of the Bible. Similarly, Valla was not afraid to label the Vulgate translation "barbarous,"[86] and both he and Erasmus frequently referred the reader to classical examples when suggesting improvements to the traditional text.

The critics of the humanists, however, denied that ordinary literary standards applied to the Bible. They claimed that "sacred matters should not be expressed in a more elegant style or more cultured speech," Brandolini reported. A century later Erasmus noted that the argument, *in divinis literis non esse recipiendam sermonis elegantiam,* "sacred writings do not admit of elegant speech," had become a commonplace argument.[87] Both Nebrija and Erasmus report that the defenders of the Bible cited the Fathers in support of their position. "They take refuge in that Gregorian dictum: Holy Writ is not subject to the rules of Donatus. A pernicious decree if it is interpreted as they suggest," Nebrija wrote. "It is true that the nature and purpose of grammar is such that it serves other disciplines, yet when it is a question of letters, syllables, and phrases, grammar is superior to them. It is in its own domain and dictates to them."[88] Similarly, Erasmus scoffs at those arguing that "God is not offended by solecisms. That may be so, but neither is he delighted by them. Augustine forgives mistakes in language, but he does not recommend them. . . . Indeed God hates arrogant solecists who persecute correct speakers and are unwilling to learn what is better or allow others to do so."[89]

The importance of language had already been discussed in the epistolary exchange between Pico and Barbaro. Pico's scholastic representative concedes that polished speech is esthetically appealing and has the force of persuasion, but he insists on a strict distinction between sacred and profane use. "We do not want our style delightful, adorned, and graceful," he says. "We want it useful, grave, something to be respected; we would have it attain majesty through rudeness rather than charm through delicateness." Barbaro agrees, but turns the argument around. Speech should match contents. "Philosophy ought to be approached religiously since it is a gift divine, holy, and associated with religion." Thus special care should be taken to adapt one's style to the exalted purpose at hand. "[Theology/philosophy] is not to be handled with unwashed hands; it must be neat, even well-cared for, and dealt with in speech that is pure, not base and muddied."[90]

Some of the views aired in the exchange between Pico and Barbaro had already appeared in the apologiae of biblical humanists. Defending his new translation against critics, Manetti adopted a moderate stand. Jerome, he noted, had not totally neglected style but "for the greater dignity of Holy Scripture embellished his translation in some measure with stylish words." He conceded that the biblical translator faced more constraints than his colleague in the secular field: "There should be a considerable difference between translators of poets, orators, and writers of history and translators of philosophers and theologians." The latter must not add to or alter the text unless considerations for clarity and idiom required it. Generally speaking, Scripture demanded "a solemn, accurate, and carefully weighed translation."[91]

Brandolini argued in terms similar to Barbaro's: an exalted subject required exalted language. His critics had their priorities wrong. They did not mind if unimportant subjects were graced by ornate words, but would not tolerate important subjects to be dignified by polished language. He rejected the argument that "divine matters are in themselves beautiful and illustrious enough; they do not need external polish and splendor." This argument made no sense, he said, and was at variance with human experience. We see that physical beauty is most effectively shown off when dressed in beautiful garments, and the natural beauty of precious gems shines more gloriously when they are set in gold. Similarly, the liberal arts appear bare when they are not dressed in polished speech. Without the embellishment of words, they cannot display their natural beauty. "Must we not conclude that divine matters are illuminated and exalted by [such embellishments], indeed, that they cannot be expressed or brought into the open without them?" Some doctrines are difficult to accept, for example, the Church's teaching about Christ's virgin birth or the Holy Trinity. "To convince people of it, one needs exceptional rhetorical power and an infinite abundance of words. And only eloquence can produce this. As you can see, therefore, eloquence is very much necessary in sacred matters, both because it brings dignity and lustre to the subject and because it has the power of persuasion."[92]

The importance of style is also discussed in Paolo Cortesi's *Liber Sententiarum* (1504), a commentary on the standard scholastic textbook, the *Sentences* of Peter Lombard.[93] Cortesi's book served as a demonstration that the subjects arranged by Peter Lombard in the scholastic fashion of questions and articles could be treated equally well in literary fashion and in a classical style. In his prefatory letter to Pope Julius II Cortesi noted that some people hotly contended "that philosophers must not bring to their studies the splendor of [classical] Latin," and that it was desirable for philosophy "to be sordid and . . . uninviting, and not pour out its wealth to the common people." Cortesi himself was not advocating artificial splendor or the use of rhetorical deception, but merely a regard for the natural beauty of speech. He made a distinction accordingly, between *fucata* and *sana* eloquence. The latter was not merely embellishment, but aided comprehension and attracted Christians to the study of theology. Cortesi's views are applauded and reinforced in a letter from Conrad Peutinger to Beatus Rhenanus, added to the Basel edition of 1513. Certain theology professors, Peutinger writes, despised eloquence. They belittled those who taught Latin and Greek literature, calling them "poets" and demanding "that they be kept from teaching the young and even driven out of town." They forget that the Fathers joined eloquence with sacred philosophy. Cortesi, following their example in his book, "rescued Holy Writ from boorish and careless language" and showed that theological writings can be stylistically improved, "which was thought impossible until then."[94]

The argument of the defenders of the Vulgate is developed, for example, by Frans Titelmans in his *Collationes* (Antwerp 1529).[95] He took issue with humanists labeling the Vulgate's language "uncouth and lacking in style, or as they are inclined to think, horrid and filthy" and reproached their fastidiousness. These critics obviously did not understand that different styles are suited to different literary genres. As he saw it, there were three types of eloquence: the effeminate language of the poet, the carefully construed rhetoric of the philosopher, and the simple eloquence of the Bible.

> There is a certain carnal eloquence, soft-spoken and flattering, sweet and feminine, born from carnal loins rather than the Spirit of God, and most pleasing to carnal and effeminate men. There is a second kind of eloquence, no better than the first, but magnificent, sublime, and grandiloquent, weighing words in a marvelously majestic manner, balancing phrases and adorning them with wonderful human conceit. The wise men of this world use this kind of style to describe their wonderful wisdom in such obscure terms that it is accessible to the smallest possible number of readers. It is that wordy wisdom—an exceptional style, in which the wise men present their doctrines to the world in magnificent fashion—that pushes aside the humility of Christ's cross. This is a style that Paul was proud not to possess, a style which he despised and left to the

princes of this world ... When the eternal wisdom of the Father came to this world, it did not choose this style. Like a new philosopher, indeed a new wise man and a new teacher, he showed those who believe in him a third kind of eloquence. It is a simple and chaste style, humble and modest, meek and good, strict and lovable, a neat and clean kind of eloquence, in which he spoke to us in the flesh and which he wants his disciples to use.

While Titelmans presents a coherent argument set within a theory of style, Cousturier offers a jumble of arguments in a highly emotional tone. It was frivolous to be concerned with form rather than content; rhetorical pomp "did not become Holy Writ." Comparing the Bible to a life-giving tree, he reproached "excessive lovers of the Latin language" who cared more for the "leaves of style" than for the "fruit of its meaning." Expanding on this simile elsewhere, he condemned their shallowness for "thinking that we should tickle our ears and take vain pleasure in the foliage of words, when we should be convinced that we must seek spiritual understanding and sweet pleasures of the mind from the rough bark of its letter." Furthermore, stylistic artifice, rhetorical bombast, and refined words were unsuited to convey the divine message. The Holy Spirit loved simplicity and humility. "He wants simplicity of style observed in Holy Writ so that the salvation of the world be attributed to divine love and to a divine miracle rather than to human eloquence and polished style." To undertake a new translation to please lovers of Ciceronian Latin was thus "vain, bold, presumptuous, scandalous, harmful, dangerous, insulting, and indeed heretical, or at least smacking of heresy."

The passages quoted so far document objections based on the principle of inspiration and on resistance to polished speech as counter to the nature and purpose of Scripture. Cousturier adds a third argument: Scripture must be accessible to learned and unlearned alike. Stylistic revisions would make the text more difficult to understand. Contrary to the humanists' claims that solecisms obscured meaning, Cousturier insisted that the familiar nonclassical Latin was more easily understood than the polished language the humanists had in mind. "If you wanted to observe [classical] Latin idiom, the majority of priests would not understand it," he wrote. The Holy Spirit had dictated the Bible in a humble style, he said, "so that Holy Writ might benefit not only Latin scholars but also common clerics who generally know little Latin." It was inappropriate to produce one version for scholars and another for the common people: "All of us, scholars or not, must be content with one common translation."[96]

Cousturier's views are echoed by Alberto Pio, an Italian nobleman who fled to France after the Sack of Rome in 1527, and devoted the remainder of his life to defending the traditional text and interpretation. The Bible must be accessible to as many people as possible, he wrote, and for this reason it was not advisable to correct its grammar and style. He preferred words that were "less proper Latin but familiar": *minus Latina sed nota verba*. There was, moreover, something pagan and heretical about classical diction. He, for one, preferred unorthodox grammar to unorthodox thought.[97] Erasmus tells us that this was a common attitude. In some people's opinion it was "heresy to speak like Cicero." "Anything elegant or embellished with Greek will be suspect and brought before the censors," he observed. His own writings were a prime target for such critics. The Franciscan Nicolaus Bureau sampled the *Praise of Folly* and pronounced it dangerous. The author was bound "to lapse into some heresy on account of his lofty style."[98]

Erasmus' reputation as a stickler for classical style under all circumstances and a relentless critic of the Vulgate was undeserved, however. His position on literary criticism of the Bible was in fact a moderate one. He stated in the prolegomena to his New Testament edition that every discipline had its "technical terminology." On this analogy it was reasonable to make allowances for biblical idiom.[99] In his annotations on the text he repeatedly observed that he had retained phrases that were objectionable from a grammatical or stylistic point of view because they "were too ingrained to be removed."[100]

In a late work, *The Ciceronian* (1528), Erasmus made a remarkable effort to come to terms with the question of a "Christian style" and to present a solution palatable to both parties in the dispute. He suffered the fate of all moderates, however, and pleased neither side. In his view, the Christian style would be neither classical nor scholastic, but "something in between the extremes of Scotuses and Ciceronian apes": a style that was "appropriate and decorous."[101] He insisted, moreover, that for Christians it was Christ, not Cicero, that set the standard of speaking. "And if your speech departs from that standard, you will prove neither a good orator nor a good man." Indeed, "the person who treats matters of the faith in the phrases of unbelievers and contaminates his Christian subject matter with pagan follies will be thought a positive monstrosity."[102] This statement may surprise modern readers, who know Erasmus only as an advocate of classical learning. They may even argue that the character in the *Ciceronianus* does not represent Erasmus' opinion. There are, however, enough supporting statements in his other writings to suggest that Erasmus was not playing devil's advocate. Thus he writes in a letter to John Claymond, an old friend from Oxford days: "I cannot but approve of those who, out of a concern for morals, prefer to acquire a limited competence in rhetoric from the writings of Christian writers; these offer the added advantage of moral benefit, rather than exceptional purity of style learned from the books of pagans, in which there is a moral risk." He linked Ciceronianism with paganism in a surprising number of passages in letters, in one case going as far as to say that "Satan would want all men to be Ciceronians rather than Christians."[103] The speaker in the *Ciceronianus* is therefore clearly expressing Erasmus' personal opinion when he concludes: "We must be on our guard lest . . . we turn out not Ciceronian but pagan." Erasmus himself professed that he "would rather be thought a Christian than a Ciceronian."[104] In reading his discussion of alternative role models to Cicero, it becomes clear, however, that Erasmus is not suggesting that Christians turn to the Vulgate or to scholastic theologians. Rather, he advocates an eclecticism informed by the principle of appropriateness. "The doctrine of *decorum et aptum* . . . is a matter of primary importance."[105] Whether a Christian is speaking of secular or religious matters, he must preserve decorum in three respects. His speech must be appropriate to the subject, to the audience, and to the time. To follow the standard of Christ is to respect the conventions of Christianity. Speaking to a Christian audience on a Christian subject, one must use *recepta Christianis vocabula*, "established Christian vocabulary." This does not give Christians license to speak ungrammatically, but requires that they adapt classical rhetoric to the purpose at hand, or, as Erasmus expresses it elsewhere, in Jerome's image, "apply Egyptian trimmings" and "spoil the Egyptians of their gleaming vessels."[106] Speaking of the need to adapt speech to the exigencies of the time, Erasmus repeatedly uses the image of dress. "One garb suits the consort of a great king, another a swaggering soldier's mistress." Thus the speech of Demosthenes and Cicero must be tailored to the new, Christian age. "The dress that suits a child is not appropriate to an old man . . . well, then, do you think the world as it is now has anything in common with the situation at the time when Cicero lived and delivered his speeches?" The Church had gone from humble beginnings to greatness; so Christian speech, once humble, should now be allowed to adopt rhetorical splendor. After all, "bishops no longer dressed as the apostles once did."[107] Erasmus' final words on Christian style combine the ideal of *imitatio Christi* with *imitatio Ciceronis*: "If you allow that a person is a

Ciceronian when he speaks clearly, richly, forcefully, and appropriately, in keeping with the nature of his subject and with the circumstances of the times and of the persons involved, then there is nothing to stop a person from speaking in a manner that is both Christian and Ciceronian."[108]

In sum, the defenders of the Vulgate Bible argued that it was an inspired text and thus flawless in every respect; others conceded that its style was humble and even unidiomatic, but insisted that this was as it should be. It reflected Christian humility, while an ornate style and the use of rhetorical conceits were evidence of pride and hypocrisy. The simple style of the Bible made it accessible to a larger readership, moreover. The biblical humanists, by contrast, argued that the language of the Bible reflected the humble social status of the writers and admitted of improvement, either because it offended the learned or because it was out of tune with the status of the Church in their own time. As for the question of accessibility, it was true that the Bible was written for the people at large, but neither Greek nor Latin was any longer a lingua franca. Only educated readers were able to consult the biblical text today, which should therefore be adjusted to their standards.

Of the various arguments advanced for and against textual and literary criticism the ones that concern us most directly in the context of the humanist-scholastic debate are those related to the consultation of original texts and the need for language studies. In this discussion the philological method championed by the humanists is weighed against the scholastic method, which involved the study of medieval commentaries and their competent defense in disputation. The discussion touched on curricular requirements. Humanists demanded that logic, the core subject of the scholastic curriculum, be replaced by language studies or at any rate share time with them. The resistance of the theologians at Paris and Louvain, which was ostensibly based on their desire to preserve tradition and safeguard the authority of the Church, was to some extent an effort to protect their own authority and stave off changes in the curriculum that might expose their shortcomings or oblige them to acquire new skills.

CHAPTER SIX

The Debate
and the Reformation

ALTHOUGH THE HUMANIST-SCHOLASTIC debate at the universities was substantially about curriculum, it was also inseparably linked to matters of faith. The polemicists did not separate professional from confessional issues. Thus humanists were often cast in the role of destroyers of Church authority; scholastics in that of guardians of orthodoxy. From the opposite vantage point, the two parties were seen as enlightened reformers and guardians of a corrupt hierarchy, respectively.

In his classic article on the relationship between humanism and the Reformation, Bernd Moeller speaks of a "constructive misunderstanding" through which the cause of the humanists was identified with that of the reformers.[1] It appears that this misunderstanding was primarily in the minds of veteran Reuchlinists. The attack of the theologians of Cologne on Reuchlin, the champion of Hebrew studies, was an ugly combination of antisemitism and power politics with pseudo-doctrinal underpinnings in the common perception of Jews as "heretics" desiring to lead Christians astray. The humanist supporters of Reuchlin focused the discussion on a matter dear to their own hearts: language studies. Their support for the cause gained momentum from the parallel efforts of teachers of the humanities to enhance their standing at the universities, for the party lines in that struggle were much the same as in the Reuchlin affair. The case wound its way through the episcopal and papal courts. It was a see-saw battle, ending with Reuchlin being fined, that is, receiving a slap on the wrist. Although humanists tended to be bullish about the outcome of the dispute, they could by no means claim a victory. Perhaps the attacks on Luther and Erasmus, coming so closely on the heels of the earlier dispute, were regarded by them as an opportunity to fight a second round. The three cases—Reuchlin, Luther, Erasmus—

are linked, for example, by Willibald Pirckheimer, here commenting on the campaign of the Louvain theologians against Erasmus: "What they are doing is nothing new . . . to pass over the perverse spirit of sycophancy and the criminal machinations with which they harassed the renowned Reuchlin, who had done so much for Germany and literature . . .—what have they not plotted against Jacques Lefèvre and against Luther?" In a similar vein, Hermann Buschius likened the role Edward Lee played as spokesman of the Louvain theologians in their dispute with Erasmus to that of Ortvinus Gratius in the Reuchlin affair: "Before he sank his teeth into Erasmus, Lee was nothing but an insignificant little master of arts; once he had ventured forth against Erasmus . . . he suddenly became a theologian dropped from Olympus." Gratius had played a similar game in Cologne, he said, "when, to advance his career, he energetically implored his Alma Mater to act against Reuchlin."[2] The connection between Erasmus and Luther was evoked by Hutten. Luther's condemnation, he wrote, set a precedent, and "one could not suppose that the men who condemned Luther would spare [Erasmus]."[3] The jurist Ulrich Zasius drew similar parallels, praising Erasmus and Luther, classical and Christian scholarship, in one breath: "Through the divine talent of Erasmus and, in part, with the help of the most learned Martin Luther . . . there is no one today who does not understand Paul. I'll say nothing of Erasmus' efforts in establishing the text of Seneca and emending Cyprian, nothing of his admirable work, the *Adages*."[4] Albrecht Dürer likewise linked the two men's work. Puzzled by Luther's disappearance after the Diet of Worms, he called on Erasmus "to take his place."[5] Such remarks would indicate that some humanists failed to differentiate between cases that shared certain ingredients, to be sure, but in very different proportions. Remarks by Bucer and Zwingli have been interpreted as signs of a similar confusion in the camp of the reformers.[6] But when Bucer wrote that "Luther and Erasmus agree in everything" and Zwingli noted that "Luther is approved by all scholars in Zurich, as is the *Ratio* of Erasmus,"[7] they did not speak of Erasmus *qua* humanist, but, rightly or wrongly, drew parallels between the two men's theological positions. Bucer's remarks are made against the background of the Heidelberg Disputation, that is, in a theological context; Zwingli refers not to some humanist manifesto but to Erasmus' *Ratio*, a proposal for a new approach to theological studies. Hence linking Erasmus with Luther in this context does not necessarily mean identifying humanism with the Reformation.

Erasmus himself immediately recognized the danger of such an association and made every effort to keep the two movements separate. He

observed with alarm that the inquisitors of Brabant persecuted humanists and heretics indiscriminately. "The imperial edict arms them, not
against the champions of letters and language studies, but against heretics," he said. "Yet they abuse their authority." Elsewhere he wrote:
"They persecute letters rather than Luther"; they insinuate that "this
whole tumult has originated with language studies and literature."[8] A
number of Erasmus' partisans subscribed to the conspiracy theory. Ge-
rard Lister, rector of the Latin school at Zwolle, wrote of the attacks on
Erasmus' orthodoxy emanating from Louvain: "They [that is, the theo-
logians] leave no stone unturned, no venture, no plot untried against the
humanities." Beatus Rhenanus was of the same opinion: Edward Lee had
been suborned "by certain silly theologians, to play the lead in this comedy, enacted for the purpose of destroying good literature root and
stem." Hutten, too, acknowledged the adverse effects of the perceived
connection between Luther and the humanists: "In this business liberal
studies have got a bad name," he wrote.[9] Guillaume Budé deplored this
effect. "Linked with unpopular doctrines, the reputation of belles lettres,
both here and abroad, is at risk," he lamented. Similarly, Heinrich Cornelius Agrippa remarked that the "scholastic theologians of our day form
a solid phalanx to fight language studies and persecute them as if they
were the causes of all schisms and heresies."[10]

Thus the "misunderstanding" of which Moeller speaks, may have
served an agenda in the scholastic camp. It was in the interest of the
theologians to promote confusion. They eagerly seized on certain humanistic elements in Luther's program—his call *ad fontes*, his support for
language studies, his denunciation of scholastic Aristotelianism—to blur
the distinctions and kill two birds with one stone: suppress the "heretic"
and saddle the humanistic upstarts at the universities with a reputation
for supporting heresy. In the event, many humanists did abandon the
established Church, but to postulate a simple cause-and-effect relationship between their studies and their religious affiliation was a piece of
scholastic propaganda.

Luther himself, although not averse to a humanistically oriented curriculum for students of theology,[11] never identified his program with that
of the humanists. He and the other reformers naturally wished to replace
scholastic theology with another theological system, not with humanistic
rhetoric.[12] Conversely, leading humanists like Erasmus had no desire to
be drawn into the Reformation controversy and had already seen the
danger of humanism becoming a target in a war in which its own aims
figured only marginally. He wrote on this matter to Luther, asking him
"not to bring my name or my friends' names into what you write in

an unpleasant way . . . your enemies seek every opportunity to make us unpopular with the princes." By "us" he meant "the authors of the new learning who are the subject of conspiracies everywhere."[13] Luther, for his part, was content to keep Erasmus (and humanism) out of the dispute. "Do not publish any attack on me, and I shall refrain from attacking you," he wrote. "The one thing to be afraid of is that you might be persuaded by my enemies to attack my opinions in your published work, and that I should then be obliged to resist you to your face." Earlier on, Hutten had made the same request of Erasmus: "If you are afraid of burdening yourself with any unpopularity, do grant me just this: . . . remain silent."[14]

Erasmus, who was under considerable pressure to write against Luther to prove his orthodoxy, kept aloof for some time. He finally entered the fray in 1524 with a treatise on free will. *De libero arbitrio* and its sequel, *Hyperaspistes*, are regarded by some scholars as signposts on the road toward the divorce of humanism from the Reformation. Stupperich saw the subject as "an unsettled question between humanism and the Reformation"; W. Maurer wrote dramatically that the polemic "tore open an unbridgeable chasm" between the two movements;[15] F. Heer called Erasmus' polemic a "manifesto of European humanism."[16] Such interpretations give undue weight to Erasmus' views and, more important, put the wrong accents on the dilemma facing humanists in the 1520s. Although Erasmus was one of the most prominent scholars of his generation, he enjoyed only a brief vogue as an opinion-maker. His refusal to jump on the Lutheran bandwagon may have hastened the decline of his popularity. But whatever the reason, by 1525 his celebrity status was tarnished and he was soon to be reduced to the level of a stylistic model. Erasmus himself was keenly aware of this development, writing in 1523: "Time was when hundreds of letters described me as the greatest of the great, prince of the world of literature, bright star of Germany, luminary of learning, champion of humane studies, bulwark of a more genuine theology. Now silence greets me, or I am painted in far different colors."[17]

In his attack on Luther, Erasmus deliberately entered the polemic not as a humanist but as a theologian. He pointedly observed in a letter to Melanchthon, informing him of the publication of *De libero arbitrio*: "I kept the cause of the humanities separate from Luther's cause."[18] Accordingly, he did not focus his inquiry on an issue central to humanism—the dignity of man—but on a theological issue—the justification of the sinner. As a result, *De libero arbitrio* lacks that telltale humanist pride in the moral and intellectual potential of the human being, the triumphant, celebratory tone of Pico's *Oration*, or the proud symbolism of Vives' *Fable of Man*, which places the human being among the Olympic gods. Instead we find a self-deprecatory tone characteristic of St. Augustine, who saw the human potential reduced after the Fall to a flicker rekindled by the grace of God. Erasmus, likewise, reduces the human will to its lowest possible level and would have relinquished it altogether in deference to God's omnipotence, had he not considered it necessary to uphold the concept of a divine justice in terms comprehensible to the human mind. In his disquisition, Erasmus postulates the existence of the will only as a necessary corollary of personal responsibility; he devoutly accepts the idea of a human nature weakened and corrupted by original sin and redeemed not so much by human effort as by divine aiding grace.[19] Since doctrinal disputation was not an Erasmian forte—indeed he seemed at times out of his depth—his contribution to the debate over free will remained ineffectual. The dispute between Luther and Erasmus, though highly publicized, determined nothing on the doctrinal front, let alone on the humanist front.

Although *De libero arbitrio* was a theological treatise concerned with "a fundamental question of the Christian religion" (as Melanchthon noted),[20] it was not devoid of humanistic elements. It was certainly a humanistic notion that one could have a civil exchange about doctrinal matters.[21] Erasmus' treatise was no headstrong *Assertio* (the title of the Lutheran treatise at which he was taking aim) but a polite *diatribe*, that is, a discourse exploring various solutions to a given problem. He would have been content to let his inquiry end in suspended judgment, had not the Church, "to which [he] everywhere freely submitted [his] own judgment" already pronounced on the question of free will, thus obliging him to favor one side over the other. The treatise might therefore be said to deliver a lesson in humanist method, but it did not act as a catalyst. Humanists did not see their dilemma as one of a choice between Erasmus and Luther.[22] The choices to be made were between professions (literature or theology) and confessions (traditional or reformed church), not between humanism and the Reformation, movements that were not intrinsically incompatible.

Bernd Moeller coined the phrase "Ohne Humanismus keine Reformation" ("No humanism, no Reformation"), an aphorism that should be expanded to "A humanistic education may have made some people more receptive to the ideas of the reformers but did not necessarily lead them to join their ranks." It is true that there are many examples of humanists turning Protestant and few died-in-the-wool scholastics embracing the reformed church. Yet any conclusions about the relationship between humanism and the Reformation must be heavily qualified. First, geographical distinctions need to be made. It mattered a great deal whether the city or principality in which the individual lived gave the reformers official standing or consistently repressed them and threatened their followers with death, exile, or confiscation of property. Only in the first case can we make a clear distinction between supporters of the old and new faith and draw conclusions about the relationship between their cultural and religious orientation. In the second case the undoubtedly large number of Nicodemites will skew any statistic. It is presumably for this reason that James Tracy limited his survey of humanists joining the Reformation to those born in Germany, Switzerland, and the Low Countries between 1450 and 1510.[23] He finds an impressive number of humanists among the reformers in this period, but an even larger number of converts among the younger generation born after 1480. Even with this chronological division, the statistics operate on a coarse grid. After all, the conditions varied considerably for those born between 1450 and 1470, whose advanced age in the crucial years 1517–1521 would have made a conversion extremely unlikely; those born between 1470 and 1490, who would make decisions under the most difficult circumstances, that is, in the middle of their careers and before Protestantism was given official standing; and those born after 1490, whose decision was not burdened by the ballast of the traditional scholastic education, and who had the prospect of legitimate careers in Protestant cities.

Tracy himself invites scholars to investigate individual biographical data since certain questions are not answered by statistics. They concern practical and psychological considerations. How many of those who remained Catholic drew their income from benefices or depended for their livelihood on patrons with Catholic sympathies? How many sympathized with the Reformation but lacked the moral strength to act on their principles? These factors, which would of course influence an individual's decision, are difficult to document and evaluate. Mutianus Rufus (1470–1526) is one of the few who mentions practical considerations. In June 1521 he wrote to Johannes Lang, apologizing for not openly declaring his Lutheran sympathies. He was "in agreement with the Lutherans," he said, but they were causing disturbances in Gotha—"doors were pelted with stones, windows were rattled. We are surrounded by barbarity. I would be a fool to declare that I am on the side of the tumultuous Lutherans." "If you were in my place, good people, would you act differently?" he asked with touching candor.[24] *Beata tranquillitas* was Mutianus' guiding motif. Beatus Rhenanus (1485–1547) was a kindred spirit.

He did not declare his sympathies for the Reformation, his biographer Johann Sturm explained, because he was a man of peace: *propter ingenii placabilitatem*. He acknowledged that "some people blame [Beatus] for having been weak in matters of religion. He approved of our belief but did not take our side." Caspar Hedio, another contemporary of Beatus, commented: "There is no doubt that he [Beatus] cherished the true religion, but he conformed to the rites of his native city" (Catholic Sélestat). Hedio made much of the fact that Bucer was with Beatus at his deathbed, but it was by coincidence that Beatus died in Strasbourg on his way home from Baden, where he had taken the baths, and does not amount to a deathbed conversion.[25] Thus Beatus' position remains unclear. After all, he moved to Sélestat when Basel was gripped by religious strife. In other words, he voted for Catholicism with his feet, as did his friend, Erasmus. The latter, too, was in search of tranquility. He moved from the aggressively Catholic Louvain to the more liberal Basel to escape peer pressure, but left Basel when it officially joined the Reformation and moved to Catholic Freiburg. The actions and attitude of Henricus Glareanus (1488–1563) mirror those of Erasmus: like him he moved from Basel to Freiburg. In each of these cases, men who had given indications of sympathy for Luther remained Catholic. Whatever this may have meant in the context of their personal beliefs, it meant reducing friction with the outside world.

Humanists turned Protestant engaged in similar manipulations and/ or migrations to safe places. Wolfgang Capito (1478–1541) and Justus Jonas (1493–1555) openly professed their support for a reformed church but continued to guard their (Catholic) posts. Jonas did not relinquish his canonry in Erfurt until he was assured of a career in Wittenberg; Capito, "not one needlessly to jeopardize his position," retained his prebend until a crisis obliged him to choose between the Gospel and the Catholic Church.[26]

Many humanists were professional teachers—traditionally a highly mobile group—and they went where their religious preferences enhanced their careers or at any rate did not create obstacles for them. Hermann Buschius (c. 1468–1534) left the conservative University of Cologne and, after some wanderings, obtained a position at Protestant Marburg. Willem Nesen (1493–1524) left then-Catholic Frankfurt for Wittenberg but did not live to benefit from the move. Johannes Sapidus (1490–1561) gave up his post in Catholic Sélestat and was made welcome in Strasbourg. Conradus Pellicanus (1478–1556) moved from Basel to Zurich, where the Reformation was already established.

Practical considerations may also have determined Willibald Pirckheimer's (1470–1530) position vis-à-vis the Reformation. After clear expressions of support for Luther and glowing praise for the University of Wittenberg, "which had begun after so many centuries . . . to depart from the degenerated method of philosophizing that was setting it apart from Christian philosophy," he found his name on the papal bull and was obliged to recant.[27] Whether this represented a genuine return to the Catholic fold is a matter of dispute among modern scholars. W. Fuchs, for one, declares: "This was no devout turning back, not even a formal recognition of the Catholic Church, but a decision reflecting political realities."[28] Whatever Pirckheimer's personal commitment at the time, he was certainly shaken by the riots the Reformation engendered in his native Nürnberg. The city officially embraced the Reformation in 1525. Subsequent demands for the dissolution of monasteries affected Pirckheimer's family interests directly, since his sisters were in orders. He became a vocal opponent of the Reformation and actively engaged in the doctrinal dispute by writing a polemic against Oecolampadius.

Conversely, there are examples on both sides of the confessional borders of hardships bravely borne and practical considerations set aside in favor of following one's conscience. Otto Brunfels (1488–1534) suffered considerably for his choice. When he was refused a dispensation from his vows, he was obliged to flee his monastery, but succeeded after some wanderings to make a new life for himself in Strasbourg. In the other camp, Jacob Wimpheling (1450–1528) was almost seventy years old and in poor health when the Luther affair broke, but he "took up the pen in his tired old age" to come to the defense of the traditional church.[29] Wimpheling's confessional stand was in agreement with the official position of his city, Sélestat, but he lost the support of his friends, who by and large sympathized with the Reformation. Conrad Peutinger's (1465–1547) loyalty to the Catholic Church, on the other hand, put him at variance with the confessional policy of his city, Augsburg. When Augsburg officially joined the Reformation in 1534, Peutinger was obliged to retire from the post of city clerk, which he had held for thirty-seven years.

There is obviously a broad spectrum of responses among humanists to the Reformation. Some moved to places more congenial to their confessional preferences; others maintained their beliefs in defiance of the official position; a third group concealed their sympathies, yielding to peer pressure. The complex pattern of motives warns us not to attempt a facile answer to the question of the relationship between humanism and the Reformation. Instead of drawing general conclusions, it may be more profitable to examine the careers of two individuals in whose lives the tensions between humanism and the Reformation can be seen "writ large," and who can teach us an object lesson: Erasmus, opting for a painful compromise between humanism and Catholicism, and Melanchthon, embodying a successful conjunction of humanism and the Reformation.

Erasmus (ca. 1469–1536)[30] was brought up on the traditional medieval fare, although Alexander Sinthen, the headmaster of the school he attended at Deventer, was a disciple of Agricola and allowed his pupils a first glimpse of the New Learning. The death of his parents obliged Erasmus to abandon plans to go to university, since his guardians disapproved of this idea. On their urgent representations he entered an Augustinian monastery instead, where he pursued his education informally by reading the Fathers and perusing the classics surreptitiously. In 1495 he was sent by the Bishop of Cambrai to study theology at Paris, but conceived an instant dislike for the scholastic method. In a letter of 1497 to his friend and pupil Thomas Grey he gave a scathing description of the "quasi-theologians . . . whose brains are the most addled, tongues the most uncultured, wits the dullest, teachings the thorniest, characters the least attractive, lives the most hypocritical, talk the most slanderous, and hearts the blackest on earth." Theology, he writes only half in jest, "cannot be grasped by a person who has anything at all to do with the Muses or the Graces."[31]

Some thirty years later Erasmus provides this thumbnail sketch of the university and the changes it was about to undergo:

> Nothing darkens the glory of that university more than that young people barely get a taste of grammar before they are rushed off to study sophistry and the disciplines that arm them for the scholastic wrestling grounds. These disciplines may be conducive to forming judgment, but a knowledge of the languages is absolutely necessary. Many people are able to judge correctly without training in dialectic, but no one can understand what he reads or hears without linguistic skills. There will be some initial resistance [to introducing language studies], but the uproar will soon die down.[32]

The passage describes both the conditions at Paris in 1527 and Erasmus' own preferences—the preferences of a humanist—for philology over dialectic.

It is not clear how long Erasmus attended formal lectures in Paris. He never earned an academic degree, although a doctorate of theology was eventually conferred on him *per saltum* by the University of Turin. His letters from the Paris days give the impression that his theological studies were held in abeyance and his prime concern was earning a living through private instruction. As a tutor, Erasmus created a humanistic enclave for himself and his pupils: "Our talk is of letters at the noonday meal; our suppers are made exquisite by literary seasoning. In our walks we prattle of letters and even our frivolous diversions are no strangers to them; we talk of letters till we fall asleep, our dreams are dreams of letters, and literature awakens us to begin a new day."[33] Not surprisingly, the fruit of these years was a number of humanistic textbooks: a letter-writing manual, a handbook of style, an anthology of proverbs drawn from classical authors.

A shift in Erasmus' interests from the humanities to theology is noticeable in the aftermath of a journey to England in 1499, perhaps influenced by John Colet. His earnest pleas may have turned Erasmus from secular to sacred studies, and his bibliocentric approach supplied a congenial alternative to the despised scholastic method, but Colet had an aversion to language studies and therefore did not inspire Erasmus' philological approach to scriptural exegesis.[34] Erasmus first conceived a desire to put the *studia humanitatis* into the service of God from his readings in Jerome's works and sought to pattern himself after the Church Father. By the time he discovered Valla's practical example of textual criticism in 1504, he had already begun to collate manuscripts and fully realized the importance of a knowledge of Greek for establishing the correct text of the New Testament. His efforts to integrate humanism into theology can be traced to a youthful poem in which St. Jerome gives his blessing to those dividing their time and interest "between Pierian bands and Holy Writ."[35] A first example of such a combination of secular and sacred learning is Erasmus' tract *De contemptu mundi*, in which a Christian theme is illustrated with quotations from classical authors. Similar motives inform Erasmus' first translations of secular Greek texts, which he designated as propaedeutic. In the preface to his Latin Libanius he emphasized that he was practicing his skills on pagan authors "to avoid learning the potter's art on a great jar." If he made mistakes in these practice pieces, he did so "at the cost of my intellectual reputation alone, causing no harm to Holy Writ."[36] In retrospect, Erasmus saw his engagement with the *studia humanitatis* as a preparation for biblical scholarship: "When in my youth I embraced the finer literature of the ancients and acquired, not without much midnight labor, a reasonable knowledge of the Greek as well as the Latin languages, I did not aim at vainglory or childish self-gratification, but had long ago determined to adorn the Lord's temple."[37] These efforts would eventually come to fruition in his *magnum opus*, the New Testament edition of 1516.

The elements defining Erasmus' work at this point in his life reflect the converging paths of humanism and the Reformation in the first decade of the century. The two movements shared a rejection of the scholastic approach as crude in form and empty in content, and a focus on language studies as the essential preliminary training to an understanding of Scripture. These concerns are exemplified in Erasmus' writings, notably in the *Antibarbarians* and the *Ratio verae theologiae*, both of which we have already had occasion to quote.[38] The *Antibarbarians* establish the value of the humanities for the formation of the Christian mind in general; the *Ratio* makes the same point with respect to the professional theologian. The connection between humanistic studies and theology is emphasized in the defiant statement:

> I am quite aware with what arrogance and disdain some people view "poetry" as a rather puerile occupation, how they condemn rhetoric and everything that is called and indeed is "good letters." Yet these much-maligned letters have given us great theologians whom it is easier to neglect than to understand or imitate . . . Would it not be more justified to find fault with the commentaries of the theologians because they are replete with Aristotle? And if someone protests that one cannot be a theologian without an exact knowledge of those commentaries, I shall find comfort in the example of so many excellent men—Chrysostom, Cyprian, Jerome, Ambrose, Augustine, and Clement—in whose company I would rather be the meanest of orators than a theologian in the company of those who think they are above mere mortals. . . . It is more to the point, in my opinion, to teach our tyro doctrines in summary form drawn principally from the fountainhead of the Gospels and secondly from the apostolic letters, so that he might have a definite standard against which he might check what he reads . . . But someone may object: "What are you saying? Do you think Holy Writ is so easy and its meaning so evident that it can be understood without commentary?" Yes, it is—at least as far as we need to understand it for sound teaching rather than a theatrical display of learning.[39]

Here Erasmus promotes ideas that combine the catchphrases of humanism and the Reformation: he rejects scholastic commentaries; he expresses a preference for patristic theology; he recommends focusing on Scripture. For some time Erasmus had seemed to edge closer to the reformers. His first reaction to Luther was one of cautious approval, but soon it became clear that his own sense of tradition and his strong belief in consensus prevented him from joining a movement that appeared to head for schism and that denied the teaching authority of the Church.

Deference to the Church and its institutions forms a steady theme in Erasmus' writings from 1520 on. In his reply to Edward Lee, who had questioned his comments on auricular confession, Erasmus replied: "If the Church affirms in an unequivocal decree that this form of confession is based on divine law, if she believes that it was instituted by Christ himself, if she believes that it cannot be abolished, I do not contest the judgment of the Church but adapt my view to its definitive pronounce-ment, however much it may differ from my own." After his annotations on the New Testament had been attacked, he added an apologia to the revised edition of 1522, *Summary points against captious and morose critics*, in which he assured readers that "I wish to have it attested throughout that I never willingly depart even a finger's breadth from the judgment of the Church."[40] In 1525 he repeatedly professed his readiness to sub-mit his findings to the judgment of the Church: "I do not contest the verdict of the Church, I adapt my interpretation to its oracular voice, even if it goes against the grain"; "I submit my conjectures to the judg-ment of the Church."[41] In an apologia *Against the Spanish Orders* of 1527, he insisted that his researches did not go against the Church but were subject to her approval: *non contra ecclesiam, sed sub ecclesiae judicio*. In his defense against the censures of the University of Paris in 1531, he stressed the same point: "If the Church commands us to believe this, I gladly submit my interpretation to the verdict of the Church"; "I merely give my opinion without prejudice to the constitutions and customs of the Church."[42]

His willingness to submit to the Church circumscribed his research as a scholar and defined for him the relationship between humanism and theology. The limitations this definition put on his findings made it im-possible for Erasmus to graft humanism on to the Reformation. To the modern, secular mind this may be an unacceptable compromise of scien-tific principles and a violation of scholarly integrity; to the pious mind nourished on the ideas of the *Devotio moderna* it was an acceptable limita-tion. Erasmus' willingness to yield to the Church is not only the result of personal piety but also part of an intellectual construct. Central to his attitude toward the magisterium of the church is his definition of "ar-ticles of faith." There are three tiers of doctrine, he explains:

First, there is that which the Catholic Church holds without con-troversy and by a large consensus, such as the doctrines expressly stated in Holy Scripture and in the apostles' creed, to which I am willing to add the decrees of councils properly constituted and following proper procedure. Secondly, there are doctrinal matters on which Church authority has not yet clearly pronounced and about which there is dispute among theologians even today. Thirdly, there are those doctrines which are pressed on us as if they were the oracular pronouncements of the Church, whereas they are the opinions of men and often lead to strife and dissent, contributing little or nothing to piety. As far as the first category is concerned, there is nothing which I have not sincerely professed in all my writings. As for the second category, if I feel certain about something I say so openly, if I am in doubt, I neither approve nor disapprove of it. If I object to it and see no good coming from my objections but rather upheaval, I keep silent. If I see that it would do some good, I speak up. . . . I have said a great deal about the third category and have proposed material for discussion to scholars. But they are looking for a certain and definitive pronouncement on every single point. It is obviously not pious for me to pronounce on matters which are clear and have been handed down by lawful and public authority and have been accepted by the Church. Concerning the rest—matters on which the Church has not yet expressly given judgment—it is not my task to pronounce, for I have neither the learning nor the public authority to do so. With respect to the third category, my inexperience likewise excuses me from making a pronouncement . . . I would ask those who demand this from me to join me in embracing unquestioningly what the Church—indisputedly inspired by the Holy Spirit—has handed down to us; and in doubtful matters either to consult those who are foremost in knowledge and authority or else join me in awaiting the verdict of the Church, suspending their own judgment.[43]

One of the key words in this full statement on doctrine is *consensus*, which Erasmus consistently employs as the touchstone by which orthodoxy may be distinguished from heresy. This consensus, however, must be of long standing and prevail among a significant number of people. In the *Explanatio symboli*, Erasmus offers this answer to the catechumen asking how he may recognize the voice of the Church among so many sects: "There are many indications, . . . [but] the foremost is the authority of the ancient synods approved by the lasting consensus of so many centuries and nations. To this is added the authority of the exegetes whose sanctity the Church blessed . . . thirdly, one must consider the range, for no heresy is as widespread as is the [orthodox] Catholic doctrine."[44]

Erasmus declares repeatedly that he cannot join the reformers because they do not manifest the telltale consensus. "The preaching of the apostles inspired trust because their teaching always agreed," he writes to the Strasbourg reformers, "whereas you not only disagree among yourselves, but individuals are inconsistent with themselves concerning rites and doctrines . . . If I could convince myself that you are all following the genuine Gospel, I would already be in your camp. But the dissensions among you clearly show that this is not the case." He rejects the remonstrations of the Lutherans with the same arguments, writing to Conradus Pellicanus: "Why these threats? Because I refuse to depart from the public verdict and the consensus of the Church and am not convinced by a dissenting opinion? You are fighting among yourselves." To Bucer he wrote in the same vein: "You say that you are convinced that what you profess is the teaching of Christ. If I could convince myself of that, no one among you would profess it more readily than I. But if you are convinced, how it is that you cannot agree among yourselves?" Similarly he taunted Luther that he was calling him to join a congregation that was divided among itself: *disgregatam congregationem et undique dissectam sectam.*[45]

Erasmus' pacifism is well known. "The Church is shaken to its very foundations by menacing factions," he laments, "on every side the seamless coat of Jesus is torn to shreds." In one of his last works, a Psalm commentary subtitled "On rebuilding the concord of the Church," he makes a plea for peace, linking it to his other criteria—consensus and tradition: "It ought to be a deep conviction of everyone that it is neither safe nor helpful in fostering peace to brashly abandon those positions which have been established by the authority of our ancestors and confirmed by the practice and agreement of generation after generation."[46]

Clearly, Erasmus did wish to put his skills as a humanist into the service of theology, but as a Catholic humanist he was prepared to accept the magisterium of the Church and the curtailment of individual liberty this entailed. I say this as a twentieth-century scholar: Erasmus himself would not have defined his position in the negative terms of "curtailment." He saw it in the positive light of *docta pietas* or *pia curiositas*— the term he uses in the *Ratio*. There he describes the approach a Catholic humanist should take to research:

> He must have the simple, dove-like eye of faith which sees nothing but what is of heaven. He must have an ardent desire to learn . . . In approaching the sacred threshold he must shed all pride, all arrogance. These qualities are at variance with the Spirit, which takes

joy in meek hearts far removed from headstrong minds. The palace of this Queen is grand once you have penetrated to the innermost chambers, but the entrance gate is very low. You must bow your head, if you want to be admitted. Stay away from that most noxious plague, the thirst for glory, which is generally found in headstrong minds. Stay away from tenaciousness, the parent of strife, and even more so from blind temerity . . . distrust your own judgment, submit yourself to the Holy Spirit, our teacher, that He may shape and form your judgment . . . Embrace what is placed before your eyes; adore with simple faith and venerate from afar what is kept hidden from you. Keep away from impious curiosity . . . If you read anything that appears to be at variance with Christ's teaching, take care not to misinterpret the text; rather, assume that you have not understood what you were reading, or that there is some underlying figure of speech, or that the text has been corrupted. . . . Be sober and temperate in disputation; make it look like a comparison of points rather than a conflict. Frequently interrupt your reading to pray and give thanks—pray and implore the help of the Holy Spirit; give thanks for God's favor when you feel that you have made progress.[47]

The road to Christian humanism which Erasmus outlines here was not easy to follow. The conjunction of learning and piety he envisaged meant accepting rather than confirming doctrine. To many this appeared to be an unserviceable approach. They interpreted Erasmus' spirit of compromise as lack of moral courage and personal commitment. His call for moderation was doomed in an era that was characterized by a polarization of opinions which ended in schism.

Philipp Melanchthon (1497–1560) belonged to a younger generation of humanists.[48] His studies at Heidelberg and Tübingen brought him in contact with both scholasticism and humanism, and although his inclination toward the latter became apparent early on, it was not immediately accompanied by a sharp rejection of scholasticism. For some years Melanchthon kept his criticism of the scholastic method muted. In his preface to the *Epistolae virorum clarorum* of 1514 he avoided the subject altogether, although the context would have afforded him an occasion to comment on the scholastic theologians of Cologne. Similarly, he did not condemn dialectic in the oration *De artibus liberalibus* (1517); rather, he praised it generously as an essential skill.[49] The new subjects he championed on this occasion—history and poetry—were meant to be additions to the curriculum rather than replacements of any existing subject. Veiled criticism of the scholastic method can be found in the preface to the edition of Terence (1516), where Melanchthon contrasts "nugatory" academic exercises with the kind of inquiry that is "most useful in the formation of character." But it was only in 1518, in the preface to his Greek grammar, that he rejected the scholastic approach to learning in terms typical of the humanist-scholastic debate, speaking of pseudo-philosophers who teach nothing but "the rudiments of quarrel and strife."[50]

These sentiments are expressed in a more definitive form in the oration that inaugurated his lectures in Wittenberg in the fall of 1518. There Melanchthon openly condemned the scholastic method, "which our barbarian forefathers brought from Scotland to France and from France to Germany," tracing the decline of learning to the devotion of the scholastic theologians to a "corrupt and truncated Aristotle." These "teachers of ignorance" taught a method that did not deserve the name of dialectic. They themselves had been taught in a corrupt fashion and perpetuated a worthless method, "capering like old men in their second childhood." The scholastic system, Melanchthon said with disdain, "produced men like Thomas, Scotus, Durandus, the Seraphic and the Cherubic doctors, and all the rest—a progeny more numerous than the Cadmean brood." He made a point of the fact that his criticism of scholasticism was based on personal experience: "I am entitled to speak freely in this respect because I suffered the grind for six whole years."[51]

Melanchthon did not merely criticize the scholastic method but also proffered his own views, recommending a humanistically oriented curriculum: "Grammar, dialectic, and rhetoric should be studied to the extent of equipping you to speak well and pronounce judgment, so that you do not rashly embark on higher studies. Greek must be added to Latin studies, to enable you to understand the philosophers, theologians, historians, orators, and poets whom you encounter at every step, and to understand the essence of the matter, not just its shadow." Equipped with these resources, the student was ready to turn to philosophy and theology.

Even at this early point in his career, Melanchthon linked the *studia humanitatis* with ecclesiastical reform, repeatedly associating the decline of learning with a decline in piety. "When the old disciplines were deserted . . . holy matters were neglected." "As soon as good letters were replaced by bad, pristine piety underwent a change as it was subjected to ceremonies, human customs and laws, decretals, chapters, addenda, and glosses twice removed." A humanistic curriculum, by contrast, would help to restore theology to its pristine condition. It would guide the theology student back to the very sources of Christianity and aid his understanding of the literal meaning. "Next, after we have understood the letter, we shall examine the meaning of things. Let us be done with all the frigid little glosses, the concordances (or rather discordances), and all the other hurdles that hold back the mind. When we turn our minds to the sources, we shall begin to have Christ's wisdom. His instructions shall become clear to us and the nectar of the blessed divine wisdom will be poured on us."[52]

In the *Encomium eloquentiae* of 1523 Melanchthon makes another statement on the importance of the humanities in the training of the theologian and the unwillingness of the scholastic theologians to accept this idea:

> For the sake of being regarded great theologians, they look down on the humanities . . . But this is a pretext for mental sloth, for they are far from being the theologians they profess to be. They are too lazy to learn pure diction and to bother reading difficult authors and exercising their style (for a knowledge of letters is not achieved without keen study); instead, they come home well soused, read a little sermon from which they pluck the nauseous stuff they produce, and hold forth at dinner parties (for that's when they are at their best). Because the common people applaud, they think they are practically perfect theologians, whereas they discuss matters of the highest importance without respect and with a filthy mouth.[53]

Learning and piety go hand in hand, Melanchthon notes repeatedly: "The Church was deprived of letters, and ignorance of sacred matters ensued"; "ignorance of letters is accompanied by public impiety"; "it is clear that with the help of some good men the knowledge of letters must be restored in theology."[54] At the same time, Melanchthon acknowledges the importance of vocation, the divine calling of the theologian. "I am not of the mistaken opinion that sacred matters can be penetrated by the earnest application of the human mind. There are elements in the sacred Scriptures that no one can understand without God's help, nor does Christ reveal himself to us unless we are taught by the Holy Spirit." The scholastic theologians, however, were neither inspired nor learned. "They drew up articles in Paris, which the world adored as if they were divine laws; nothing was pious except what they dreamed up. And these wonderful men who had no learning to teach them wisdom, brought forth a foolish, sophistical theology." As a result, "theology has been completely buried in silly and impious questions. They want to be professional philosophers and they don't even understand the meaning of the word philosophy."[55]

Thus far Melanchthon repeated well rehearsed slogans of the humanist-scholastic debate, but his writings soon showed a creative reworking of these ideas. The integration of humanism into a theological system is already apparent in his first doctrinal work, the *Loci communes*, the title of which invokes the precepts of classical rhetoric and serves notice to the reader of the author's departure from the scholastic method.[56] Although medieval writers occasionally employ the term *loci* in Melanchthon's sense of doctrinal commonplaces or principal points— Thomas Aquinas' use in the *Summa* is probably the best-known instance[57]—the more common terms are *maximae* or *sententiae*. Alanus of Lille is the first medieval writer to make the connection between the rhetorical *loci communes* and principal theological doctrines in his *Regulae theologicae*. He begins his preface: "Every science is based on its own rules or foundation ... just as dialectic has rules called *maximae* and rhetoric *loci communes*, and ethics *generales sententias* ... so theology does not lack its maxims."[58] Melanchthon introduces his *Loci* in similar fashion: "Each discipline usually requires certain *loci* which contain the sum of the discipline and on which we focus our studies as on a target."[59] Significantly, he acknowledges his debt to medieval predecessors only in passing and in a critical tone.[60] It was more in keeping with his own cultural orientation and the direction taken by the Reformation to acknowledge links with the Fathers, as he did in the preface to the revised *Loci* of 1535.[61] Conversely, it may have been politic not to mention Erasmus, although the Dutch humanist was likely one of Melanchthon's sources of inspiration.

In his *Education of the Christian Prince* of 1516 Erasmus recommends that the teacher put together a collection of doctrinal commonplaces: "What must be implanted deeply and before all else in the mind of the prince is the best possible understanding of Christ; he should be constantly absorbing His teachings, gathered together in some convenient form drawn from the original sources themselves."[62] In the *Methodus*, also published 1516, Erasmus actually uses the term *loci* in describing such a collection. The passage sounds remarkably like a prescription for Melanchthon's *Loci communes*:

> Now I shall speak of a method which may be of exceptional benefit if it is used dexterously. It is the method of devising a number of theological commonplaces *(locos theologicos)*, either thinking them up yourself or taking up those provided by someone else, and arranging what you read under these headings, in pigeon holes, so to speak, so that when you need to put your finger on what you want,

it will be readily available. For example, you might jot down something on the subject of faith, fasting, suffering evil, helping the sick, on ceremonies, on piety, and on other things of this kind.[63]

In his *Ratio* of 1519, the expanded version of the *Methodus*, Erasmus elaborates on this section, suggesting additional headings, "on bearing with impious magistrates, on avoiding offense to simple minds, on the study of Holy Writ, on obligation toward parents or children, on Christian charity, on respect for those in charge, on envy, on slander, on chastity."[64] Although his categories do not parallel those of Melanchthon except in two or three cases, they point in the direction pursued by the reformer.

Reformed theology and humanism are linked in Melanchthon's *Loci* in the sense that he employs a classical rhetorical concept in a book on Christian doctrine. The two currents are also conceptually linked in Melanchthon's theory of the *duplex regimen* or twofold order, first developed in the *Themata ad sextam feriam discutienda* of 1522. Melanchthon's distinction between the spiritual and the corporeal order and his discussion of their relationship could serve as a model for the relationship between sacred and secular letters, or between reformed theology and humanistic studies. In Melanchthon's system education belongs, together with the ordering forces of family, state, and the institutional church, to the *regimen corporale*. Just as custom and law support the divine order, so secular learning forms a support system for theology—not merely in the traditional sense of being a "handmaiden of Queen Theology" but in filling the more significant propaedeutic role of creating the external framework for spiritual progress. A humanistic education established certain norms which were "pedagogical" in the Pauline sense of laws being "schoolmasters to bring us unto Christ" (Gal.3:24), a passage which Melanchthon expressly applied to the *regimen corporale* in his *Epitome ecclesiasticae doctrinae* of 1524.[65] The connecting and distinguishing points between humanism and the reformed theology are made clear in this question: "If the humanities have not been taught, what kind of theologians will we create?"—carefully qualified by "but I know how much to attribute to the humanities, lest anyone think I am detracting anything from the Holy Spirit here."[66] The same distinctions and connections appear in the *Ratio discendi* of 1522:

You must know that languages and literature are from heaven. When in former times the Gospel had to be spread over the whole world, the apostles received the gift of tongues. The same obtains today: the Gospel is reborn and, simultaneously, the study of languages is restored and with its help we learn the Gospel. . . . Eloquence was once dead. Now that God has restored it to life, we must guard the divine gift in every way. For you know what chaos the collapse of eloquence brought with it. Theology and piety died with it . . . I know that not only languages, but the Spirit is required in treating of sacred letters. But one needs the help of the other, and there is a friendly exchange. I require both Spirit and languages. And Paul required that they speak in languages and prophesy. And so I implore you with all my power to ready your minds for the study of Latin and Greek literature, lest your efforts in sacred literature be in vain.[67]

Melanchthon's urgent admonition contains several key statements linking reformed theology with learning and, more specifically, with the humanistic curriculum. Both sacred and secular learning are seen as divine gifts (coelestes demum linguae ac literae sunt; illam [eloquentiam] restituerit Deus); the decline of eloquence is said to have led to the decline of religion and theology (collapsa illa . . . theologia, pietas simul cecidere); the revival of language studies and letters is seen as part of a divine plan. Just as the apostles were once equipped with the gift of tongues that they might spread the Gospel, so at this junction in the history of the Church languages are once again destined to play a crucial role in the dissemination of the reformed doctrine: cum renascitur evangelium, simul illae [linguae et literae] restituuntur, quarum adminiculo evangelium discamus.

The humanistic ingredient—the emphasis on learning as the basis of a correct understanding of Holy Writ and thus piety—remains constant in Melanchthon's writings and is expressed just as vividly in his later writings, for example, in the *Oratio de studiis linguae Graecae* of 1549. Again he links learning (in this case a knowledge of Greek) with piety. "God entrusted the New Testament to the Greek language . . . Therefore this language is absolutely necessary to help us read and correctly understand the New Testament , which contains the message of Christ . . . Thus I have said that the Greek language is the teacher and, so to speak, the fountainhead not only of the celestial doctrine but of all learning."[68]

Melanchthon's official pronouncements suggest that he effortlessly combined humanism with the Reformation and fused the tasks of the humanist and reformed theologian in himself, but there are indications that even Melanchthon was unable to overcome completely the tensions between the two movements. He was curiously ambivalent about teaching theology, seeing himself merely as a stand-in for Luther and his lectures as *opera vicaria*.[69] It is significant, moreover, that Melanchthon did not proceed to a doctorate in theology and continued to teach arts courses. When Luther urged him to relinquish his philological lectures and concentrate on theology, he justified his preference by saying that there were many qualified theologians but few philologists.[70] In 1521 he wrote that he would "rather leave off" teaching theology; in 1523 he stated that he had looked at his lectures in theology merely as a partial requirement for the degree of a bachelor of theology and never expected them to turn into a permanent duty.[71] In his study of the theological faculty at Wittenberg, K. Aland therefore asks the provocative question: "Is Melanchthon to be regarded a theologian?"[72] Melanchthon, however, was only reluctant to teach, not to write theology. And this may well provide us with a key to understanding his approach. It is important to remember that he professed to have engaged in theology "for no other reason than to correct [his] life."[73] His overriding goal, then, was self-improvement. The teacher's task, by contrast, cannot be exclusively self-centered; it is altruistic by definition and involves reaching out to others. The intellectual process is one of giving to the student and, as every teacher will confirm, a "draining" experience. Conversely, the process of writing a textbook or developing a theory, which involves discovery and the ordering of one's thought, is a learning process. Although publication, which makes a writer's thoughts accessible to others, may convert scholarly findings into a teaching tool, a book remains in the first instance the record of an internal dialogue. Melanchthon's statement that he studied theology for the purpose of self-improvement suggests that the conversion of the results of his private quest into a handbook of doctrine for others was incidental, so to speak. Lutheran anthropology may also have affected Melanchthon's approach to teaching theology. After all, Luther denied the possibility of synergism in the process of salvation and thus intrinsically weakened the rationale underlying the teaching of theology. However, in the absence of any definite statement from Melanchthon himself, the motives for his reluctance to teach must remain vague. It is notable, though, that a certain rekindling of his interest in the teaching of theology in later years was accompanied by a softening of his position on predestination.[74]

The choice of Erasmus and Melanchthon as examples illustrating the relationship between humanism and the Reformation was determined by their high profile and the large corpus of their writings, which provide more evidence for their intellectual and spiritual progress than we are able to gather for lesser figures of the period. They are, however, only examples of the kind of thought processes to which every humanist in the sixteenth century had to submit in order to reach some sort of accommodation between his intellectual and religious life. Although Erasmus' and Melanchthon's experiences make the issues concrete, it would ultimately be wrong to draw general conclusions from the public lives of these two men about a matter that is essentially private and personal and often remained, because of the intoleranz of the age, unstated or disguised.

The sublimation of the humanist-scholastic debate into the Reformation leads us to examine some examples of the debate in the 1520s and 1530s, that is, the climactic period of the Reformation, for the purpose of commenting on the literary qualities of the polemic at that stage. Two works are especially suitable for our purpose, affording us an opportunity to juxtapose Reformation polemics with entries composed in the fifteenth century. They are Franz Burchard's re-casting of Barbaro's reply to Pico (1534), and Frans Titelmans' dialogue *Collationes* (1529).[75] Burchard's composition invites comparison with Barbaro's second letter to Pico, on which it attempts to improve; Titelmans' *Collationes*, contrasted with Bruni's *Dialogues*, exemplify the changes that occurred within that genre.

In the original exchange between Pico and Barbaro dating from 1485,[76] Pico's scholastic rejects the use of rhetoric in philosophical discussions, contending that truth needs no adornment. Nor do philosophers offend against the rules of grammar, he notes; rather, they have devised their own rules or conventions—a legitimate practice, since grammatical norms are nothing but an arbitrary set of rules agreed upon by a group. The scholastic concludes his arguments with a diatribe against "certain grammaticasters [who] turn my stomach, who when they have made a couple of etymological discoveries become such show-offs, so tout themselves, so boastfully strut around, that as compared with themselves they would have philosophers esteemed as nothing. They say, We do not want these philosophies of yours. Well, small wonder. Neither do dogs care for Falernian wine." Barbaro begins his second, elaborate reply to Pico by emphasizing that their dispute is an intellectual exercise. He is delighted with Pico's clever conceit, allowing a barbarian to defend scholastic barbarisms in the most exquisite style, and continues the game by introducing a "real" scholastic who rejects the defense of scholasticism proffered by Pico's pseudo-scholastic in the most contorted and inconclusive terms.

Fifty years later, a student of Melanchthon, Franz Burchard, expressed dissatisfaction with Barbaro's reply and composed what he considered an improved version. In his dedicatory letter to the jurist and historian Justinus Göbler he noted that Barbaro had not in fact refuted Pico's arguments, speculating that he may have held back on purpose because the subject was not suitable for a letter. To deal with it in epistolary form was rather like depicting a colossus on a tiny canvas. "When I came to realize this myself, I began to write with less enthusiasm, and reined in my course, as it were. However, I have briefly shown the sources of Pico's arguments so that youthful readers may find it easier to assess where he goes off course, so to speak, and maintains absurd ideas in jest."[77]

While Barbaro in his original letter has ample praise for Pico's genius, Burchard's praise is only perfunctory. He is clearly not delighted that Pico has put his eloquence at the service of the scholastics and questions the practice of defending a worthless cause even as a rhetorical exercise: "I would not have them armed with the authority of your name, nor equipped with your weapons against the most eminent arts" (53).

In the original letter Barbaro imitated Pico's conceit of having a fictitious scholastic philosopher argue against eloquence by introducing a contemporary scholastic to carry on the argument. This "Paduan" is annoyed at being defended by a "grammarian" who "uses examples, stories, yarns, and proofs from the poets . . .I am a philosopher [he declares], I want conclusive proof, the rest I leave to the orators" (29). He proceeds to discuss the relationship between philosophy and rhetoric, citing the arguments of the humanists without, however, refuting them conclusively. Rather, his point is that the humanists are merely offering "commonplaces that may perhaps be argued against us as much as for us" (37). Their loose handling of these *topoi* and their faulty process of reasoning leads nowhere. "When Pico says, 'The discourse of an orator is soft and dainty,' it is called false in every part, for there is neither regression nor transposition, that is, there is neither antistrophe nor anastrophe. When he says 'Rude and mean discourse is full of majesty,' it is called wholly false because it is neither invertible nor convertible" (37). What the Paduan wants instead is a proper syllogistic treatment: "Let the matter be taken up by men who have no art of speaking, that is, men who with heart and tongue are our partisans." He may be beaten in such a disputation, but "it will be less annoying to be beaten fairly, and besides, a victory sought with enemy help cannot be sweet and good to look upon" (38). In his reply, then, Barbaro makes no serious effort to refute Pico but has composed a persiflage, ridiculing the scholastics' preoccupation with formal modes of inference.

Burchard's Barbaro, by contrast, answers Pico in earnest and in his own words, eschewing the conceit of citing a third person. Moreover, while the "Paduan" merely considers the logical probability or conclusiveness of a proposition, Burchard considers its substance. Significantly, his letter focuses on ethical rather than logical considerations. He speaks of rhetoric not merely as an academic discipline or professional skill, but as a moral power: neglect of rhetoric has had an adverse effect on religion, he claims (53). Eloquence has both an esthetic and an ethical dimension. "It makes it possible for great things to be magnified and for things needing abasement to be humbled" (55). Language, moreover, is the cement of society; it cannot be reduced to "a game or a pack of tricks" (56). The scholastic jargon, by contrast, serves no moral purpose: "Of what use to the commonwealth is this obscure speech? Can it be used in teaching men? In guiding or expounding religions? In the exercise of justice? In short, in managing the whole of our public and private life?" (57) The moral urgency of Burchard's reply stands in marked contrast to Barbaro's letter of 1485. The earlier writer offered a playful reply, criticizing scholasticism implicitly by presenting an amusing caricature of scholastic foibles. Instead of this, Burchard substituted an explicit argument representing his personal convictions. Although his letter was a rhetorical exercise and was published as an appendix to Melanchthon's manual of rhetoric, epideixis was not the author's ultimate goal. The exercise clearly served an educational purpose. It was to teach the student correct thinking along with correct speaking.

The purpose of Burchard's reply to Pico is also borne out by the material he chooses for discussion. He responds to the elements in Pico's letter that specifically concern theology or may be applied to it rather than to philosophy in general. Pico's scholastic says that eloquence is out of place "in questions about natural and celestial things" (17). Burchard effectively turns "questions about natural and celestial things," that is, natural philosophy and metaphysics, into a specific reference to scholastic theology: "As for those masters of yours, Thomas and Scotus, . . . how can one imagine anything more stupid than for those men to present themselves as teachers of churches and guides of life—without eloquence!" (58) Pico's scholastic notes that philosophers do not aim to please: "We do not expect the applause of the theater because a rounded or a rhythmical period has caressed the audience's ears" (18). Burchard turns the philosophers into theologians. "Would, dear Pico, that likewise your theologians might spurn other pleasures, just as they scorn elegance of discourse" (61). Pico's scholastic contrasts Lucretius with Duns Scotus, concluding that "no doubt Scotus philosophizes better than the other man, who speaks more elegantly" (24). Burchard suggests a more pertinent comparison, namely, between Jerome and Scotus. "Which do you think has served the Church better? The one who by his eloquence illuminated the Holy Scriptures and diligently expounded many dogmas, or Scotus who, while he elucidated no dogma, brought into the Church the most trifling disputations?" (64). Burchard's final criticism of the scholastics is pointedly anachronistic and quite obviously aimed at the scholastic theologians of his own time:

> They do not understand the discourse of the Scriptures, they have no knowledge of ancient history, their poverty of judgment makes them incapable of handling the controversies and ideas of antiquity. In consequence, they have spread in the Church many impious and pernicious opinions. How stupid are their interpretations of the prophets and of Paul! In this matter especially it is absurd for dialecticians and men who have spent a lifetime in that one art never to see (and this is the very business of dialecticians) what David or Paul is saying, what are the beginnings of their arguments and what their ends. But your commentators of Scripture are, as the common saying goes, clowns at a feast. So it is that because they cannot understand a discourse, they build a new edifice of theology . . . All sane-minded men admit that disputatious theology has gone so far in vanity that Christian doctrine ought to be called back to its sources. To effect this the study of eloquence will be profitable. If ever our people begin to cultivate it, I hope some Hercules will rise up to free the earth of those monsters and restore the native beauty of philosophy and Christian doctrine.   (67)

Significantly, Burchard also introduces a concern that is central to the Reformation but has no parallel in Pico's letter: the call to by-pass scholastic theology and return to the source, that is, Scripture. He concludes with another catchphrase of the sixteenth century, a reference to the "plot" of the theologians to suppress the humanities, "an amazing conspiracy . . . to prevent the possibility of a reflowering of the better studies" (68).

Burchard's reply is thus an opinion piece masquerading as a rhetorical exercise. Barbaro's original letter presents the opposite case. It contains two levels of conceits. The argument he pursues is posed artificially, for (as he notes) there is no disagreement between himself and Pico. What is presented as an opinion piece is therefore really an intellectual exercise. Furthermore, Barbaro devises a "Paduan" scholastic to refute the defense of scholasticism proffered by Pico's fictitious champion. This is clearly a spoof, designed to entertain the reader with clever paradoxes.

Burchard, conversely, adopts the format of a rhetorical exercise, but clearly presents his own heartfelt views on the present state of things. The literary veneer on his composition is thin. We find Barbaro's pleasant, almost jocular tone replaced by what Burchard himself apologetically calls "sharp" and "vehement" argumentation. Thus what passes for a variation on Barbaro's theme is actually an independent entry into the humanist-scholastic debate.

The same pedagogical tightening of purpose is apparent in Frans Titelmans' *Collationes*, which might be contrasted with the *Dialogues* of Bruni. Titelmans (1502–1537), a Franciscan and member of the theological faculty at Louvain, was a protégé of Jacques Masson and continued his mentor's polemics against Erasmus. For his dialogue he chose a historically impossible scenario, "mingling the dead with the living," as Erasmus observed.[78] The characters are Titelmans himself, Lorenzo Valla, Jacques Lefèvre, and Desiderius Erasmus. Valla's lifetime does not overlap with any of the other speakers; the rest are contemporaries, but Titelmans was personally acquainted only with Erasmus. Given these difficulties, it is not surprising that the author had the four characters meet in a geographical vacuum—no description of place is provided. However, the reader is given a sense of the passage of time. The conversation takes place over a period of five days, interrupted by a feast day (Ascension of the Lord) and a Sunday. Except for one malicious detail (Erasmus "forgets" about the feast day), the speakers are devoid of personal features and do not emerge as literary characters. They seem to be reciting from their works, to be refuted by Titelmans in an atmosphere of forced cheer and perfunctory expressions of good will. Thus the *Collationes* are a pale reflection of Bruni's *Dialogues*, with their detailed and historically plausible setting. They offer nothing comparable to the lively atmosphere created by the Italian humanist, the cordial relations between the speakers that override their disagreements, and the leisurely pace of conversation that allows for contradictions and reversals of opinion. For Bruni's convivial discussion, which is savored by all as a form of spiritual refreshment, Titelmans substitutes a dialogue that is carried on as a Christian duty. Accordingly, each day in the *Collationes* ends with expressions of fatigue, the only realistic touch. Titelmans concludes the discussion of the first day: "I suggest that we end our labor now that we might return with a fresher mind to a similar work of disputation, lest the tedium of a conversation protracted too long burden and blunt our minds" (54 recto). The others respond with similar sentiments. They want "to pause in their work and recover," "stop in their work while it is not yet too hard" (ibidem). In the context of the discussion, each man is expected to bear his colleague's admonitions in the spirit of Christian meekness: "It becomes Christians to accept the corrections and even reproaches of true friends with equanimity and a more joyous heart than the bland kisses of flatterers . . . for a friend's correction and, when so required, his harsh reproaches are a principal aid to a virtuous life and self-knowledge," Titelmans pontificates (137 recto–verso). While Bruni's speakers take pleasure in learned companionship, Titelmans emphasizes moral obligation. The discussion in the *Collationes* is not undertaken for pleasure but as a Christian duty. From the beginning the reader is made aware of what constitutes the correct view. There is no question who will win the argument, and no playful exploration of the opposite point of view. Bruni presented a discussion among friends and equals for the purpose of intellectual stimulation, in which the pursuit of truth was central while truth itself remained elusive. In Titelmans' *Collationes* the object is to establish the truth or truthful interpretation of the Bible, from the author's point of view. He pursues his goal singlemindedly, giving such marginal attention to the literary setting that one wonders why he did not simply present his work as the disquisition it is. Perhaps Titelmans felt obliged to adopt what he considered a humanistic format, since he wanted to engage in discussion with humanists, just as Pico in his *Apologia* adopted a scholastic style to be able to communicate with scholastics.

Neither Titelmans nor Burchard are successful in their attempt to archaize—if that was their purpose. Their compositions have an unmistakable sixteenth-century flavor and are representative of the humanist-scholastic debate as carried on in the shadow of the Reformation. Comparing Titelmans' and Burchard's entries with earlier pieces, we see how the debate has been transformed over a period of a hundred years. The literary epistle of the fifteenth century has turned into a sermon; the dialogue into a disputation. And the scholarly gentlemen and dilettantes have given way to professionals, whose purpose is not intellectual recreation but the salvation of the soul.

Humanist Critique
of Scholastic Dialectic

MODERN SCHOLARS ARE DIVIDED on whether humanism acted as a retardant or a stimulant to the development of Renaissance philosophy. Some see it as an impediment in the linear path leading from scholasticism to the scientific revolution, others think it breathed life into a moribund system.[1] The most recent studies have emphasized the complex interaction between humanism and scholasticism and the methodological advances made as a result of this cross fertilization. The branch of philosophy that is of particular relevance to our subject is logic, or more specifically, dialectic, the core subject of the scholastic curriculum. The humanists voiced their opposition to the scholastic method on several counts, as we had occasion to observe: its excessive reliance on Aristotle; the separation of rhetoric from dialectic and the exaggerated attention given to formal proof at the expense of other modes of inference; and the use of technical jargon accessible only to a narrow clique of professionals.

The humanists' opposition to Aristotle did not aim at complete emancipation from his authority. The point was to steer away from the slavish devotion to Aristotle, which allowed no objection to the argument *ipse dixit*, "He said so." The humanists claimed, moreover, that his medieval interpreters had misrepresented and corrupted Aristotle's teaching, and hence insisted on the need to consult the text in its original language. Alternatively, they suggested that Aristotle be approached through humanistic translations and commentaries, which showed greater historical sophistication than did their medieval forerunners. Whatever the nature of their criticism, however, it is significant that their own proposals for a humanistic dialectic remained a modification of medieval Aristotelianism rather than an original construct, a reaction to an existing system or curriculum rather than a completely new initiative.[2]

In the teaching of the three branches of the *scientia sermocinalis*—grammar, rhetoric, and dialectic—the medieval curriculum placed the emphasis on dialectic. The need for grammar was acknowledged, but it was considered a rudimentary art. To be called a *grammaticus*, a grammar teacher, was accordingly regarded an insult by serious scholars. The value of rhetoric, on the other hand, was questioned by some. Its purpose was suspect in their opinion because it produced belief rather than knowledge and addressed emotion rather than reason. Conversely, polemicists held a perception, or perhaps one should say a pretense, that dialectic showed the way to an objective truth. Medieval textbooks of dialectic clearly promised to teach a method of *probabiliter disputare*, arguing with plausibility,[3] but in the academic world, obtaining the agreement of the opponent or gaining formal victory over him in a disputation was accepted as the criterion transforming *probabile* into *probatum*, a plausible argument into proof. Indeed, the flaw lay not in the process of reasoning, which guaranteed a valid conclusion from valid first principles, but rather in the method of establishing first principles. This did not deter scholastic theologians, since their first principles were supplied by the Church in the form of articles of faith that needed no further confirmation. Over this point there could be no quarrel between believers, humanist or scholastic. But once it was acknowledged that the validity of a conclusion rested, in the final instance, not on reason but on authority—in theological disputations, on the authority of God as revealed in the Bible and interpreted by the Church—it was difficult to maintain the superiority of dialectic over rhetoric. Neither could lay claim to presenting the audience with finite proof, each asked the hearers to "believe," that is, to take certain premises for granted. The scholastics themselves revealed the weakness of their system by producing formally correct arguments which concluded in patent nonsense. Thus Prantl in his history of logic characterized scholastic logic after Ockham as "formalistic, obscure, and—we must say—nonsensical."[4] In the context of logic a purely formalistic approach resulted in a lack of personal conviction in the defeated protagonist despite a formal concession of victory to the opponent; in the civic and religious spheres, such argumentation left people "cold," a simile often used by reformers complaining of the adverse effects of a "frigid" scholastic theology on the spiritual and moral state of Christianity. Humanists were interested in a philosophy that was applicable to life. Their criticism of scholastic argumentation was informed by concerns for ethics and the demand for a method that was of use in decision-making rather than in academic disputation. They therefore demanded effective rather than formally valid arguments, conclusions to which the hearer would give not merely his cerebral but also his emotional assent, since the latter translated into action more readily.

The discussion over method of argumentation led many humanists to claim that the distinction between dialectic and rhetoric was artificial, that both subjects drew on the same material for their proofs. The corollary of this conjunction of disciplines was the demand that both use the same language and terminology. For humanist attacks on the scholastic jargon, Erasmus' *Praise of Folly* provides the locus classicus:

> They dwell in a sort of third heaven, looking down from aloft, almost with pity, on all the rest of mankind as so many cattle crawling on the face of the earth. They are fortified with an army of scholastic definitions, conclusions, corollaries, and propositions both explicit and implicit ... they quibble about concepts, relations, instants, formalities, quiddities, and ecceities, which no one could possibly perceive unless like Lynceus he could see through blackest darkness things which don't exist ... These subtle refinements of subtleties are made still more subtle by all the different lines of scholastic argument, so that you'd extricate yourself faster from a labyrinth than from the tortuous obscurities of realists, nominalists, Thomists, Albertists, Ockhamists, and Scotists—and I've not mentioned all the sects, only the main ones. Such is the erudition and complexity they all display that I fancy the apostles themselves would need the help of another Holy Spirit if they were obliged to join issue on these topics with our new breed of theologian.[5]

Lampoons and tirades against the language of the scholastics are frequent in the literature of the debate, but serious intellectual arguments against the need for a specialized language are found less often. Conversely, scholastics failed to defend their need for a technical language effectively. They protested that all specialists used technical terminology, that literary Latin was not precise enough for their purposes, that they were concerned with content rather than form. They might have argued more cogently that logic was different from other disciplines using language as a medium because it was wholly about language, but I know of no scholastic who advanced the idea of a meta-language in the context of the humanist-scholastic debate.[6] Although it would have been more difficult to deny the need for a technical notation if it had been presented in these terms, humanists could of course still have objected (as they did) to the type of analysis needing a meta-language, that is, to an analysis concerned with structures of language rather than the meaning of terms. The former method did require a kind of scientific notation to test arguments; the latter analyzed arguments in terms of usage. Indeed, if an analysis of meaning rather than structure was desired, philological rather than logical skills were called for.

After these preliminary thoughts, let us consider the humanist response to traditional scholastic dialectic in more detail. A brief survey of works in which significant alternatives were presented will be in order here.

The first humanist to go beyond verbal sparring to offer constructive criticism of scholastic logic was Lorenzo Valla (1407–1457). He laid the foundation for what might be called a humanistic dialectic by fusing the rhetorical and dialectical methods and focusing attention on compelling argumentation rather than demonstrative proof. The work that interests us in the present context is his *Dialectic*, first drafted in 1439 under the title *Repastinatio dialecticae et philosophiae*.[7] The keyword in the title of the prototype, *repastinatio*, has been variously interpreted as a "re-laying," "ploughing over" or "re-digging" of the foundations of traditional logic.[8] However, Valla may have had in mind the more specific meaning in which the word was used by Tertullian:[9] "cutting back" or "weeding out," terms which aptly describe his approach to Aristotelian logic, as we shall see. Although Valla worked on the book for some twenty years, the text, first printed in 1499, lacks the smoothness of a final version and often requires the reader to interpret what is merely implicit in the text. New avenues of thought are explored more often than developed, and inconsistencies or traces of parallel thought remain throughout. Valla himself believed that he had at any rate provided his readers with the means of escaping from the confines of medieval Aristotelianism:

> May the dialecticians and philosophers hereafter refrain from persevering in the ignorant use of their own terminology, and turn instead to the natural speech commonly used by scholars, for if they persist they will achieve nothing now that I have revealed the great number of words in which they stray from the truth, so that now it will be self-evident. What they will do is their decision, however. Certainly those who are not followers of their school have been supplied by me with the weapons to defend the camp of wisdom from the enemies (or rather, deserters) of truth.[10]

Valla's critique of scholastic dialectic was given textbook format, so to speak, by Rudolf Agricola (1444–1485). The title of his book, *De inventione dialectica*,[11] is indicative of Agricola's emphasis on the process of invention, that is, the discovery of appropriate *loci*—"receptacles or store-houses," as he called them, "in which all the instruments of establishing belief are laid up" (1.2, p. 9). Throughout the book we find indications of the author's didactic purpose. We hear the teacher's voice in the statement: "It is not enough to memorize the commonplaces; rather one should keep them ready, practiced, in view, so to speak, and at hand" (2.26, p. 354). It is Agricola's stated purpose to help those who are "of a slower cast and cannot see things and are able to discover what to say about each subject either late or never" (1.1, p. 2). He deliberately expressed himself in a simpler fashion, he explains, because he saw merit in "bringing Cerberus up from the Underworld, that is, to draw into the light and lay out for all to see what is abstruse and hidden in the inner core and recesses of things. I want to explain this to the crowd, that is, to those who are less sophisticated and rather inexperienced, for the learned need no teacher" (1.3, p. 14). Elsewhere he reiterates this purpose: "If my discussion is less subtle, I will succeed at any rate in making the matter plain—and that will fulfill my intentions" (1.3., p. 180). He concludes the book with another reference to the didactic purpose of his work: "I could have led on by a shorter, but rougher, more difficult path strewn with obstacles, but I thought it better to take the roundabout way, which is more pleasant and commodious and less beset by thorns." He expresses the hope that readers will appreciate his effort, for it was for "their benefit and advancement" (3.16, p. 455). Readers responded enthusiastically. The forty-three editions published between 1515, when the *editio princeps* appeared, and 1543 are striking testimony to the success of Agricola's book.

Sixteenth-century humanists consistently paid homage to Valla and Agricola as sources of inspiration. Among those who transmitted and elaborated on their ideas are Juan Vives, Philipp Melanchthon, Petrus Ramus, and Marius Nizolius.

Juan Vives (1492–1540) entered the field in 1519 with a diatribe *Contra pseudodialecticos* which, he emphasized, was based on his own experience with the scholastic curriculum at Paris. Thus no one could accuse him of "condemning what he did not understand."[12] The short oration is effective because the bitter criticism it contains is seasoned with wit and humor. It is clear that Vives' aim was not only to fill his audience with indignation but also to move it to laughter with examples of bizarre questions and absurd conclusions proffered by the scholastics.

More detailed criticism of Aristotelian logic can be found in Vives' *De causis corruptarum artium*.[13] There he briefly acknowledges his predecessors Valla and Agricola. His references to the former are not without barbs, however. "Lorenzo Valla began to rebuild dialectic, disagreeing with Aristotle and both the old and the modern Aristotelians; yet in a few cases his counsel is incorrect; in many matters he slips up, for he was full of passion and rushed to conclusions ... his arguments are not shored up with strong reasons, nor were they accepted by anyone as doctrines of dialectic."

In his oration *Contra pseudodialecticos*, Vives had expressed the intention to complement his criticism of Aristotle with a theory of his own: "If by God's favor I shall live for another ten years in reasonably good health, I shall rid their minds of this error, not by arguments, but by example" (76–78). A work entitled *Dialectices libri quatuor* (Paris, 1550), published after Vives' death, does not fill the bill. It takes a traditional approach and appears to be a youthful work, evidently not considered fit for publication by the author himself.[14] More in line with Vives' projections in *Contra pseudodialecticos* are two essays composed in 1531 on judgment (or proof) and invention respectively: *De disputatione* and *De instrumento probabilitatis*.[15] Both tracts continue the trends initiated by Valla and Agricola, using nontechnical Latin and moving away from syllogisms.

Vives' contemporary Philipp Melanchthon produced what is perhaps the best Renaissance handbook of dialectic. His *Erotematum dialectices libri ... scripti ut iuventuti utiliter proponi possint* (published in its first version in 1520) was, as the subtitle indicates, conceived as a textbook "written such that it can be usefully presented to young people."[16] The book has all the merits of a modern manual of instruction. The material is concise, clearly structured, presented in a convenient question-and-answer format, and elucidated with down-to-earth examples. The feature that sets Melanchthon apart from his predecessors is the Christian thrust of his exposition. He uses examples with a predominantly Christian moral—a notable departure from the examples of the "Roe and Doe" kind found in earlier handbooks. Like Agricola, Melanchthon demands that students understand rather than memorize the rules. He notes that some students use technical terms "like magical incantations." They must be directed "not only to recite the figures and moods [of syllogisms], but to think about the reasons for the logical connections" (593).

Petrus Ramus (1488–1567) first gathered his thoughts on the teaching of dialectic in *Dialecticae partitiones*, published in 1543 (a slightly revised version appeared in the same year under the title *Dialecticae institutiones*). Highly rhetorical in style, the book at times gives the impression of being a *laus disciplinae* rather than a handbook. A lack of structural divisions and lengthy digressions made Ramus' first dialectic a cumbersome tool for the classroom; a handier, more lucid version appeared in 1546 under the title *Dialectici commentarii*. Since Ramus' books had been banned by a royal decree because of their polemical nature, this edition was published under the name of his colleague and collaborator, Omer Talon. After the royal decree was revoked, Ramus translated a streamlined version into French (*Dialectique*, Paris, 1555). Latin adaptations (with Talon's commentary) entitled *Dialecticae libri duo* appeared in several editions until 1572. The system of bracketed, dichotomized tables generally associated with Ramist dialectic was fully developed only in the posthumous editions of Freige.[17]

Marius Nizolius (1488–1567) published his *De veris principiis et vera ratione philosophandi contra pseudophilosophos* in 1551.[18] The Parma professor of rhetoric was well known for his Ciceronian lexicon, which saw more than fifty editions in the sixteenth century, but his book on dialectic fell into oblivion almost immediately, to be rescued in the seventeenth century by none less than Leibniz. Re-editing the work in 1670, the great scholar of the Age of Enlightenment pronounced it "right for the times" and expressed the hope that it would "contribute something to the restoration of modern philosophy."[19] In twentieth-century literature, however, Nizolius has been treated, until recently, with contempt as the purveyor of homespun truths and bourgeois platitudes.[20] Neither as simplistic as his modern critics would have him, nor as relevant to our age as Leibniz found him to be in his, Nizolius is nevertheless of interest to us in the present context because his emphasis on experience and sense perception marks the transition from the scholastic method and its humanistic alternatives (which, whatever innovation they suggested, were still rooted in the Aristotelian system) to a more critical scientific method.

After this brief introduction to the proponents of a humanistic dialectic, let us proceed to examine their views on the principal points under discussion: their opposition to Aristotelian logic; their views on the relationship between dialectic and rhetoric, and in this context their attitudes toward the question of technical terminology and formal proof; and finally, their pronouncements on the purpose of studying/teaching dialectic.

In this group of proponents of a humanist dialectic, Valla, Ramus, and Nizolius were the most outspoken critics of Aristotle. In Valla's estimate, Aristotle was not worth the hero-worship accorded him. His sphere of activity had been rather limited, Valla noted in the proem to his *Dialectic*. Aristotle had not engaged in pursuits beneficial to mankind: "giving public counsel, administering provinces, developing therapeutic treatments, administering justice, issuing decrees, writing history, or composing poems" (Zippel 5:20–24). While some disciples of Aristotle admired the quantity of his output, Valla was not impressed by it. "What if Aristotle wrote more than others? Did he write better books?" (6:12). Valla furthermore implied that Aristotle's work lacked originality. "He wrote more than the rest, but he also compiled more [from other sources]. And you can judge his lack of integrity from the fact that he does not acknowledge his debt to those from whom he took the material, but boasts of it as his own. Yet if he thinks they made a mistake somewhere, he cannot keep their names to himself any more than he could keep a burning flame in his mouth" (6:19–24). Although Valla is sharply critical of Aristotle himself, he reserves his sharpest rebukes for his followers. "It is embarrassing to relate the initiation rites of his disciples. They swear an oath never to contradict Aristotle—a superstitious and foolish lot, who do a disservice to themselves. They deprive themselves of an opportunity to investigate the truth" (7:4–8). Not only did these people follow their idol slavishly, they expected the same devotion from others. "Those modern Peripatetics are intolerable. They deny a person who does not adhere to any school the right to disagree with Aristotle" (2:16–18). They have closed their minds firmly to all arguments. "They regard all other philosophers as nonphilosophers and embrace Aristotle as the only wise man, indeed the wisest—not surprisingly, since he is the only writer they know. If one can call it 'knowing,' for they read him, not in his own language, but in a foreign, not to say corrupt, language. Most of his works are wrongly translated, and much that is well said in Greek is not well said in Latin" (4:10–16).

The main thrust of Valla's efforts was toward "simplifying" the Aristotelian system, as can be seen from his treatment of the categories, transcendentals, and modal terms. He reduces the ten categories (substance, quality, quantity, relation, place, time, action, affection, state) to substance, quality, and action. Similarly he collapses the six transcendentals (being, quiddity, thing, unity, truth, and goodness) into "thing" by resolving "being" into "quiddity," and "quiddity" into "thing." To the rest he "denies the honor of being transcendentals" (18:10). The six modal terms (possible, contingent, impossible, necessary, true, false) he reduces to three: possible, impossible, true. Valla's efforts to prune traditional logic are not without medieval precedents. The question whether the ten categories of Aristotle were necessary or could be reduced or combined was well rehearsed and makes its appearance in summaries such as Ockham's *Expositio aurea*.[21] The number of modal terms is critically examined in Abelard's *De partibus categoricorum*.[22] Similarly, the number of transcendentals was discussed by Thomas Aquinas. There is however a significant difference in the arguments proffered by the scholastics and by Valla. While all of them argued by logical inference, Valla adds examples from classical literature to clinch his argument. Thus in the process of reducing Aristotle's ten categories to three, he argues that in ordinary speech quality and quantity are often combined in one phrase, indicating their synonymous nature and thus a conceptual overlap. He draws his proof from Virgil's *Aeneid*, quoting the lines "like Polyphem in his cave" (*qualis quantusque*; 2.592) and "as she is accustomed to appear" (*qualisque . . . et quanta*; 3.64) in which terms denoting quantity and quality respectively are used as synonyms (139:26–30). He employs a similar process in discussing the transcendentals, mixing logical arguments with examples drawn from common usage and employing metaphor to make his proposal more plausible. Thus he argues logically at first: "'Something-thingness' is . . . 'some thing'; 'otherness' the equivalent of 'other thing,' 'sameness' of 'same thing,' 'nothingness' of 'no thing.' Thus if 'being' is resolved into 'that which is' and 'that which is' into 'this thing,' then 'being' is resolved into 'this thing which is'" (14:1–5). To this Valla adds a discussion of the meaning of *res*, thing, referring to common usage to show the broad range of the term: "*Res* can mean 'quarrel' or 'business,' as in *res est mihi cum homine furioso*, or it can mean 'deeds,' as in *res Augusti multi scripsere*, . . . or it can discreetly denote sexual intercourse, as Thais says in Terence, *Miles cum quo tum rem habebam* . . . or it can stand for 'usefulness,' as in *e re est, in rem tuam est*" (16:22–17:10). Valla's whole argument is wrapped in metaphor: "We shall inquire which of these six words [the six transcendentals] . . . is the general and king, that is, the most powerful . . . In my view, of these six, which now contend for the kingdom, as it were, 'thing' will be king as surely as Darius, son of Hydaspes, was designated king by those six Persians who permitted fate to decide the kingship" (11:18–12:2). He continues with this metaphor after concluding his logical argumentation: "To bring the inquiry to an end and no longer to deny all those clamoring nations their king, since (as I have already indicated) the horse of our Darius neighed, not on account of his servant's trick,[23] but on account of reason and God's assenting nod, there will be no further controversy about the kingdom. As for the other five—quiddity, being, unity, good, and truth—let them do as the Persians did, get off their high horse and humble themselves before 'thing,' which is special among the six—just as the five Persians prostrated themselves before Darius whom they had acknowledged as their king" (15:11–18).

It is interesting to compare Valla's frilly treatment of the question with

Thomas Aquinas' spare and sober discussion of the terms "good" and "being" and the relationship between the transcendentals in general:

> Being can in no way be understood apart from the true, for being is known only in so far as it is true. Therefore, the true and being do not differ conceptually . . . And they do not differ in any other ways, for they must belong to some common genus. Therefore they are entirely the same. If they were not entirely the same, the true would add something to being. But the true adds nothing to being, even though it has greater extension than being . . . The true includes both being and non-being; since it does not add anything to being, it seems to be entirely the same as being.

This is followed by arguments to the contrary and their refutation. In this manner, that is, in purely logical terms, Thomas leads his readers by degrees to the conclusion that "being, the true, the one, and the good are such that by their very nature they are one in reality."[24]

The juxtaposition of the two passages demonstrates at one glance the striking differences between the scholastic and the humanistic approach and, at the same time, explains the impatience of the scholastics with arguments that necessarily struck them as silly chatter and examples of fuzzy thinking.

We have noted Valla's references to "corrupt" translations of the Aristotelian corpus. The authenticity of the texts in circulation was a matter of lively discussion in the Renaissance. Vives alluded to their corrupt state in *De causis* (1.4). Ramus, according to his biographer Freige, defended in his master thesis the proposition "Whatever is circulating as said by Aristotle is trumped up *(commentitia)*." Nizolius likewise devoted a chapter to the same topic in his *De principiis*, contending "that the books which are read today under Aristotle's name are in their majority not truly his, but surrogates and forgeries" (II 165). Ramus' thesis is not extant, but a critic describes its contents as a denial "that the works of Aristotle which have come down to us were by Aristotle, on the grounds that you [Ramus] could not find in them the golden river of eloquence which Cicero so often says he found in Aristotle. You maintained that these works were the productions of some other upstart and crotchety sophist."[25]

Ramus' critical attitude toward Aristotle found its fullest expression in his *Aristotelicae animadversiones* of 1543, aptly described by Ong as "a whirlwind tour of the Aristotelian *Organon* . . . [which] has as its objective not explanation but annihilation of the text to which it is addressed."[26] Ramus spoke of the errors, confusions, and fallacies found in the Aristotelian corpus, and of the "chaos" and "darkness" of his teaching. His precepts did not produce honest disputants, but "pertinacious, captious sophists and impostors" (65–66).[27] Although Ramus' own dialectic uses some of the Aristotelian elements, his structure differs significantly. He arranges the material under three headings or "steps" (*gradus*): nature, theory/teaching, and practice. This combination of ingredients of success can be found in classical sources going back to Plato, Isocrates, and the Greek Sophists, and reappears in the pedagogical writings of humanists in the same sense. In Ramus, too, the three criteria determine success—in finding the truth, that is—but nature is used here not in the sense of an individual's ability but of the natural ability to reason that is inherent in all human beings. "Nature laid the groundwork for disputation; theory (*doctrina*) equipped these beginnings with appropriate and fitting counsel; equipped with theory, practice applied it and rounded it off."[28]

Ramus' treatment of the third part, practice, is the most original. Here he applies the rules of dialectic to classical literary texts taken from Virgil, Ovid, and Martial, that is, uses dialectic as a method of literary criticism or exercise in comprehension. The process involves "cutting out from the parts of the continuous discourse the many syllogisms which you see in it," peeling away the rhetorical ornaments, "and forming the sum total of the discourse into one syllogism." We also find in this first edition of Ramus' dialectic a "summary and universal partition of the dialectic art . . . for the eyes to see," that is, displayed in chart form—a technique which did not originate with Ramus but became his trademark.[29]

Nizolius, as we have noted, shared Ramus' suspicions about the authenticity of the Aristotelian texts current in his time. In *De principiis* he wrote: "Someone made extracts of the genuine works and reduced them to the epitome or compendia we have now. . . . Much material has been added, subtracted, and changed at the pleasure of the person who reduced them to this form" (II 173). Nizolius accordingly ridicules the disciples of Aristotle who are so fascinated by their idol that "the claim 'Aristotle said so' has more credibility with them than rational arguments" (I 33). The Aristotelian system had already been attacked by Valla, Nizolius acknowledged, but Valla had merely "lopped off some branches, leaves, and shoots of dialectic, doing some damage, . . . but leaving stem and roots intact" (I 35). Nizolius, who was familiar with earlier humanistic critics of Aristotle, citing Valla, Agricola, Vives, and Melanchthon, declared that it was his intention not only to criticize Aristotle, as his predecessors had done, but to root out the whole system. In the event, however, his bark was worse than his bite. He criticized Aristotle in great detail, but left many of his constructs in place.[30]

Where he differs most radically from Aristotle is in the doctrine of universals, and, in consequence, of demonstrative proofs based on an innate knowledge of the universals. Nizolius advocates a crass nominalism. He attacks first of all the traditional notion of the abstract, insisting that abstract nouns were no more than collective terms, *omnia singularia unius cuiuslibet generis simul comprehensa* (I 78). Thus he substitutes *comprehensio* (comprehension in the literal sense of a "gathering together") for the notion of abstraction, which carries with it the ballast of realism. "In place of abstraction we must put a truly philosophical and rhetorical process of gathering together, which brings forth and creates, so to speak, those universal premises on which rests the tradition of the arts and sciences, and on which (as I have shown) proof and syllogisms are truly founded."[31] The "pseudo-philosophers" (the Aristotelians), however, prattled of universals "which are not found in the true nature of things, and which are totally false and fictitious" (I 61).

While Valla, Ramus, and Nizolius show strains of a rather virulent anti-Aristotelianism, Agricola, Vives, and Melanchthon are more restrained in their remarks on the teachings of Aristotle and his medieval interpreters. Agricola conducts only a mild polemic against the philosopher, "a man of the highest talent, learning, eloquence, practical experience, prudence—in a word, a great man, but a man after all. It is possible, then, that he remained ignorant of some things, that he did not discover everything but left some things for others to discover . . . so that I think we may justly excuse those who believed that they need not cling to him in everything everywhere as to a rock and who did not give up on their own intelligence" (*De inventione* 1.3, p. 15). What Agricola criticized primarily in Aristotle was his complexity, "so that in addition to the difficulty presented by the obscure subject matter, he added more obscurity himself" (ibidem).

Agricola's reworking of the Aristotelian system is announced in a statement at the beginning of Book II of his *De dialectica inventione*:

> The one task proper to dialectic is, then, the ability to present a plausible argument, so far as the nature of the subject permits. This process, as I said before, consists of two parts: one, called invention, shows how to devise the argument; once the argument is devised, the other teaches a form of argumentation, that is, a fixed rule for exploring the argument, by which it is, like a coin, proved either valid or false and deceptive. This part is called judgment. Whereas

the former has an advisory function and deliberates about what needs to be said about each subject, the latter argues the thesis to be proved in a sort of exploratory way and brings it to the point of establishing conviction in the listener.

Agricola is speaking of the materials presented in Aristotle's *Topics* and *Prior Analytics*, respectively, but he reverses the order in which they appear in the *Organon* and in which they were conventionally taught. Instead, he suggests teaching commonplaces before syllogisms. He notes, moreover, that the choice of commonplaces is as important as formal proof in arguing plausibly. Aristotelian dialecticians failed to take this into consideration.

> These learned men (for thus I shall politely call them) do not understand that no argumentation is cogent because it is derived from species or genus or any other of the *loci;* for one can derive inept and inconsistent conclusions from any of them. An argument is cogent only when things are related in a manner that allows their being cast in the form of a syllogism or other accepted type of argument, which permits the conclusion that things are internally consistent and necessarily connected. (2.1, p. 179)

It is important to choose material appropriate to the subject and to the listener: "Internal consistency is one thing, establishing belief is another." In order to be convincing, the proof presented must be meaningful and relevant: *cognatum esse oportet illi cui probando adhibetur* (1.2, p. 7). Because it is difficult to reduce this process to hard-and-fast rules, Agricola decided to make it the focus of his book. The Aristotelians, by contrast, had their priorities wrong: "Following Aristotle, everything is full of teaching about the part that concerns judgment, although it is the part that gives less trouble since it consists of fixed rules, and those neither very difficult nor very numerous. The method of invention, on the other hand has, as far as I know, never been committed to writing by anyone worth reading after Boethius" (2.1, p. 181).

Vives' remarks on Aristotle indicate a certain change in his attitude over the years, the later works evincing less tolerance. In *Contra pseudodialecticos* he made a point of distinguishing between Aristotle and his medieval interpreters, which permitted him to be more benevolent toward the former. Thus he allowed that Aristotle's Greek moved within the bounds of common usage and blamed his translators for having vitiated his language (36, 68). He also blamed medieval interpreters for making Aristotle's doctrine unnecessarily complex and obscure with their accretions. Aristotle's own teaching was straightforward, he claimed.

The logic of Aristotle consists in its entirety of a few brief precepts, namely the nature of terms as taught in the books of the *Categories;* the force of propositions in the *On Interpretation;* formulas for syllogisms in the *Prior Analytics;* their demonstration in the *Posterior Analytics;* the uses of persuasion and invention in the *Topics;* and subtle argumentation in the *On Sophistical Refutations.* Equipped with this *Organon,* that is, tool, the young student proceeds to the other arts and sciences, since disciplines that are learned for the sake of other disciplines (and logic is one of them) should not occupy the student for too long a time, but only as long as is necessary to prepare him for other disciplines. Aristotle does not embroil and detain his pupil in frigid and senseless suppositions, extensions, restrictions, and other petty terms. This great genius, the inventor of all those forms and syllogisms and indeed of all logic itself, did not consider such things necessary for a training in logic.   (68)

Vives was prepared to make allowances for Aristotle's place as pioneer in his field. "No art is invented and perfected at once . . . therefore I shall say no more about Aristotle, whom I admire, as one ought to, and with whom I disagree with due respect" (124). He was less forgiving toward the philosopher's medieval interpreters. "What Aristotle handed down in Greek was not bad, but was badly corrupted by our people who translated it into Latin" (125). Medieval interpreters spoiled rather than expounded their source: "They do not even know who Aristotle is. They have no first-hand knowledge either of his natural or moral philosophy, or even of his logic, which they shamelessly profess to teach without having laid eyes on any of his books of logic" (80). He maintained similar views in *De causis.* Errors accumulated in the books of the medieval interpreters "as in a ship's bilge." The resulting dialectic was unnatural. "I am surprised they don't have nightmares about it and are not afraid to speak about it in the dark, for it is such a monstrous thing."[32]

In later works Vives attacks Aristotle himself. His misgivings center on the concept of first principles. In *De causis* he objects to Aristotle referring the dialectician for safe premises to "self-evident" propositions. "In this way the whole doctrine of proof is inane and useless," he remonstrates with Aristotle.

You never seem to have turned your eyes to nature, for you refer first principles *(immediatas propositiones)* to us. In this matter, then, no one needs instruction. Teaching human beings, you will have no single unchanging proof to offer, for each person has different first principles. Some are persuaded by what is only probable; others, like the Academicians, do not accept even what is most evident and attested by the senses; others again, like the Epicureans, accept all sense perceptions. Thus your proof will be like the proverbial Lesbian Rule which adjusts to the curve of a structure rather than adjusting the structure to itself.

This objection appears to be at variance with Vives' pronouncements in *De disputatione*, where he accepts the idea of innate, self-evident first principles. The mind, he says, brings to its cogitations "natural information, axioms, so to speak, and notions which are imprinted and engraved on everyone's mind, on which science rests." Any judgment based on these axioms will be true; that proceeding from probable premises will only be plausible. However, the axioms of which Vives is speaking here are not Aristotle's first principles[33] but the certainties of divinely instilled knowledge. He therefore rejects the notion of Aristotelian syllogisms as a reliable method of inference. Even if formally correct, they may produce invalid conclusions, for they are not based on axioms: "A syllogism can be good [that is, formally correct], even if it is based on false premises." In discussing the degree of certainty with which a conclusion can be drawn from probable premises, Vives introduces a gradation that is significant for his overall approach to dialectic as a Christian humanist. He accords the lowest rank to sense perception, followed by ratiocination/prudence, experience, and human authority. Above these, in a category of its own, is revelation. This last tier is beyond the realm of argumentation. "There are things that can be known only to God or are revealed to us through his prophets and thus do not admit of argumentation and proof."[34]

Melanchthon's textbook on dialectic was largely nonpolemical. He acknowledged the conventional nature of his teaching: "I shall recite the rules as did the other dialecticians."[35] He was generous in his interpretation of the teachings of medieval dialecticians and went so far as to defend some of their concepts. For example, the Aristotelian square of opposites, a standard item in medieval textbooks, was not, as some alleged, "an inane game." It had practical applications, for example, in mathematics. "It is the rules of conversion that prove that $4 \times 5 = 20$, therefore $5 \times 4 = 20$."[36] Melanchthon shows no animosity toward Aristotle and frequently refers students to his works. In a review of pagan philosophies evaluated from a Christian vantage point, only Aristotelianism comes in for praise, the rest are roundly condemned. Aristotle, says Melanchthon, "has the true, uncorrupted, and genuine dialectic."[37] Accordingly, the material he presents in his handbook on dialectic is largely the traditional Aristotelian corpus with a few medieval accretions. Through-out the book, however, Christian faith colors classical doctrine. With respect to the theory of commonplaces, for example, it is obvious that Melanchthon's approach is governed by considerations for the authority of the Church:

> We often use the commonplaces, not in investigating, but in choos-ing things. Their list is fixed, since with the Church as our teacher, things must not be invented. After all, we do not create doctrine. Rather, when a section of the heavenly teaching is considered as a proposition, the prudent exegete chooses certain principal points, and the commonplaces show in what order these are to be ex-plained, the definition that needs to be sought, the partitions to be made, the causes to be found out, the effects of indication.[38]

Melanchthon's selection of subject matter shows a humanist's bias. He keeps the material added by medieval Aristotelians to a minimum.[39] Conversely, he expands on informal modes of inference, putting their importance in perspective: "Syllogisms have a predominant role in proof and in the most serious cases, and are not as fragile as the other kinds of argumentation. Yet the forms and application of the latter must be shown as well, because enthymemes especially are very frequent in ordi-nary speech and numerous in the brief counsels of the prophets and apostles."[40]

The search for an alternative to Aristotelian dialectics led humanists to examine the relationship between rhetoric and logic. While they dis-agreed on the conceptual differences between the two disciplines, they generally held that a strict division was untenable in practice. They agreed, moreover, that the two disciplines shared a common method of argumentation, that formal and informal modes of inference must be placed on an equal footing, and that invention and judgment were of equal significance in the process of argumentation.

Valla first formulated his views on the relationship between rhetoric and philosophy in *De voluptate* (first redaction ca. 1430). Following Quintilian, he spoke of the philosophers as "thieves" from whom the orator must reclaim "whatever rhetorical gear he finds in them—and everything in which philosophy takes pride belongs to us."[41] He likened the position of philosophy to "a soldier or tribune under General Speech." This idea is further developed in the *Dialectic,* where Valla de-nied that the orator was limited to certain methods of argumentation. Some people claimed that syllogism was a method used exclusively by the dialectician. Valla objected: "How so? Does the orator not use syllogisms? Of course he does. And enthymemes and epicheiremes as well, and also induction." The difference was one of style. The dialectician "uses a bare syllogism"; the orator one that is "clothed and equipped and embellished with gold, purple, and gems." Thus rhetoric was the more comprehensive discipline, dialectic merely a poor cousin. Indeed, "poverty becomes the dialectician, if he is a proper one" (Zippel 175:23–176:4). His task was restricted to teaching, whereas the orator not only taught but also moved and delighted his audience, "which is sometimes more effective than proof itself" (176:6–7). Valla was referring to the three tasks of the orator—*docere, movere,* and *delectare*—as defined by Cicero.[42] Restricting the dialectician to the first, he reinforced the message of *De voluptate:* dialectic was merely an aspect of rhetoric, that is, "a soldier of General Speech."

The fusion of the two disciplines, or more precisely, the subordination of dialectic to rhetoric, is signaled in many ways by Valla. We have already noted that he is in the habit of adding philological observations to logical argumentation or couching his arguments in rhetorical terms. More evidence for his conjunction of the two disciplines comes in the form of frequent references to authorities on rhetoric, especially to Quintilian. Valla aggregates, or, on occasion, substitutes their teaching for Aristotelian doctrine. Thus he replaces Aristotle's "A definition is an expression signifying what something is," which responds to the needs of the logician, with Quintilian's rhetorically oriented "A definition is a statement worded appropriately, lucidly, and concisely, and consisting primarily of genus, species, differences, and properties."[43] He ends the first book of the *Dialectic* with a homage to Quintilian, likening him to the Homeric hero Achilles and himself to Achilles' friend and stand-in, Patroclus: "I am his [Quintilian's/Achilles'] driver, and armed with his weapons, I climb into his chariot, daring to advance on the serried ranks of the Trojans, ... that I might encourage and raise the spirits of the other Greeks thrown back on their last resources."[44]

Book II of Valla's *Dialectic* is substantially informed by the teaching of Quintilian. Valla takes over his treatment of the theory of commonplaces verbatim, explaining:

> I attribute so much to this man that I cannot imagine anyone being able to add anything to his words, or take anything away, or change them in the least, and I confess that I myself was unable to do so, although I often tried. The more closely I inspect his work, the more this author fills me with admiration or rather astonishment, so that I have come to believe and am convinced that no one could

speak with such intellectual vigor and eloquence as Quintilian did, unless he were a god, so to speak. And he wrote with such discernment about things that I know I cannot achieve his excellence. Yet I am not a man of low self-esteem, and there is no "authority," as we call them, whom I have not dared to criticize in some respect.[45]

Basing his thinking on the premise that dialectic and rhetoric use the same kind of argumentation, Valla extends the range of his discussion to nonformal proofs. Notable is his treatment of *coacervatio* (*soros* in Greek), which is barely touched on in classical handbooks.[46] It is an effective argument, though of problematic validity. Valla offers this example: "My mother goes along with my wishes; Themistocles goes along with my mother's wishes; the people go along with Themistocles' wishes—therefore, the Athenian people go along with my wishes" (306:18–20). This is a cogent argument, Valla says, so long as each step is carefully examined and one stays away from vaguely defined terms or obvious fallacies, such as the following: "Curtius should not die for A, Curtius should not die for B—therefore Curtius should not die for his country" (308:27–28). "Even the greatest men are caught out," he says, "by being careless in their speech" (328:16–17). In other words, Valla sought—no doubt raising the hackles of all logicians—to equate logical consistency with consistency of terms, and rigorous argumentation with precise language.

The delineation of grammar, rhetoric, and dialectic is also a recurrent topic in Agricola's *De inventione dialectica*. He begins with the traditional division of logic into three subject areas: grammar, which teaches clear and correct speech and "makes the meaning of the speaker comprehensible"; rhetoric, which teaches ornate and pleasing speech and "effects that the words spoken are heard with pleasure"; dialectic, which teaches us to say what is probable about any topic and "produces belief in the listener" (2.1, p. 192, repeated 2.25, p. 316). Although Agricola accepted the traditional tripartition of logic and considered it the principal task of the dialectician to instruct, he subscribed to the thesis that the perfect speaker will combine all three tasks: instructing, moving, and delighting his audience.[47] Agricola connects the three tasks in the following manner: it is possible for a speaker to instruct without moving or delighting the audience, but it is not possible to move and delight without also instructing.[48]

In his *Oration in praise of philosophy* Agricola also postulated a practical connection between rhetoric and dialectic. He noted that invention belonged to dialectic, arrangement and embellishment to rhetoric, but in making a speech the orator must combine the two disciplines. Whereas

Valla uses the simile of the philosopher-thief, Agricola makes the orator the trespasser: "Whatever the orator usurps for himself in the process of invention belongs properly speaking to dialectic."[49] It is clear, however, that Agricola approved of such trespassing. His own treatment of invention is informed by the principle that "the commonplaces on which we draw in arousing emotion are the same on which we draw in teaching" (2.4 p. 201). Moreover, while the title of his book suggests that it is concerned with *dialectical* invention, its text covers large areas traditionally associated with rhetoric. Book III is almost completely given over to rhetoric, discussing strategies of manipulating emotions and of giving the audience esthetic pleasure. Chapter headings include: "On delighting [the hearers]: how it is done; and a method of digressing from the proposed subject" (chapter 4) and "On copious speech, and how it is effected" (chapter 5). Agricola therefore appears to sanction mutual trespassing or even an erosion of borderlines between dialectic and rhetoric. Unlike Valla, who reserves only a small corner of the rhetorical domain for dialectic and calls any encroachment "thievery," Agricola recognizes the two disciplines as separate areas but proposes joint tenure.

Rhetorizing dialectic in this fashion, Agricola focuses on invention rather than proof and moves from demonstrative logic toward probabilism. He associates plausibility with perspicuity, which consists in clarity of words and clarity of things. Grammar and rhetoric govern the former. "Perspicuity of things, however, lies partly in their nature, partly in their treatment . . . [the former] does not pertain to speech, because it is carried into the speech with the subject matter (whatever its status may be). The latter is achieved by order and disposition of things" (2.2, p. 198). Yet a formally correct proof does not guarantee validity. "One can speak plausibly about things that are at variance with the true nature of things and with common sense"—this has to be taken into consideration in formulating a definition of dialectic. "It is the art of speaking plausibly about any subject, *as far as its nature admits*" (2.2., p. 197).

Vives' definition of the respective tasks of grammar, dialectic, and rhetoric suggests that he too believed that they could not be separated without detriment to the quality of speech. "Grammar cuts the timber and brings the stones; dialectic erects the house; rhetoric creates the community," he wrote, interpreting the simile: "Grammar goes as far as the conjunction of words; dialectic as far as argumentation; rhetoric progresses toward continuous prose and, what is more demanding, oration." Modern dialecticians were wrong to neglect rhetoric, Vives said. They boasted that their art sharpened the mind, but their "thorny dialectic makes the mind contentious and morose rather than lively and perceptive of beauty; it sharpens the mind all right, in fact it pares it down until there is nothing solid left; it thins it, trims it, pushes it down, so that, once crushed, it cannot easily be lifted up to noble things."[50] Like Valla, then, Vives saw logic as an impoverished and impoverishing discipline.

Discussing the cogency of argumentation in *De causis*, he notes that formal syllogisms do not necessarily ascertain the truth. Dialecticians played a fatuous mechanical game in which victory went to the person who left the opponent without a counterargument. Thus the response of the opponent was elevated to a criterion of truth: "Contradiction is their sole measure; it is the only reason for which a doctrine is rejected." Everything else, however senseless and paradoxical, must be accepted because the contestant cannot refute it. In *De disputatione* Vives spends little time on syllogisms, therefore, broadening his discussion to include nonformal proofs and focusing on invention. He recognizes that no hard-and-fast rules can be devised for the selection and application of commonplaces and compares *loci* to the letters of the alphabet: "There are no rules by which one can teach what letters need to be used for what words; custom and usage teaches that."[51]

Melanchthon follows Valla's example in making style the distinguishing mark between dialectic and rhetoric. The former is concise *(propriis verbis nude proponit)*; the latter uses ornate language *(addit ornatum)*. He restricts the scope of rhetoric, however, noting that dialectic deals with all subjects, whereas "not all subjects admit of rhetorical splendor. It would be inept and ridiculous, for example, if the geometrician played the orator and wanted to add rhetorical flourishes to his demonstrations . . . but in ethics those glossy words and figures are prominent, for the listener must be moved and his mind directed to dwell on one idea for a long time, or he may have to be terrified or motivated with the thunder of words" (CR XIII 515). In practice, the dialectician often had to shore up his arguments with the help of rhetoric. "The concise nature of a dialectical argument does not strike the listener (especially when he is unsophisticated) and [the thesis] cannot be immediately grasped. Therefore one ought to embellish individual sections to give a close-up view, so to speak. Thus the art of rhetoric benefits both the speaker and the person forming a judgment" (642). Unlike Valla and Agricola, Melanchthon does not "stray" far from his subject proper into rhetoric, but he refers readers to Cicero and Quintilian for further instruction (642). The concluding paragraphs of his *Dialectic* reinforce this recommendation. It is necessary to combine dialectic with rhetoric to make the former more effective: "Let the students bring their knowledge of figures to dialectic; let them join rhetoric with it" (751).

Melanchthon's theory of argumentation is firmly grounded in his Christian faith. As a Christian, he rejects probabilism, for

> God wants some things to be certain, firm, and immutable—the guidelines of our life. He wants to be known by us in some form; He wants our knowledge of numbers and figures to be clear and firm; He wants some unshakable moral laws. We must not listen to the Pyrrhonists or Academicians doing away with certainty and contending that everything is uncertain and doubtful . . . Such madness gainsays the principal divine gift of truth; it undermines the arts which are the bulwarks of life; it confounds our knowledge of God, however tenuous it may be in human beings, which ought to be illuminated and strengthened by true reasoning rather than extinguished . . . It is a crime to seek out tricks to slip away from statements which God wants us to embrace without doubting. (645–646)

Melanchthon therefore refers students to the Stoic criteria of truth—universal experience, innate first principles, and rational discernment of order—but immediately anchors the pagan philosophy in Christian doctrine. To doubt universal experience is "to declare war on God," the Creator of the physical world; the first principles have been "divinely implanted" in us; and human beings are born with a sense of order that allows them to recognize the disposition of an argument (647–648). In addition to these three criteria, the Christian must embrace a fourth: revealed truth. "All rational creatures must assent to the statements revealed by God, even if they are against their rational judgment. Just as we affirm without doubting that two times four is eight, so we must firmly state that God will raise the dead and honor His Church with eternal glory and cast the impious into eternal punishment" (650–651). This firm belief, Melanchthon says, must extend also to biblical explanations of natural phenomena. A particularly pungent example of Melanchthon's Christianized dialectic is the statement: "Our intellect comprehends that the earth stands still and the sun moves. But when we hear that this knowledge has been handed down to us by God, we give it our firmer assent" (651).

Ramus' definition of dialectic does not give us a clear indication of his views on the relationship between logic and rhetoric. The formulations he uses—*ars disserendi* or "art de bien disputer"—focus on verbal skills.[52] Ramus' interpreters, however, introduced another dimension. An adaptation of the *Dialectique* (1576) defines dialectic as "l'art de bien raison-ner," and Johann Piscator in his commentary on Ramus' *Dialectic* (1580) notes: "Speech teaches, reason learns; therefore Dialectic is the art of teaching and learning."[53] The Latin term *disserere* is thus interpreted by Ramus' commentators in the sense of logical argumentation, both men-tal and verbalized. More light is shed on Ramus' views concerning the relationship between rhetoric and dialectic in his *Rhetoricae distinctiones in Quintilianum* (1549). There he distinguishes in the traditional manner between grammar, rhetoric, and dialectic but emphasizes that all three disciplines must be combined in practice: "In use these should be united, so that the same oration can expound purely, speak ornately, and express thought wisely. However, the precepts of pure diction, ornate delivery, and intelligent treatment must be kept separate and should not be con-fused."[54] He expresses similar views in *Aristotelicae animadversiones*: "Al-though dialectic and rhetoric each have its proper procedure *(ratio)* and the heart is not situated in the mouth or the mouth in the heart, the tasks of heart and tongue are nevertheless most closely linked by nature. Therefore rhetoric and dialectic ought to be combined in exercise and practice" (78 recto). Ramus' own textbook on dialectic bears out this recommendation. Book III of the *Dialecticae institutiones* (1543) concerns the explication of literary texts, clearly demonstrating that Ramus did not wish to limit dialectic to its traditional field but broadened it sub-stantially to include rhetoric. Ramus' critic Pierre Galland exaggerates, however, when he claims that Ramus wanted to eliminate all distinction between rhetoric and dialectic. Criticizing Ramus' "mixed-up and con-fused presentation," he noted that he himself was not against individuals combining wisdom with eloquence, but philosophy and rhetoric must be *taught* separately: "He who attempts to secure for himself a knowl-edge of philosophy and of speaking well, all at the same time, will suc-ceed in neither." The examples Ramus cited, of famous men in classical antiquity or the Fathers who had combined wisdom with eloquence, were irrelevant. At issue were not the private accomplishments of indi-viduals but the type of curriculum that would foster such achievements. And Ramus could not cite a single example from history of a person "who learned or taught the disciplines in this [confused] manner; rather they joined the two pursuits in their lives."[55] Galland's indignation ap-pears spurious, for, as the quotations from Ramus' work show, the two men's views did not differ significantly.

We have already noted that Ramus approached his subject under three headings or aspects—nature, theory, and practice. In Book II of his *Dia-lecticae institutiones*, which is devoted to theory, he discusses invention and judgment. Adopting the order suggested by Agricola, Ramus proceeds to list and briefly explain first the commonplaces (which he conceives as being arguments rather than the seats of arguments), then the methods of proof. He makes no distinction between rhetorical and dialectical commonplaces, creating a kind of master list for finding the middle term in a syllogism.

As for judgment, Ramus distinguishes three levels, which he terms first, second, and third judgment respectively. The first consists simply of arranging the *loci* in the form of a syllogism; the second is more complex, involving the concatenation of a number of syllogisms; the third allows the human mind to draw near to divine wisdom. At this stage the human being "discerns what is true and what is false in things by the light of his [intellectual] power; he puts the most obscure and confused things in clear order and, as closely as he may, approaches to that wisdom of his heavenly father." To illustrate this progression to the light of truth, Ramus recasts Plato's cave simile in a Christian form. As in the classic tale, human beings living in a subterranean cave are so fettered that they can discern only shadows. One of them is freed and enabled to see the sun and the objects it illuminates. Ramus' philosopher is, however, more successful than his Platonic predecessor in finding proselytes among his fellow prisoners on his return. And Ramus ends the fable with an appeal to all: "Let us light the fire brought down from that heavenly light, let us free ourselves from the fetters, loosen the images from the darkness of their shadows, and meditate the truth . . . dialectic shall be our leader."[56]

Nizolius' proposals for a combination of rhetoric and dialectic are the most radical. His approach to the question of the relationship between dialectic and rhetoric is founded on his separation of science into two branches: philosophy, which deals with the knowledge of all things, and rhetoric, which deals with the knowledge of all signs. Neither is complete without the other, for "philosophy and rhetoric are not two separate faculties but one composed of words and things just as living beings are composed of body and soul; . . . philosophy cannot be perfect without the aid of words: rhetoric cannot be perfect without being founded on things" (II 33). The Socratic separation of philosophy and rhetoric, "of heart and tongue" (as Cicero put it), was unwarranted. As for dialectic, Nizolius said, it was an artificial category. It had no sphere of operation distinct from rhetoric. He examined the disciplines according to three criteria—method, subject matter, and purpose—and declared that a strict distinction could not be maintained in any of these areas. Both rhetoric and dialectic dealt with all subjects, and both used syllogisms, induction, enthymeme, and example. Both argued with probability and aimed at persuading the hearer. Even if certain methods such as syllo-gisms and questions were associated more closely with dialectic, it was only in the sense of dialectic being a special area of rhetoric.

> It is included in the definition of rhetoric—not in that given by Aristotle in the first book of his *Rhetoric*, which is wrong ... but in that given by Cicero and Quintilian and all sound rhetoricians: "Rhetoric is the art of speaking well on all subjects" ... This in-cludes dialectic, which is the art of discoursing with probability on both sides of a proposed question, for no one can discourse with probability on both sides of any matter without speaking well about everything, for speaking well about everything is the more compre-hensive category.   (II 63).

The connection Nizolius makes between language and knowledge in general is clear from the principles of philosophical inquiry stated at the outset of his book. According to Nizolius, scholars in quest of the truth need (1) a good grounding in Greek and Latin to enable them to consult the sources in the original; and (2) a good knowledge of grammar and rhetoric to allow them to state their theses persuasively and clearly.[57]

Propounding his theory of argumentation, Nizolius follows Agricola's lead in specifying that the teaching of invention must precede that of judgment, "for by nature the invention of arguments precedes the expo-sition of the argument found; no one explains something he has not yet discovered" (II 135). Regarding judgment, Nizolius denies the possibil-ity of demonstrative syllogism. This denial is based on a theory of knowledge elaborated in Book III of *De principiis*. Nizolius begins with a discussion of the word *scientia*, which he notes is used in three senses. First, there is the knowledge that governs our everyday actions, "which is easy to have and is acquired in no particular fashion." Second, there is knowledge "of what is worthwhile and difficult and not known to the average person"—the academic disciplines. Finally, there is knowledge of "what is necessary, what cannot be created or corrupted, and is eter-nal" (II 13). Plato and Aristotle would admit only the last as true knowl-edge, but Nizolius "completely rejects the third type of knowledge" (II 14) and mocks the mystical air which the Greek philosophers give to it (*sancte colent et observant*, II 14). He returns to this subject in his discus-sion of methods of argumentation, since rejection of the third type of knowledge leads to the rejection of demonstrative syllogisms and deduc-tive reasoning in general.

To Nizolius the demonstrative syllogism is "complete fiction and, to speak frankly, an Aristotelian fairy tale pure and simple" (II 148). According to Aristotle, the premise of the demonstrative syllogism is "true, primary, immediate, prior, and known," but there is no such premise, and Aristotle fails to provide a single example of it. Nizolius expressed his surprise that so many people were taken in by these theories, "that they could read this stuff and were so foolish and blind as not to see that this whole book of Aristotle dealt with things that neither existed nor could exist, and that such blathering could deceive humanity wholesale and make fools of them" (II 150).

It is evident from the passages quoted that humanists, whether upholding a theoretical division between dialectic and rhetoric or declaring one to be an aspect of the other, advocated that the two disciplines be combined in practice. Accordingly, they incorporated material traditionally associated with rhetoric in their handbooks on dialectic, or at any rate encouraged dialecticians to seek instruction in rhetoric to enhance their performance. If the borderline between the two disciplines was to be erased, a joint theory of argumentation had to include both formal and informal modes of inference. There was no agreement, however, among the proponents of a humanistic dialectic on the possibility of formal demonstrative proofs. At one end of the scale, Nizolius completely rejected it; at the other end, Christian humanists like Vives and Melanchthon asserted the possibility of absolute knowledge.

The fusion of the two disciplines advocated by the humanists in theory or practice had another important consequence: the demand for a common standard of language, variously designated as "natural language" or "common usage" or "scholarly usage."

Valla affirms the close connection between truth and common usage, *veritas et consuetudo* (Zippel 46:8), and criticizes scholastic dialecticians for divorcing them by using language that was against custom and nature. He furthermore links natural with scholarly usage in the demand that dialecticians "adopt a diction that is natural and generally in use among scholars" (278:26). Usage in turn is linked with grammar: "What can be better than to use the art of grammar, especially when it is confirmed by usage?" (331:27). In Valla's ideal world, then, grammar accords with general/scholarly usage, which reflects nature. It is not clear whether Valla's pronouncements are based on a coherent philosophy of language. There is a brief statement on the relationship between words and things embedded in a chapter of his *Dialectic* entitled "On the qualities which are apprehended by the senses" (Book I, chapter 14). Things are known first, Valla says, words to describe them were invented thereafter. Finally, letters were devised, "dumb words, so to speak, or images of words, just as words are images of meanings" (123:13–14). He then reflects on the special case of the words "word" and "thing."

> The word "thing" signifies thing. The latter is signified; the former is the sign. One is not a word; the other is a word. Therefore we arrive at the definition: "thing" is a word or name embracing in its meaning all names . . . but the signified thing is above the signified word; the word is also a thing and one specific thing, but it signifies all things.

A leap of thought is required to go on to the remainder of the sentence. The reader must supply the transition:

> [word is both sign and signified; both genus (of all words, including "thing") and species (of thing)] and it makes no difference whether we say "what is wood (or stone, iron, man)?" or "what does wood (or stone, iron, man) signify?" but none of this applies to thing, for in the questions "what is thing?" and "what does thing signify," "what" is resolved in "what thing" . . . But if I ask what word is 'thing' you will rightly respond: it is a word signifying the meaning or sense of all other words.   (123:23–124:16)

One would rather like Valla to elaborate on this statement, but he leaves readers guessing how (or indeed, whether) he incorporated this piece of insight into a more general theory of language.[58]

Throughout the *Dialectic* Valla criticizes the scholastic dialecticians for diverging from general usage. Although he himself occasionally employs scholastic terminology, for example in his section on the figures and moods of syllogisms, he uses these conventional terms with obvious distaste. "Oh, peripatetic household enamored of nonsense!" he exclaims (298:14–15).

> . . . It is as if you wanted to invent new letters other than the ones that help our language to express meaning! . . . like shameless women who prefer to speak cant with their lovers rather than using clean language. To crown their perversity, the dialecticians offer a kind of geometry or mathematics, using letters rather than examples. In my opinion they act no differently from merchants who have a low opinion of their wares and therefore try to display them to buyers in semi-darkness, or mothers who want to marry their ugly daughters off to a husband and trot them out at night and by artificial rather than by the natural light of day. They [the dialecticians] likewise think they can pass their precepts off as something

more valuable if they are less obvious and exposed to scrutiny, just as those things that are made safe with multiple locks are thought more precious. But does it make sense to add darkness to what is obscure in itself, and to add bitterness and bile rather than spice to food that is in itself harsh, disgusting, and sickening? (299:28–300:8)

In a similar burst of impatience he inveighs against the terms associated with the traditional cross of oppositions—terms which are idiomatic in Greek but, literally translated, result in awkward Latin compounds:

"Not-someone does not read, not-man does not walk, someone non-man jumps, someone non-man does not jump"—what kind of terminology is this, I ask you—the speech of crows and grackles ... What kind of man is this "non-man"? But perhaps you are an illustration of it, a man, uttering non-man's words like crows and grackles! ... What is the purpose of this ludicrous and barbarous heap of terms, some man non-man reads, not someone man walks, every man is not-just, not-Socrates is not non-just—these are monsters of speech not words, ... Is there such a dearth of material for jokes that you want to appear as liars and jokers in a discipline concerned with the truth, as you boast (for every discipline is seeking the truth)? We must speak according to grammatical norms, and not only grammatically but in Latin, that is, not merely according to the precepts of the art but according to the usage of scholars and those who speak the language in its pure form.   (216:14–217:12)

A practical reason why Valla counsels the dialectician to use standard language is its clarity. Unidiomatic usage is confusing, he notes. Common usage allows the reader to pinpoint the sense of an ambiguous phrase.

The same phrase does not always have the same meaning ... as for example: "A bad man deserts a friend on no account" and "A good man deserts a friend on no account" (or "would desert" or "will desert"). In this case the same phrase is used concerning the bad and the good man, but it is understood that the bad man will desert the friend ["on no account"=] without provocation; the good man will desert the friend ["on no account"=] not even on provocation. And why is it understood? Because of usage. If a speaker diverges from it, he must be ejected from the circle of literate people just as a man who disdains law and order must be ejected from the state. (219:7–17)

In some cases the argument from usage served to simplify not only language but also concepts. Valla's discussion of the concept of *materia* may serve as an example of this process. He suggests the simplification: "Let us give both truth and usage their due and let us speak more distinctly and more lucidly by adopting the following practice: when we speak of a thing that consists of two components [*materia, forma*] according to the Aristotelian convention, we shall term it *substantia*; when we speak of the Aristotelian *materia*, we shall term it *essentia*" (46:8–13).

Here as well as in other instances, Valla's suggestions appear amateurish or simplistic, but perhaps this was the image he wanted to project. He repeatedly professes "not to understand" the logicians. "I don't see why Aristotle says that some things grow although they are not changed" (133:3–4); "I don't understand why a point is something, but has no quantity" (145:17–18). Sometimes this display of ignorance turns into a little farce:

> Aristotle denies that one is a number . . . Once two women had a dozen hens and a rooster in common and had an agreement that of the eggs laid every day one would have the odd-numbered, the other one the even-numbered. If one day a single egg is produced, which woman will get it, pray tell me? Neither one? Of course not. It will belong to the one who gets the odd-numbered eggs. And therefore one is a number. Thus foolish women sometimes know more about the meaning of words than the greatest philosophers. For they employ words for a purpose, the philosophers for sport. An example of this kind of sport is Aristotle's assertion that numbers are counted or countable. I—and the foolish women—deny that this is intelligible. (216: 14–217:12)

While Valla's emphasis is on simplification of Aristotelian logic, Agricola's approach to dialectic is determined by his concept of the word as a means of communication, a bridge between minds that makes teaching or persuasion possible. Speech "is the sign of things which the speaker understands in his mind; clearly, its proper task is to show and explain this to the person to whom the sign is directed" (1.1, p. 1). It is in this sense that Agricola criticizes the dialectician's lack of attention to language, and thus to communication. Mentioning Raymond Lull as an example, he complains of the scholastic's "great obscurity of speech and his *horror incultus*" (2.1, p. 145). Generally speaking, dialectic is taught in such a "complex and obscure manner that this art, which ought to open up the others to us, is more deeply covered with darkness and must be dug out of more remote hiding places" (2.1, p. 164).

Similar complaints can be found in Vives' *Contra pseudodialecticos*. He joins the chorus of humanists demanding that the logicians follow common usage: "The teacher of logic should use words and statements which will be intelligible to anyone who knows the language in which he is speaking, not only to specialists" (34). In this context, Vives states what Valla merely implied: grammatical rules reflect common usage. "Languages are not twisted to suit the rules; rather the rules follow the pattern of the language. We do not speak Latin in a certain way because Latin grammar bids us so to speak." The grammarian does not prescribe but describe—correspondingly, the logician does not devise the rules of logic but "merely transmits what the consensus of speakers ... approves" (38–39).

Unwilling to concede to logicians some form of technical language, Vives alleges that they want to hide their incompetence behind specious terms. By using "words contrary to the customs and conventions of mankind . . . they win a sham victory in debate by making themselves incomprehensible." The true logician, by contrast, uses common language, which is like "common currency" (38–40). If the pseudo-dialecticians spoke plainly and according to common usage, the difficulties they created artificially would disappear. "In the simple, genuine, true, and direct manner of speaking there is no room for caviling, which is the primary goal of their investigation" (52).

Like Valla, Vives compares the scholastics unfavorably with common folk and portrays them as inferior to them, because "they are lacking in common sense" (36). After all, the function of language is communication: "If raillery, jokes, jeers, witticisms, insults, and injuries are expressed in words that are privately invented by the speaker and unknown to anyone else, that would be ridiculous enough, but if their meaning is obscure, they are utterly absurd and pointless and are worth nothing at all" (52). The pseudo-dialecticians claimed that their arguments were too subtle to be treated in the ordinary language; they must be discussed *ad rigorem*, by more rigorous standards. In reply, Vives again accuses them of incompetence. "The reason that they are insisting on this distinction [between *ad rigorem*, rigorous proof, and *ad bonum sensum*, common sense] is that they are lacking the latter" (54). He contrasts this artificially created rigor with the rigorous requirements of idiom, "an exact and unchanging norm of speech" (56).

Melanchthon similarly discredits the usage of the scholastic dialectici- ans. Like Vives, he implies that they deceive and are deceived by their obscure terminology. "They cannot even express their thoughts"; "They cannot even understand the import of the precepts about which they contentiously dispute." Agricola, he says, was the first dialectician "to recognize the flaws and opt for a better kind of speech."[59]

Ramus does not say much about style in his *Dialecticae institutiones*, but he makes key statements in his critique of Aristotle, *Aristotelicae animad- versiones*. There he follows Valla in quoting Horace on the people as ar- biters of speech: "in them is vested the judgment and the right and the norm of speaking."[60] Ramus elaborates: "It is agreed, then, that words are used not at the pleasure of lazy people, but that they must be defined by common usage and natural speech." He criticizes scholastic dialec- ticians for diverging from common usage *(consuetudo)*, "for where, except in the schools of those sophistic ranters, is this kind of language spo- ken?" (10 verso). The translators and commentators of Aristotle should have considered that students are "drawn to the text on account of the beauty and smoothness of expression, motivated by the great conve- nience, captivated by its perspicuity and thus led to study Aristotle," but instead, they were "alienated by its barbarous filth, deterred by the wretchedness of the task, crippled by the obscurity of the text, and led to dislike dialectic."[61]

Nizolius placed a similarly high value on common usage. We have noted that the second of his five principles or prerequisites of a success- ful quest for the truth is a knowledge of grammar and rhetoric. The "philosophasters," by contrast, use language that is barbarous, unintelli- gible, and against common usage (contra communem omnium loquendi consuetudinem).

> They reply that they are not speaking grammatically or rhetorically, but dialectically or logically or metaphysically—as if the truth of things could be investigated more successfully and human cogita- tions expressed more clearly in barbarous and unusual terms than in familiar Latin, and in dialectical and metaphysical rather than grammatical and rhetorical terms. I in turn reply: to speak gram- matically and rhetorically is to speak correctly, according to com- mon usage, and in a form adapted to everyone's understanding; to speak dialectically or logically or metaphysically is nothing but to speak boldly and without consideration, or rather, to spout words . . . to prattle and offend human ears by speaking in the manner of crows and grackles. (I 25–26)

Strongly disapproving of the language of the dialectics, Nizolius stands Zeno's famous dictum on its head: "In my opinion [Zeno] would have done better to compare dialectic with an open hand and rhetoric with a closed fist," for the open hand better designated the unregulated, barbarous language of the dialecticians, whereas the closed fist better represented the rules followed by the orator (II 54).

Nizolius' third principle requires the scholar to read the classics, the "approved Greek and Latin authors," and to be acquainted with their language as well as the language of the people. Like Valla and Ramus, he quotes Horace in support of this theory (I 26). He also shares Valla's (and Vives') idealistic view of common usage, not as the corrupt language of the people but as natural (and therefore timeless) language whose rules are recorded by the grammarian. Dialecticians, as we have seen, defended their terminology in more realistic terms, defining correct language as language following rules drawn up and agreed upon by a group of people, and legitimizing their own technical language as defined by rules drawn up by a group of professionals.

The passages quoted show the humanists in full agreement concerning the language of the scholastics. They refused to exempt them from the rules of grammar and the norms of scholarly diction or common usage. The aspect of scholastic dialectic which the humanists found most unsatisfactory was its low potential for application in life. Much was accordingly said by the proponents of a humanistic dialectic concerning the purpose of training in logic and the "uselessness" of the traditional system. Their criticism of scholastic dialectic focuses on three aspects: the role of dialectic in moral decision-making; the related question of its role in the curriculum of theology students; and the propaedeutic nature of dialectics which suggests that the time allotted to it should be curtailed. The goals set by the humanists also shaped the relationship between teacher and student or between participants in a disputation. If the purpose was moral education and edification, there was no room for a spirit of contentiousness—an accusation often brought against the scholastics.

Agricola wanted the disputant to be a concerned teacher rather than a competitive wrangler. Both teacher and polemicist aimed at proving a thesis, but "the teacher acts in good faith toward the one who offers himself to be taught; the polemicist offers proof if possible—if not, he is content with the appearance of proof. For he is after victory, which he prefers to win by the force [of his argument] if possible, but if the subject does not permit this, he will fight with cunning and set traps" (2.7, p. 211).

Concerned about the inability of dialecticians to convey a moral message, Agricola objected to the central place logic had been given in theology:

> And what can one say about theology? What is left of it nowadays after you take away the metaphysical, physical, and dialectical elements? A naked and destitute discipline that cannot live up to its name. Thus when it comes to teaching the people and turning them to religion and justice, they drag up from the depth of their inextricable arts a disputation that wastes time and strikes the ears of their listeners with inane noise. And so they teach, proposing childish riddles, leaving instructor and instructed alike without a grasp of what is being taught. (2.1, p. 179)

Agricola sees dialectic as a propaedeutic art, a skill that should be learned not for its own sake but to advance knowledge. It is properly used as a tool (*ministerio et usibus aliarum sit addicta*, 2.1, p. 180). But the dialectic taught in his day was "not only useless for learning the other disciplines but in fact posed a significant hurdle" (ibidem). Agricola complained that it "nailed the mind to the ground," so that the student could never take a free step again. Asked what purpose dialectical studies served, some people claimed that they sharpened the mind; others were more candid and admitted that they served little purpose but were kept up for the sake of tradition. Thus dialectic was "learned only for its own sake . . . whereas it should benefit all studies" (ibidem).

Vives repeats many of Agricola's concerns in *Contra pseudodialecticos*. He directs his criticism squarely at the most conservative university in Europe: "Who is not familiar with the current saying that in Paris our youth are taught nothing save to rant and rave in displays of endless verbosity? Other institutions have their useless and futile branches of learning, but much that is substantial as well; only in Paris does one encounter the most idiotic and frivolous froth to the exclusion of all else" (28). The specious reasoning taught at Paris had no practical use and could not be employed in everyday conversation. Anyone trying to do so would only succeed in "frightening and chasing off all his hearers, as if he had pronounced words of bad omen. The only audience [the pseudo-dialectician] has for his delirious ravings are the poor two-penny disciples who are used to these mysterious utterances, sitting in their louse-ridden corners, amid stench and squalor" (82).

The dialectician is helpless in real life, Vives notes, painting a lively picture of the retired teacher of logic. Unlike other specialists, he has no application for his art and lapses into "a frigid and stultified silence" (82).

The real world is foreign to such people. "Their speech as well as their manners and actions are so alien to humanity that you would see no resemblance in them to other men except for their external appearance. The result is that in the conduct of business, fulfillment of duties, administration of public or private affairs, and in questions of personal feelings, they are as inept as men of straw" (84).

Vives' concerns are, however, not only practical but also ethical. He is therefore particularly concerned about the central role given to dialectics in scholastic theology. Great damage is done to souls when religion is polluted with sophisms, he says. Yet members of religious orders "are not ashamed to embrace these corruptions of the mind, often with more fervor than laymen. There are some theologians who think that there can be no exactitude of speech if it is not seasoned with this most bitter of condiments, adorned with horrid and rank barbarity, and stuffed with the vain devices of sophistry" (70–72).

Vives sees dialectic as a tool needed to handle other disciplines. Since it is propaedeutic, he advocates curtailment of the material taught and the time spent on it: "Only that knowledge of the art of logic should be imparted which is necessary to insure that the other arts will not be harmed by an insufficient knowledge of logic" (79–80).

While other humanists merely complain that dialectic lacks a moral purpose or application, Melanchthon sets out to remedy the situation by giving an ethical slant to his teaching. Accordingly, he enriches his textbook on dialectic with examples that will edify as well as instruct the student. Thus the text illustrating the division of propositions is taken from the Gospel of John (CR XIII 582–583); in the section on modal terms, "necessary" is illustrated by a discussion of the concept of God's omnipotence (591–592). The various examples for the figures and moods of syllogisms have a decidedly Christian message. The syllogism "Camestres" is illustrated in this fashion:

—Only the elect are in the assembly of the called, as Paul says: "Whom he elects, he also calls";
—There are no followers of Mahomet in the assembly of the called;
—Thus none of the followers of Mahomet are elected.

Another illustration has a programmatic slant:

—Peter did not rule;
—Peter had the keys of the Church;
—Thus the keys of the Church are not equivalent to ruling. (611)

The syllogism "Cesare" is illustrated by the example:

—Nothing sinful must be honored;
—God commands us to honor lawful holders of office;
—Thus it is not sinful to hold a lawful office.   (613)

Another syllogism contains a brief catechism:

—Because of His Son, God gratuitously remits the sins of all who
repent their sins and ask for forgiveness;
—I repent and through faith ask for the remission of my sins;
—Therefore it is certain that I shall be received, and my sighs will
be heard because of [Christ] my intermediary.

These examples clearly demonstrate that Melanchthon's purpose was not only to transmit a method but also to form in students a Christian attitude and to habituate them to applying dialectical reasoning to moral and religious questions. In this approach he combines the humanist's desire for practical applicability with the missionary zeal of the reformer.

A key statement of the purpose of dialectic and the moral and intellectual benefits to be derived from the subject when taught in the right manner can be found at the end of the section on syllogisms: "The practice of dialectic has many uses. First, if suitably chosen material is proposed to the young pupils, their judgment will be formed concerning many questions of general interest, an understanding of which is useful in life: for example, material from science, ethics, and also theology as far as it is suitable for that age." This approach serves a multiple purpose: it forms the pupil's character, sharpens his mind, and improves his language. Moreover, dialectic can be entertaining as well as instructive: "Our judgment is honed; . . . speech too is formed, because one sentence must be expressed in several ways until the smoothest, most appropriate and perspicacious formula has been discovered. Finally such practice is not only useful, but a rather pleasant game for those who have a good mind." The teacher, working with students and correcting their syllogisms, will improve their understanding of the subject matter as well as their style:

He will teach students to express what they formerly said in a rather vulgar manner more appropriately and more meaningfully, and accustom them to love the truth while they are dealing with noble subjects that can be applied to public life. Dialectic should not be applied only to inane and ridiculously captious themes such as "No one and No person bit themselves in the sack," the type that blighted the use of dialectic in the past and subsequently corrupted the other disciplines and the teaching of religion. Let them take their examples from true and useful causes, and let them agree with the common patterns of those who speak correctly. When such methods are used, the usefulness of the art will be evident. I myself am following this principle and have cut out many rules and many ridiculous examples. (615)

It is important to circumscribe the scope of dialectic properly and avoid going beyond its useful and legitimate function:

> Those who have taught dialectic in the right way see limits within which one must stay in defining and arguing . . . Nor do tricks and contentious argumentation deserve to be praised as acumen and subtlety, since they have nothing good in them and have no useful application to life. A good mind displays its brilliance by applying the art [of disputation] to the exposition of the good and useful. Thus certainty will be found in true statements, since that is within the bounds of dialectic. Likewise, falsehoods can certainly be refuted by showing up inconsistencies. Just like the other arts, dialectic has been established and developed for creating certainty . . . the person who is skilled in teaching dialectic and has gained more confidence by being able to confirm or refute a thesis, sees the rationale behind his work and with his mind at ease embraces truth more firmly. He gives thanks to God for the light of the intellect, refraining from imitating the Pyrrhonists who work out tricks to destroy the truth. (616)

Melanchthon's statement of purpose is built on the principles of a humanistic pedagogy and at the same time evidences the dogmatism of a religion that categorically forbade doubts in matters dealt with in Scripture, and that could not imagine a world without moral certainty.

The concluding section of Melanchthon's book, which deals with fallacies, affords him occasion once more to lash out against the corruptors of dialectic. "For sophistries are not merely a competitive game played by boys in school, as many think. . . . No, sophistries have invaded life, horribly sowing and implanting false opinions in the Church, in the curia, in politics, giving rise to great discord, war, and the ruin of mankind. Mind and soul must be well fortified against this dire plague" (715).

Usefulness in the sense of effectiveness is a prominent concept in Ramus' writings as well. He wants dialectic to be useful, that is, to be an instrument to advancing studies in other disciplines; and he wants his books about dialectic to be useful, that is, to provide an effective method of acquiring knowledge in a given field. The traditional method of teaching dialectic rendered it useless as a tool. "When students set foot outside the precincts of the university, they cannot think of any way to apply it," Ramus wrote.[62] How could it be that it never occurred to the dialecticians who are "stuck in this wretched mud for so many years" to examine the purpose of their teaching and ask "in what contexts their precepts can be used, what benefit accrues from them?"[63] His own *Dialecticae institutiones* offered concrete examples of the applications of the art: for example, to literary criticism. As Ramus developed his methodology further, he wanted to convert dialectic into a master tool. His aim was to provide a unified method that would be applicable to all fields of learning. Accordingly, he states in the *Animadversiones:* "Let us look at it in terms of usefulness: there ought to be and there could be one type of invention . . . such that it could answer all questions." He was thinking of a method by which "young people could learn an art much more easily and with a few instructions learned by heart, rather than with great effort and labor run through a disorganized doctrine scattered over many books." In his *Dialecticae institutiones* Ramus spoke only vaguely of a way "that leads by a straight course to that one point at which the mind of the learner aims." A fuller treatment appears in the 1546 edition published under Talon's name. There he explains that the method consists of "descending from universal and general principles to the underlying singular parts." There are two methods, the method of theory or teaching *(doctrina)* and the method of prudence. The former "shows us the one simple method which locates the universal and general things first, then the special and secondary afterwards."[64] The alternative method, guided not by *doctrina* but by *prudentia*, is used when arguing in a nonacademic setting before an audience on which pure syllogisms would be lost.

There are considerable difficulties with Ramus' concept of a master method. For one thing, Ramus' terminology is constantly in flux, which makes it difficult to follow the development of his thought.[65] In addition, there is the problem of reconciling Ramus' bi-partition with his simultaneous claim that there is only one method, applicable to all disciplines.[66] Ramus' critics ridiculed his obsession with discovering a single method, "a subject thrashed out to the last grain"—as Adrien Turnèbe put it. Pierre Galland, too, snubbed Ramus' efforts as a case of the proverbial "fitting everyone with the same boot."[67]

Nizolius introduced the notion of utility among the criteria by which all disciplines were to be measured. He listed truth, usefulness, necessity, and relevance to the subject (I 24). The "pseudo-philosophers" concerned themselves only with the first, and had little success even in that area: "They are wrong, for the most part, and if not wrong, then at any rate useless, and if not useless, then at any rate superfluous, and if not superfluous, at any rate irrelevant" (I 25). Nizolius' critical remarks are distinct from those of other humanists, however, in that moral considerations do not enter in his argument. Elaborating on his negative verdict, he concentrates on two points: dialectic is useless because it is outdated, and superfluous because its subject is covered by rhetoric. "Its use and application have become obsolete. Why should anyone labor and fatigue himself over learning an art for which there is no use anywhere and which is no longer practiced in the manner it once was?" (II 64) If instruction in dialectic were abandoned, students of the humanities and of true philosophy would suffer no disadvantage. "Whatever useful and valid material is lost by eliminating dialectic will be recovered by studying rhetoric [which presented this material] in a richer and more plentiful manner, for arguments and argumentation and everything else related to discourse and disputation is taught much better and more clearly by rhetoricians than by dialecticians" (II 65).

Our examination of the humanistic approach to dialectic reveals a number of common characteristics: a critical attitude toward Aristotelian doctrine; rejection of medieval technical terminology; a shift from formal to informal modes of inference; and a concern for the practical applicability of dialectical skills. Humanist criticism of traditional dialectic did not, however, issue in significant new constructs. It is therefore only marginally correct to speak of a "humanist dialectic." It would be more accurate to call it a critical review of Aristotelian dialectic, or more specifically, of Aristotelian dialectic as modified by medieval scholars. To purists, the humanist contribution to dialectic was no dialectic at all but a method of argumentation for orators. The dividing line between dialectic and rhetoric had always been vague, even in antiquity, and both subjects were traditionally regarded as an aspect of "logic" in the literal sense, that is, the science of words. The humanists tried to shift the balance in favor of rhetoric, whether to erase the dividing line between the two subjects or to subordinate dialectic to rhetoric. "Humanist dialectic" therefore consists in a redeployment of resources or restructuring or trimming of traditional material more than in the development of new theories. Nizolius, who vowed to destroy Aristotelianism root and stem, failed to make good on his promise; most critics professed less radical goals and were content to filter Aristotelian doctrine through Cicero rather than Peter of Spain. They themselves typically claimed credit for clarification and simplification rather than innovation. Defenders of the traditional system, by contrast, accused them of diluting the substance of dialectic and producing a doctrine that was "lightweight, weak, defective, and enervated."[68]

The two areas in which the humanists departed farthest from the medieval model were language and pedagogical purpose. Their efforts to introduce a purer idiom into textbooks were largely successful and became part of a general trend toward classicizing diction in scholarly circles. They also made significant progress in the area of producing "user-friendly" textbooks. The Renaissance had awakened a considerable interest in the philosophy and methodology of education. Flogging schoolmasters may have remained a reality, but in pedagogical literature and in textbooks we find a more sympathetic approach to learners, a manifest concern for facilitating the process of learning and making it appealing to students. In moving away from the authoritarian approach it also became important that students internalize and creatively use rather than mechanically reproduce the material taught. Such concerns are evident also in the humanists' approach to dialectic. Thus while it may be argued that there was no "humanist dialectic" in the strict sense of the word but merely an Aristotelian/medieval dialectic modified and adapted to humanistic concerns, the changes advocated by the humanists are significant in the context of curriculum development and form an important chapter in the history of education.

In the event, however, both humanist and scholastic dialectics were soon to be superseded as tools in the search for the truth by the new scientific method based on experiment and sense perception. Early evidence of the trend and how it affected approaches to logic can be found in Bartolomeo Viotti's *De demonstratione*, published at Paris in 1560. The case of Viotti, who taught logic and medicine at the University of Turin, is similar to that of Nizolius. In his own time he was better known for his book on spas, *De balneorum naturalium viribus*, than for his work on logic, but the latter was resurrected in the seventeenth century in the Leibniz circle. It saw two editions at Helmstedt (1661) and Braunschweig (1685) and was given honorable mention by Leibniz in a letter appended to his edition of Nizolius.[69] In *De demonstratione* Viotti takes both scholastic and humanistic dialecticians to task for their inept treatment of demonstrative proof. In his preface he announces that "we have either no knowledge of the truth, or we acquire it through demonstration," but he found traditional accounts of the process confusing. He tackled the problem both as a professional teacher searching for an effective method of presentation and as a philosopher searching for an effective tool in his personal quest for the truth. "I began to try various new systems and methods, in many cases adding material, introducing new matter, and by using different forms of exposition to fashion my own concept of demonstration, so as to instruct first myself and then others."[70] To this end Viotti studied the works of Aristotle, his scholastic interpreters, and their humanistic critics, but found all of them lacking. Aristotle's doctrine was "so immersed in thickest darkness that it was impossible to understand his method of demonstration, either from his own words or those of his commentators, or to teach it with a view to practical application." If Aristotle's method was nothing but a "chimaera," the scholastic and humanistic dialecticians did not even make an effort to arrive at certainty, teaching instead how to argue plausibly. Their method created doubt rather than certainty, Viotti said, and could lead only to suspended judgment. He included in his sweeping criticism the humanists Valla, Agricola, and Melanchthon, as well as the standard scholastic textbook authors Peter of Spain and Paul of Venice. They succeeded in teaching only one thing: that we know nothing. "What else do you teach, my clever Rodolphus? What else do they teach who preceded and followed you—I mean Valla, [George of] Trebizond, Titelmans, Caesarius, Melanchthon, and similar authors of [books on] dialectic, not to mention Peter of Spain, Paul of Venice, Tartaretus, and John Major?" Knowledge cannot be gained "either through dialectical syllogism, which generates only opinion, or through example and enthymeme, which are the tools of orators rather than philosophers, and have been devised for the purpose of persuasion rather than discovering the truth." Certain knowledge can only be derived from ratiocination based on first principles that need no demonstration, principles that are derived from what can be clearly apprehended by the senses and by the mind: *ex sensui et intellectui perspicuis citra probationem*. In this context, Viotti makes a strong plea for the reliability of sense perception: "We cannot benefit from our senses if we do not trust them. For we take our first beginnings from them. They are the starting line and the initial point from which all demonstrative reasoning takes its departure . . . and principles are deduced from them. For they [sense perceptions] are specific, whereas principles are universal." Our capability for demonstrative reasoning is a gift from God, Viotti says. "The first principles of all demonstration are innate in us through the grace of God . . . Man is the image of God and a world in miniature" (63). In a derivative sense (since God is the creator of nature), these principles can also be said to be natural, "given to us by nature herself."

It is a sign of the times that Viotti makes a decided effort to break away from reliance on authorities. "The authority of writers . . . makes us obedient like slaves. . . . One should consider, not who said it but what is said and the rationale used to corroborate it." Proper sequence must be observed in the search for the truth: "We must begin with the nature of the thing itself . . . not with the authority of writers." The search for truth involves a number of steps: investigating appropriate common-places, checking them against sense perception and intellectual appre-hension, and examining them for consistency. The most significant as-pect of judgment, however, is practice and application: *judicii summam et potissimam partem in exercitatione et longo usu sitam arbitror.*[71]

We have in Viotti an early indication of the direction which logic took in the Cartesian age. The humanists did not emancipate themselves from authority, but they made a first breach into the Aristotelian for-tress. Both their approach and the scholastic method which they criti-cized were found wanting, however, by another generation, which added observation to the traditional tools of scholarly investigation. Thus Vi-otti's peculiar combination of ideas—the rejection of authority, the insis-tence on innate and evident principles, and the twinning of observation and ratiocination—points to future developments in European intellec-tual history.

Conclusion

LIKE ALL FUNDAMENTAL CONTROVERSIES, the humanist-scholastic debate remained unresolved in its own time. This reincarnation of the historical debate over the relationship between word and thing and the classical dispute over rhetoric and philosophy metamorphosed into a debate over philological versus dialectical methods. The original protagonists—the Socratic circle and the Sophists—found intellectual heirs in the scholastics and the humanists, but the terms of reference were changed significantly by the presence of an institutionalized church which had become a pervasive force in the Middle Ages. The Christian context of the debate in the Renaissance weighted the questions discussed by the polemicists.

The ancients compared and contrasted the philosopher's search for knowledge and conviction with the orator's quest for belief and persuasion, but no one doubted that knowledge was higher on the scale measuring the progression toward the truth. The debate was not about the desirability but the possibility of absolute knowledge; not its status but its practical advantage and applicability to everyday life. In the Renaissance, the superiority of knowledge over belief was no longer considered self-evident, for belief in the Word of God, as revealed through the prophets and evangelists, was likewise associated with certainty. Thus ratiocination, the traditional method of validation, was discounted by faith. The quest for knowledge, proclaimed in antiquity the quintessential purpose of life and inseparably linked with the definition of the human being as a rational animal, became the privilege of a small professional group and subject to the magisterium of the Church. The domain of Christians at large was faith. The professionalization of institutions of higher education and the attendant compartmentalization of learning placed further restrictions on an individual's intellectual enterprise and fostered the competitive spirit that fed the humanist-scholastic debate in its later phases.

Within the Christian value system—the constellation dominating the European horizon—the humanist-scholastic debate was illuminated by lesser systems: a movement toward curricular reform at the universities, and a crescendo of voices calling for ecclesiastical reform. Reflecting the continuum of Christian values as well as these professional and confessional concerns, the debate underwent several permutations. Beginning in Italy in the late fourteenth century, it passed through a polite literary phase, ripened into inter-faculty feuding at Northern universities where humanists rivaled scholastic theologians, and was swallowed up in the confessional struggles of the Reformation. The literary genres chosen by the protagonists in the debate underwent a parallel change. Dialogue and other forms that allowed the author to appropriate several voices and present arguments on both sides of a question yielded to apologiae of an academic more than a literary cast. The mood shifted as well: eloquent compositions were succeeded by scholarly disquisitions; jeux d'esprit by scurrilous invective and caustic satire.

In its initial stage, the debate had a certain elegance and purity, as intellectuals with no urgent ideological or professional agenda pondered the moral value of pagan learning, the relative importance of style and content, the effectiveness of rhetoric and dialectic. The participants in the debate converted an internal dialogue into an epideictic exercise. As the controversy moved from Italy to Northern universities, the intellectual debate turned professional and became entangled in power struggles and career politics. Although the polemicists focused their arguments on moral and intellectual issues, considerations of professional competency and rank formed a barely concealed subtext. The debate, which had already deteriorated from a gentlemanly exchange of opinion into uncouth rivalry, turned into a full-fledged war under the auspices of the Reformation. Christian doctrine had always played a subliminal role in the debate, as evidenced in mutual accusations of paganism (both Aristotle, the hero of the scholastics, and Cicero, the idol of the humanists, made their acolytes vulnerable to the charge) and in efforts to exempt revealed texts from the scrutiny of humanist philology. Biblical humanists, charged with unwarranted interference in the business of theologians in the fifteenth century, became the scapegoats of the Catholic Church battling Lutheranism. Scholastic theologians, charged with obscurantism, became the butt of Protestant reformers attacking the Church establishment.

For a few years at the beginning of the sixteenth-century Europe saw an alignment between the forces of humanism and the Reformation. The two movements appeared to march in lockstep, but the alliance proved unstable. The Reformation was fundamentally about doctrine, not about methodology. The schism between Catholics and Protestants separated the humanistic camp into those committed to the Reformation and pressing for spiritual renewal and others aiming for curricular reform and esthetic renewal. Although the reformers went their separate ways, the focus on the biblical text that devolved from the humanistic call *ad fontes*, and the emphasis on language studies associated with it, remained a plank in the Protestant ideology. The struggle for curricular reform involved questions of methodology and pitted philologists against dialecticians. Their dispute was overshadowed, however, by the rise of the Scientific Age and its development of a third option—observation and experiment—to add to the traditional tools of investigation, language analysis, and logical inference.

Humanism itself underwent a profound change. An elitist literary movement in the fifteenth century, it emerged from the debate as a broad scholarly/pedagogical current and, as such, successfully reshaped educational institutions and esthetic values in Europe. It failed to coalesce into a philosophy with a coherent epistemology and unified body of teachings, but it formed an arterial link between the medieval and modern mind sets.[1] Scholasticism, though past its prime, experienced a certain renewal under the pressure of humanist criticism. Neither humanism nor scholasticism, however, was allowed to triumph, as both faced the challenge of new movements—rationalism and empiricism, intellectual currents that came to dominate the next centuries.

Bibliography

Notes

Index

Bibliography

PRIMARY SOURCES

Agricola, Rudolph. *De inventione dialectica.* Repr. Nieuwkoop, 1967.

Agrippa of Nettesheim, Heinrich Cornelius. *De incertitudine et vanitate scientiarum declamatio invectiva.* Cologne, 1531.

———— *Apologia adversus calumnias propter declamationem de vanitate scientiarum et excellentia verbi Dei.* S. l., 1533.

———— *Opera.* Repr. Hildesheim, 1970.

Adrianus, Matthaeus. *Oratio* in H. de Vocht, *History of the Foundation and the Rise of the Collegium Trilingue Lovaniense, 1517–1550,* I, 537–542. Louvain, 1951–1955.

Alonso de Cartagena. *Liber Alphonsi episcopi Burgensis* in A. Birkenmajer, "Der Streit des Alfonso von Cartagena mit Leonardo Bruni Aretino," *Beiträge zur Geschichte der Philosophie des Mittelalters* 20–5 (1920): 162–186.

———— Preface to Alonso's translation of Aristotle in M. Menéndez y Pelayo, *Historia de las ideas estéticas en España,* Appendix II, 597–603. Buenos Aires, 1889.

Advertissements sur la censure qu'ont faicte les bestes de Sorbonne. Anon. [Paris], 1547.

Barbaro, Ermolao. *Letters to Pico* in Qu. Breen, *Christianity and Humanism,* 11, 14, 25–38. Grand Rapids, 1968.

Beatus Rhenanus. *Der Briefwechsel des Beatus Rhenanus.* Eds. A. Horawitz and K. Hartfelder. Leipzig, 1886.

Bebel, Heinrich. *Commentaria epistolarum conficiendarum.* Pforzheim, 1508.

Béda, Noël. *Annotationum . . . in Des. Erasmum Roterodamum liber.* Paris, 1526.

———— *Requête . . . au Parlement de Paris contre les lecteurs royaux.* Ed. J. Farge in *Le parti conservateur au XVI siècle: Université et Parlement de Paris à l'époque de la Renaissance et de la Réforme,* document 7. Paris, 1992.

Biel, Gabriel. *Correctorium circa quattuor libros Sententiarum.* Ed. H. Rückert. Tübingen, 1973.

Boccaccio, Giovanni. *De genealogia deorum* in *Boccaccio on Poetry.* Trans. Ch. G. Osgood. New York, 1956.

Brandolini, Aurelio, "Epitome in sacram Hebraeorum historiam," MS Bibl. Vat. Ottob. Lat. 438.

Brunfels, Otto, *Confutatio sophistices et quaestionum curiosarum.* Sélestat, 1520.

Bruni, Leonardo. *Dialogi.* Trans. G. Griffiths, J. Hankins, D. Thompson in *The Humanism of Leonardo Bruni: Selected Texts.* Binghamton, 1987.

Bucer, Martin. *Correspondance de Martin Bucer.* Ed. J. Rott. Leiden, 1979.

Budé, Guillaume, *Opera omnia.* Repr. Farnborough, 1966.

Buschius, Hermannus (Hermann von dem Busche). *Praestabili et rare eruditionis viro Martino Mellerstat . . .* Leipzig, 1502.

———— *Vallum humanitatis.* Cologne, 1518.

Cano, Melchior. *De locis theologicis.* Padua, 1734.

Carvajal, Luis. *Dulcoratio amarulentiarum Erasmicae responsionis.* Paris, 1530.

Celtis, Conrad. *Oratio.* Ed. H. Rupprich. Leipzig, 1932.

———— *Selections from Conrad Celtis (1459–1508).* Ed. L. Forster. Cambridge, 1948.

Colet, John. *Lectures on Corinthians.* Trans. J. H. Lupton. London, 1874.

Cortesi, Paolo. *In sententias.* Basel, 1513.

Cousturier, Pierre. *De tralatione Bibliae.* Paris, 1525.

———— *Antapologia.* Paris, 1526.

Dialogus novus et mire festivus ex quorundam salibus cribratus. Anon. in Hutten, *Opera,* ed. Böcking, in Supplement I.

Dominici, Giovanni. *Lucula Noctis.* Ed. E. Hunt. Notre Dame, 1940.

Dorp, Maarten van. *Orationes.* Ed. J. IJsewijn. Leipzig, 1986.

Eck, Johann *Oratio . . . pro venerando patre Stephano priore Eberspergio.* N. l., 1512.

Erasmus, Desiderius. *Opus epistolarum Des. Erasmi Roterodami.* Ed. P. S. Allen. Oxford, 1906–1958. Henceforth cited as Allen.

———— *Ausgewählte Werke.* Eds. A. and H. Holborn. Munich, 1933.

———— *The Poems of Erasmus.* Ed. C. Reedijk. Leiden, 1956.

———— *The Colloquies of Des. Erasmus.* Trans. C. Thompson Chicago, 1965.

———— *Opera omnia.* Amsterdam, 1969–. Henceforth cited as ASD.

———— *The Collected Works of Erasmus.* Toronto, 1974–. Henceforth cited as CWE.

La Farce des théologastres. Anon., ed. C. Longeon. Geneva, 1989.

Ferber von Herborn, Johann. *Paradoxa seu theologicae assertationes.* Paris, 1534.

Ficino, Marsilio. *Opera.* Repr. Turin, 1962.

Flaccius Illyricus, *Clavis Scripturae.* Basel, 1580.

Galland, Pierre, *Contra novam academiam Petri Rami oratio.* Paris, 1551.

Gerson, Jean. *De mystica theologia.* Ed. A. Combes. Verona, 1958.

———— *Oeuvres complètes.* Ed. P. Glorieux. Paris, 1960–1973.

Gratius, Ortvinus. *Lamentationes obscurorum virorum* in Ulrich von Hutten, *Opera,* ed. E. Böcking, Supplement I.

Hasardus Angianus, Jacques. *Hasardi Angiani Apologia.* Louvain, 1520.

Hessus, Eobanus, *Dialogi tres.* Erfurt, 1524.

Hoest, Stephan, *Reden und Briefe.* Ed. and trans. F. Baron. Munich, 1971.

Hoogstraten, Jacobus. *Destructio Cabbalae.* Cologne, 1519.

Hutten, Ulrich von. *Opera.* Ed. E. Böcking. Leipzig, 1859–1870.

Lee, Edward. *Annotationes in annotationes Erasmi.* Paris, 1520.

Lefèvre, Jacques. *Epistolae divi Pauli apostoli.* Paris, 1515.

—— *The Prefatory Epistles of Jacques Lefèvre d'Etaples.* . . . Ed. E. Rice. New York, 1972.

Locher, Jacob. *Theologica Emphasis.* [Basel], 1496.

—— *De studio humanarum disciplinarum et laude poetarum* [Freiburg, 1496]

—— *Vitiosa sterilis Mulae ad Musam roscida lepiditate praedicatam comparatio.* Nürnberg, 1506.

López de Zúñiga, Diego (Stunica, Lopis). *Annotationes contra Erasmum Roterodamum in defensionem tralationis Novi Testamenti.* Alcala, 1520.

Mair, John. Prefaces in Appendix, *History of Greater Britain.* Ed. A. Constable. Edinburgh, 1892.

Manetti, Gianozzo. *Apologeticus.* Ed. A. de Petris. Rome, 1980.

Masson, Jacques (also Latomus, Jacobus). *Opera quae praecipue adversus horum temporum haereses conscripsit.* Louvain, 1550.

—— *Dialogus de tribus linguis* in *Disputationes contra Lutherum,* ed. F. Pijper. The Hague, 1905.

Melanchthon, Philipp. *Melanchthons Werke in Auswahl.* Ed. R. Stupperich. Gütersloh, 1951–.

—— *Opera quae supersunt omnia* in *Corpus Reformatorum,* vols 1–28. Halle, 1834–60, repr. 1963. Henceforth cited as CR.

—— *A Melanchthon Reader.* Ed. R. Keen. New York, 1988.

Mexia, Pedro, *Diálogos o Coloquios.* Seville, 1562.

More, Thomas. *The Complete Works of Thomas More.* Vol. 15, ed. and trans. D. Kinney. New Haven, 1986.

Mosellanus, Petrus, *Oratio de variarum linguarum cognitione paranda.* Leipzig, 1518.

Muret, Marc-Antoine. *Adversus quosdam litterarum humaniorum vituperatores oratio* in *Orationes XXIII.* Venice, 1576.

Murmellius, Johannes. *Didascalici libri duo.* Cologne, 1510.

Mutianus, Rufus. *Briefwechsel.* Ed. C. Krause in *Zeitschrift des Vereins für hessische Geschichte und Landeskunde* NF Supplement IX, 1885.

Nebrija, Elio Antonio. *Apologia earum rerum quae illi obiiciuntur.* S. l., 1516?

—— *Introducciones latinas.* S. l., [1488].

Nesen, Willem. *Epistola de magistris nostris* in H. de Vocht, *History of the Foundation and the Rise of the Collegium Trilingue Lovaniense,* I:585–596 Louvain, 1951–1955.

—— *Dialogus bilinguium et trilinguium.* Trans. P. Pascal in CWE 7:335–347.

Nizolius, Marius. *De veris principiis et vera ratione philosophandi,* 2 vols. Ed. Qu. Breen. Rome, 1956.

Pace, Richard. *De fructu qui ex doctrina percipitur/The Benefit of a Liberal Education.* Ed. and trans. F. Manley and R. Sylvester. New York, 1967.

Petrarca, Francesco. *Le familiari.* Ed. V. Rossi. Florence, 1933–1942.

—— *Rerum memorandarum libri.* Ed. G. Billanovich. Florence, 1943.

———— *De otio religioso.* Ed. G. Rotondi. Citta del Vaticano, 1958.

———— *On His Own Ignorance and That of Many Others.* Trans. H. Nachod in *The Renaissance Philosophy of Man,* ed. E. Cassirer et al. Chicago, repr. 1975.

———— *Contra medicum.* Ed. P. G. Ricci. Rome, 1978.

Pico della Mirandola, Giovanni. *Letter to Barbaro,* trans. in Qu. Breen, *Christianity and Humanism,* 15–25. Grand Rapids, 1968.

———— *Opera omnia.* 2 vols. Repr. Turin, 1971.

———— *Conclusiones.* Ed. B. Kieszkowski. Geneva, 1973.

———— *Apologia.* Ed. and French trans. H. Crouzel, *Controverse sur Origène à la Renaissance: Jean Pic de la Mirandole et Pierre Garcia.* Paris, 1977.

Pico della Mirandola, Gianfrancesco. *Opera omnia.* 2 vols. Repr. Turin, 1972.

Pio, Alberto. *Responsio accurata et paraenetica.* Paris, 1529.

Pirckheimer, Willibald. *Epistola apologetica* in *Piscator.* S. l., 1517.

Polich of Mellerstatt, Martin, *Laconismus tumultuarius . . . in defensionem poetices.* Leipzig, 1500.

Pontano, Giovanni. *Dialoge.* Ed. and trans. H. Kiefer. Munich, 1984.

Ramus, Petrus. *Aristotelicae animadversiones.* With an introduction by W. Risse. Repr. Stuttgart, 1964.

———— *Dialecticae institutiones.* Stuttgart, 1964.

———— *Rhetoricae distinctiones in Quintilianum.* Ed. and trans. J. J. Murphy and C. Newland. De Kalb, 1986.

Reuchlin, Johann. *Defensio contra calumniatores suos Colonienses.* Tübingen, 1513.

Rhegius, Urbanus. *Opusculum de dignitate sacerdotum.* Augsburg, 1519.

Salutati, Coluccio. *Epistolario di Coluccio Salutati.* Ed. F. Novati. Rome, 1905.

Sbruglio, Riccardo. *In quosdam theologastros Lovanienses sycophantas carmen extemporale* in *Flores et Elegantiae ex diversis libris Hochstrati . . . collectae.* S. l., s.a.

Seitz (Seicius), Johann. *Ad praestantem et magne eruditionis virum magistrum C. Wimpinam pro defensione sacre theologie et theologice veritatis.* Leipzig, c. 1500.

Sturm, Johann. *Partitiones dialecticae.* Lyons, 1554.

Titelmans, Frans. *Collationes quinque super epistolas ad Romanos.* Antwerp, 1529.

———— *Epistola apologetica.* Antwerp, 1530.

Valla, Lorenzo, *Opera omnia.* Repr. Turin, 1962.

———— *Antidotum primum.* Ed. A. Wesseling. Amsterdam, 1978.

———— *Repastinatio dialectice et philosophie.* Ed. G. Zippel. Third redaction in vol. I. Padua, 1982.

Varii. *Illustrium virorum epistolae.* Haguenau, 1519.

———— *Epistolae aliquot eruditorum virorum.* Basel, 1520.

———— *Correspondance des Réformateurs dans les pays de langue française.* Ed. A.-L. Herminjard. Geneva-Paris, 1866–1897.

———— *Urkundenbuch der Universität Heidelberg.* Ed. E. Winkelmann. Heidelberg, 1886.

———— *Chartularium Universitatis parisiensis.* Eds. H. Denifle and Ae. Chatelain. Paris, 1897.

——— *Letters of Obscure Men.* Ed. H. Holborn, trans. F. G. Stokes in *On the Eve of the Reformation.* New York, 1964.

——— *Cartulario de la Universidad de Salamanca* vol. VI. Ed. V. Beltrán de Heredia. Salamanca, 1973.

Viotti, Bartolomeo. *De demonstratione.* Braunschweig, 1685.

Vives, Juan, *Opera omnia.* Ed. F. Fabian y Fuero. Valencia, 1785; repr. Farnborough, 1964.

——— *In pseudodialecticos.* Ed. and trans. Ch. Fantazzi. Leiden, 1979.

——— *Somnium.* Ed. and trans. E. V. George. Greenwood, 1989.

Wakefield, Robert, *On the Three Languages.* Ed. and trans. G. Lloyd-Jones. Binghamton, 1989.

Wimpina, Conrad. *Apologeticus in sacre theologie defensionem.* Leipzig, 1500.

——— *Responsio et Apologia Conradi Wimpine contra laconismum.* Leipzig, 1502.

Wimpheling, Jacob, *Contra turpem libellum Philomusi theologie scholastice et neotericorum defensio.* Nürnberg, 1510.

——— *Pro concordia dialecticorum et oratorum* in J. v. Riegger, ed., *Amoenitates Litterariae Friburgenses,* vol. II. Ulm, 1775.

——— *Castigationes locorum in canticis ecclesiasticis et divinis officiis depravatorum* in J. v. Riegger, ed., *Amoenitates Literariae Friburgenses,* vol. II. Ulm, 1775.

——— *Jacobus Vuimphelingus Selestatinus Jacobo Philomuso poete laureato presens confessionale dicat* in J. Schlecht, "Zu Wimphelings Fehden mit Jakob Locher und Paul Lang," *Festgabe Karl Theodor von Heigel,* ed. Th. Bitterauf. Munich, 1903.

——— *Jacob Wimpfelings Briefwechsel.* Ed. O. Herding. Munich, 1990.

——— *De ortu progressu et fructu theologiae* in *Farrago miscellaneorum Conradi Wimpfelingae Fagis.* Cologne, 1531.

Zwingli, Huldrych. *Werke,* vol. VII. Leipzig, 1911.

SECONDARY SOURCES

Ashworth, E. "Traditional Logic," in *The Cambridge History of Renaissance Philosophy.* Eds. Ch. Schmitt and Qu. Skinner. Cambridge, 1988: 147–172.

Augustijn, C. "Humanisten auf dem Scheideweg zwischen Luther und Erasmus," in *Humanismus und Reformation: Martin Luther und Erasmus von Rotterdam in den Konflikten ihrer Zeit.* Ed. O. H. Pesch. Freiburg, 1985: 119–134.

——— "Le dialogue Erasme-Luther dans l'*Hyperaspistes* II," *Actes du colloque international Erasme.* Ed. J. Chomarat et al. Geneva, 1990: 171–184.

——— *Erasmus: His Life, Works, and Influence.* Toronto, 1992.

Bauch, G. *Geschichte des Leipziger Frühhumanismus.* Leipzig, 1899.

Baumgart, P. "Humanistische Bildungsreform an deutschen Universitäten des 16. Jahrhunderts," *Humanismus im Bildungswesen des 15. und 16. Jahrhunderts.* Ed. W. Reinhard. Weinheim, 1984: 171–197.

Bedouelle, G., and B. Roussel, eds. *Le temps des Réformes et la Bible.* Paris, 1989.

Bensrath, G. "Die deutschen evangelischen Universitäten der Reformationszeit" in

Universität und Gelehrtenstand 1460–1800. Eds. H. Rössler and G. Franz. Lahn, 1970: 63–105.

Bentley, J. *Humanists and Holy Writ.* Princeton, 1983.

Birkenmajer, A. "Der Streit des Alonso von Cartagena mit Leonardo Bruni Aretino." *Beiträge zur Geschichte der Philosophie des Mittelalters* 20–5 (1920): 162–186.

Boehm, L. "Humanistische Bildungsbewegung und mittelalterliche Universitätsverfassung: Aspekte zur frühneuzeitlichen Reformgeschichte der deutschen Universitäten" in *The Universities in the Late Middle Ages.* Eds. J. IJsewijn and J. Pacquet. Louvain, 1978: 315–346.

Bohatec, J. *Budé und Calvin: Studien zur Gedankenwelt des französischen Frühhumanismus.* Graz, 1950.

Bolgar, R. R. "Humanism as a Value System with Reference to Budé and Vives" in *Humanism in France at the End of the Middle Ages and in the Early Renaissance.* Ed. A. H. T. Levi. Manchester, 1970: 199–215.

Bouwsma, W. "Renaissance and Reformation: An Enquiry into Their Affinities and Connections" in *Luther and the Dawn of the Modern Era,* ed. H. Oberman (Leiden, 1974) 127–149

———— "Changing Assumptions in Later Renaissance Culture," *Viator* 7 (1976): 421–440.

Boyle, M. O'Rourke, *Rhetoric and Reform: Erasmus' Civil Dispute with Luther.* Cambridge, Mass., 1983.

Breen, Qu. "Marius Nizolius: Ciceronian Lexicographer and Philosopher," *Archive for Reformation History* 46 (1955): 69–84.

Broadie, A. *The Circle of John Mair: Logic and Logicians in Pre-Reformation Scotland.* Oxford, 1985.

Bruyère, N. *Méthode et dialectique dans l'oeuvre de La Ramée.* Paris, 1984.

Cameron, E. "The Late Renaissance and the Unfolding Reformation in Europe" in *Humanism and Reform: The Church in Europe, England, and Scotland 1400–1643.* Ed. J. Kirk. Oxford, 1991: 15–36.

Cameron, R. "The Attack on the Biblical Work of Lefèvre d'Etaples, 1514–21," *Church History* 38 (1969): 9–24.

Centi, T. M. "L'attività letteraria di Santi Pagnini (1570–1536) nel campo delle scienze bibliche," *Archivum fratrum Praedicatorum* 15 (1945): 5–51.

Connolly, J. L. *John Gerson, Reformer and Mystic.* Louvain, 1928.

D'Amico, J. *Renaissance Humanism in Papal Rome.* Baltimore, 1983.

———— "Humanism and Pre-Reformation Theology" in *Renaissance Humanism.* Ed. A. Rabil, 111: 349–379. Philadelphia, 1988.

———— *Theory and Practice in Renaissance Criticism: Beatus Rhenanus between Conjecture and History.* Berkeley, 1988.

De Jongh, H. *L'ancienne faculté de théologie de Louvain.* Repr. Utrecht, 1980.

Delph, R. "Italian Humanism in the Early Reformation: Agostino Steuco 1497–1548" PhD diss. University of Michigan, 1987.

Denley, P. "Giovanni Dominici's Opposition to Humanism" in *Religion and Humanism.* Ed. K. Robbins. Oxford, 1981: 103–114.

Di Camillo, Ottavio. *El humanismo castellano del siglo XV.* Valencia, 1976.

—— "Humanism in Spain" in *Renaissance Humanism.* Ed. A. Rabil, II: 55–108. Philadelphia, 1988.

Duhamel, P. "The Logic and Rhetoric of Peter Ramus," *Modern Philology* 46 (1948/9): 163–171.

Farge, J., *Orthodoxy and Reform in Early Reformation France.* Leiden, 1985.

Faust, A., "Die Dialektik R. Agricolas: Ein Beitrag zur Charakteristik des deutschen Humanismus," *Archiv für Geschichte der Philosophie* 34 (1922): 118–135.

Fleischer, M. "The Institutionalization of Humanism in Silesia," *Archive for Reformation History* 66 (1975): 156–173.

Fletcher, J. M. "Change and Resistance to Change; a Consideration of the Development of English and German Universities during the Sixteenth Century," *History of Universities* 1 (1981): 1–36.

—— "The Faculty of Arts" in *The History of the University of Oxford.* Ed. J. McConica, III: 157–200. Oxford, 1986.

Freedman, J. S. "The Diffusion of the Writings of Petrus Ramus in Central Europe, c. 1570–c. 1630," *Renaissance Quarterly* 46 (1993): 98–152.

Friedberg, E. *Die Universität Leipzig in Vergangenheit und Gegenwart.* Leipzig, 1898.

Friedensburg, W. "Beiträge zum Briefwechsel der katholischen Gelehrten Deutschlands im Reformationszeitalter," *Zeitschrift für Kirchengeschichte* 19 (1899): 253–258.

Fuchs, W. P. "Willibald Pirckheimer," *Jahrbuch für Fränkische Landesforschung* 31 (1971): 1–18.

Gallina, E. *Aonio Paleario.* 3 vols. Sora, 1989.

García de la Concha, V. "La impostación religiosa de la reforma humanística en España: Nebrija y los poetas cristianos," in *Nebrija y la introducción del Renacimiento en España.* Ed. V. García de la Concha. Salamanca, 1983: 123–43.

Gentile, Giovanni. *Storia della filosofia italiana.* Florence, 1969.

Gerl, H-B. *Rhetorik als Philosophie: Lorenzo Valla.* Munich, 1974.

—— *Philosophie und Philologie.* Munich, 1981.

Gerosa, P. P. *Umanesimo cristiano del Petrarca.* Turin, 1966.

Gil, L. "Gramáticos, humanistas, dómines," *El Basilisco* 9 (1980): 20–30.

—— "Nebrija y el menester del gramático" in *Nebrija y la introducción del Renacimiento en España.* Ed. V. García de la Concha. Salamanca, 1983: 53–64.

Gilly, C. "Das Sprichwort 'Die Gelehrten die Verkehrten' oder der Verrat der Intellektuellen im Zeitalter der Glaubensspaltung" *Forme e destinazione del messaggio religioso. Aspetti della propaganda religiosa nel Cinquecento.* Ed. A. Rotondo. Florence, 1991: 229–375.

Grafton, A., and L. Jardine. *From Humanism to the Humanities.* London, 1986.

Hammerstein, N. "The University of Heidelberg in the Early Modern Period: Aspects of Its History as a Contribution to Its Sexcentenary," *History of Universities* 6 (1986–7): 105–134.

Hankins, J. *Plato in the Italian Renaissance.* Leiden, 1990.

Hay, D. "Humanists, Scholars, and Religion in the Late Middle Ages," in *Religion and Humanism*. Ed. K. Robbins. Oxford, 1981: 1–18.

Heath, T. "Logical Grammar, Grammatical Logic, and Humanism in Three German Universities," *Studies in the Renaissance* 18 (1971): 9–64.

Heer, F. *Die dritte Kraft: Der Humanismus zwischen den Fronten des konfessionellen Zeitalters*. Frankfurt, 1959.

Higman, F. "Un pamphlet de Calvin restitué à son auteur," *Revue d'histoire et de philosophie religieuse* 60 (1980): Part I:167–180; Part II:327–337.

Jardine, L. "Lorenzo Valla and the Intellectual Origins of Humanist Dialectic," *Journal of the History of Philosophy* 15 (1977): 143–164.

——— "Dialectic or Dialectical Rhetoric? Augustino Nifo's Criticism of Lorenzo Valla," *Rivista critica di storia della filosofia* 36 (1981): 253–270.

——— "Humanistic Logic," in *The Cambridge History of Renaissance Philosophy*. Eds. Ch. Schmitt and Qu. Skinner. Cambridge, 1988: 173–198

——— "Distinctive Discipline: R. Agricola's Influence on Methodological Thinking in the Humanities" in *Rodolphus Agricola Phrisius, 1444–1485*. Ed. F. Akkerman and A. J. Vanderjagt. Leiden, 1988: 38–57.

——— *Erasmus, Man of Letters: The Construction of Charisma in Print*. Princeton, 1993.

——— See also under Grafton.

Joachimsen, P. "*Loci Communes*. Eine Untersuchung zur Geistesgeschichte des Humanismus und der Reformation" in *Gesammelte Aufsätze*, ed. N. Hammerstein. Baden, 1970: 387–442.

Junghans, H. "Der Einfluss des Humanismus auf Luthers Entwicklung," *Lutherjahrbuch* 37 (1970): 37–101.

Kessler, E. *Petrarca und die Geschichte*. Munich, 1978.

——— "Die Transformation des aristotelischen Organon durch L. Valla," in *Aristotelismus und Renaissance*. Ed. E. Kessler. Wiesbaden, 1988: 53–87.

——— "The Transformation of Aristotelianism during the Renaissance," *New Perspectives in Renaissance Thought*. Eds. J. Henry and S. Hutton. London, 1990: 137–147.

Kittelson, J. *Wolfgang Capito: From Humanist to Reformer*. Leiden, 1975.

——— "Humanism in the Theological Faculties of Lutheran Universities during the Late Reformation" in *The Harvest of Humanism in Central Europe*. Ed. M. Fleischer. St. Louis, 1992: 139–158.

Kittelson, J. and P. Transue, eds. *Rebirth, Reform and Resilience: Universities in Transition, 1300–1700*. Columbia, 1984.

Kleineidam, E. *Universitas Studii Erffordensis* II. Leipzig, 1969.

Knepper, J. *Jacob Wimpheling (1450–1528)*. Freiburg, 1902.

Kristeller, Paul Oskar. "Florentine Platonism and its Relations with Humanism and Scholasticism," *Church History* 8 (1939): 201–211.

——— "Petrarch's Averroists," *Bibliothèque d'Humanisme et Renaissance* 14 (1952): 59–65.

——— *Renaissance Thought*. New York, 1961.

———— "Petrarca, der Humanismus und die Scholastik" in *Petrarca*. Ed. A. Buck. Darmstadt, 1976: 261–281.

———— "Scholastik und Humanismus an der Universität Heidelberg," in *Der Humanismus und die oberen Fakultäten*. Ed. G. Keil et al. Weinheim, 1987.

Krüger, Friedhelm, "Bucer and Erasmus," in *Martin Bucer and 16th Century Europe*. Eds. Ch. Krieger and M. Lienhard. Leiden, 1993: 583–594.

Lang, A. *Die Loci Theologici des Melchior Cano und die Methode des dogmatischen Beweises*. Hildesheim, 1974.

Lavergnat-Gagnière, Ch. *Lucien de Samosate et le Lucianisme en France au XVIe siècle*. Geneva, 1988.

Lawn, B. *The Rise and Decline of the Scholastic "Quaestio Disputata."* Leiden, 1993.

Lawrance, J. "Humanism in the Iberian Peninsula" in *The Impact of Humanism on Western Europe*, Eds. A. Goodwin and A. MacKay. London, 1990: 220–258.

Lloyd Jones, G. *The Discovery of Hebrew in Tudor England: A Third Language*. Manchester, 1983.

Mack, P. *Renaissance Argument: Valla and Agricola in the Traditions of Rhetoric and Dialectic*. Leiden, 1993.

Marcotte, E. *La nature de la théologie d'après Melchior Cano*. Ottawa, 1949.

Marsh, D. *The Quattrocento Dialogue: Classical Tradition and Humanist Innovation*. Cambridge, Mass., 1980.

Matheson, P. "Humanism and Reform Movements" in *The Impact of Humanism on Western Europe*. Eds. A. Goodwin and A. MacKay. London, 1990: 23–42.

Mattioli, E. *Luciano e l'umanesimo*. Naples, 1993.

Maurer, W. "Melanchthons Anteil am Streit zwischen Luther und Erasmus," *Archive for Reformation History* 49 (1958): 89–115.

———— "Melanchthon als Humanist" in *Philip Melanchthon*. Ed. W. Ellinger. Göttingen, 1961: 116–132.

———— *Der junge Melanchthon zwischen Humanismus und Reformation*. Göttingen, 1967.

Mehl, J. "Hermann von dem Busche's *Vallum humanitatis:* A German Defense of the Renaissance *studia humanitatis*," *Renaissance Quarterly* 42 (1989): 480–506.

———— "Humanism in the Home Town of the 'Obscure Men'" in *Humanismus in Köln*. Cologne, 1991: 1–38.

M. Menéndez y Pelayo. *Historia de las ideas estéticas en España*. Buenos Aires, 1889.

Moeller B. "Die deutschen Humanisten und die Anfänge der Reformation," *Zeitschrift für Kirchengeschichte* 70 (1959): 46–61.

Monfasani, J. "Lorenzo Valla and Rudolph Agricola," *Journal of the History of Philosophy* 28 (1990): 181–200.

———— "Aristotelians, Platonists, and the Missing Ockhamists: Philosophical Liberty in Pre-Reformation Italy," *Renaissance Quarterly* 46 (1993): 247–276.

Muñoz Delgado, V. "Nominalismo, lógica y humanismo" in *El Erasmismo en España* Santander, 1986: 109–174.

Murphy, F. X. "Petrarch and the Christian Philosophy" in *Francesco Petrarca: Citizen of the World*. Ed. G. Billanovich et al. Padova, 1980: 223–251.

Nauert, Ch. *Agrippa and the Crisis of Renaissance Thought*. Urbana, 1965.

——— "The Clash of Humanists and Scholastics: An Approach to Pre-Reformation Controversies," *Sixteenth Century Journal* 4 (1973): 1–18.

——— "Humanists, Scholastics, and the Struggle to Reform the University of Cologne, 1523–1525" in *Humanismus in Köln*. Ed. J. Mehl. Cologne, 1991: 40–76.

Nikolaou, M. *Sprache als Welterschliessung und Sprache als Norm: Überlegungen zu R. Agricola und J. Sturm*. Munich, 1984.

Nolhac, P. de, *Pétrarque et l'Humanisme*. Paris, 1907.

Noreña, C. G. *Studies in Spanish Renaissance Thought*. The Hague, 1975.

——— "Agricola, Vives, and the Low Countries" in *Erasmus in Hispania, Vives in Belgia*. Eds. J. IJsewijn and A. Losada. Louvain, 1986: 99–118.

Oberman, Heiko. *Contra vanam curiositatem: Ein Kapitel der Theologen zwischen Seelenwinkel und Weltall*. Zurich, 1974.

——— *The Harvest of Medieval Theology: Gabriel Biel and Late Medieval Nominalism*. Durham, 1983.

——— *Roots of Antisemitism in the Age of Renaissance and Reformation*. Philadelphia, 1983.

——— "Initia Calvini: The Matrix of Calvin's Reformation," *Mededelingen der Koninklijke Nederlandse Akademie van Wetenschappen* 54-4 (1991): 111–147.

——— "Discovery of Hebrew and Discrimination against the Jews: The *Veritas Hebraica* as Double-Edged Sword in Renaissance and Reformation" in *Germania illustrata*. Eds. A. Fix and S. Karant-Nunn. Kirksville, 1992: 19–34.

Olin, J. *Catholic Reform from Cardinal Ximenes to the Council of Trent 1495–1563*. New York, 1990.

Olmedo, F. *Nebrija (1441–1522): Debelador de la barbarie, comentador eclesiástico, pedagogo, poeta*. Madrid, 1942.

Ong, W. *Ramus, Method and the Decay of Dialogue*. Cambridge, Mass., 1958.

——— *Ramus and Talon Inventory*. Cambridge, Mass., 1958.

Overfield, J. *Humanism and Scholasticism in Late Medieval Germany*. Princeton, 1984.

Ozment, S. "Humanism, Scholasticism, and the Intellectual Origins of the Reformation," in *Continuity and Discontinuity in Church History. Essays Presented to George Huntston Williams on the Occasion of his 65th Birthday*. Eds. F. Forrester Church and T. George. Leiden, 1979: 133–149.

——— "The Revolution of the Pamphleteers," *Forme e destinazione del messagio religioso. Aspetti della propaganda religiosa nel Cinquecento*. Ed. A. Rotondo. Florence, 1991: 1–18.

Panofsky, E., *Gothic Architecture and Scholasticism*. Latrobe, 1951.

Pascoe, L. "The Council of Trent and Bible Study: Humanism and Scripture," *Catholic Historical Review* 52 (1966): 18–38.

——— *Jean Gerson: Principles of Church Reform*. Leiden, 1973.

Perreiah, A. "Humanistic Critiques of Scholastic Dialectic," *Sixteenth Century Journal* 13 (1982): 3–22.

Prantl, C. *Geschichte der Logik im Abendlande* IV. Leipzig, 1927.

Pugliese, O. "The Power of the Text in Humanist Culture: Valla and the Donation of Constantine," *Scripta Mediterranea* 12–13 (1991/2): 157–68.

Quint, D. "Humanism and Modernity: A Reconsideration of Bruni's *Dialogues,*" *Renaissance Quarterly* 38 (1985): 423–445.

Rabil, A. "Desiderius Erasmus," in *Renaissance Humanism: Foundation, Forms, and Legacy,* Ed. A. Rabil, II: 216–264. Philadelphia, 1988.

Rashkow, I. "Hebrew Bible Translation and the Fear of Judaization," *Sixteenth Century Journal* 21 (1990): 217–234.

Raspanti, A. *Filosofia, teologia, religione: l'unità della visione in Giovanni Pico della Mirandola.* Palermo, 1991.

Rice, E. *Saint Jerome in the Renaissance.* Baltimore, 1985.

Rico, F. *Nebrija frente a los bárbaros.* Salamanca, 1978.

Risse, W. *Die Logik der Neuzeit,* 2 vols. Stuttgart, 1964.

Ritter, G. *Die geschichtliche Bedeutung des deutschen Humanismus.* 2nd ed. Darmstadt, 1963.

Robinson, Ch. *Lucian and His Influence in Europe.* London, 1979.

Rossi, P. "Il 'De Principiis' di Mario Nizolio" in *Testi umanistici su la retorica.* Ed. E. Garin et al. Rome, 1953: 57–92.

Round, N. G. "Renaissance Culture and Its Opponents in 15th Century Castile," *Modern Language Review* 57 (1972): 204–215.

Rummel, E. *Erasmus' Annotations on the New Testament.* Toronto, 1986.

——— *Erasmus and His Catholic Critics,* 2 vols. Nieuwkoop, 1989.

——— "An Unpublished Erasmian Apologia in the Royal Library of Copenhagen," *Nederlands Archief voor Kerkgeschiedenis* 70 (1990): 210–229.

——— "The Conflict between Humanism and Scholasticism Revisited," *Sixteenth Century Journal* 23 (1992): 713–726.

——— "Epistola Hermolai nova ac subditicia: A Declamation Falsely Ascribed to Philipp Melanchthon," *Archive for Reformation History* 83 (1992): 302–305.

——— trans. *Scheming Papists and Lutheran Fools: Five Reformation Satires.* New York, 1993.

——— "A 'Petition' and a 'Papal Rescript': From the Pen of Willibald Pirckheimer?" *Archive for Reformation History* 85 (1994): 309–316.

Saccaro, A. P. *Französischer Humanismus des 14. und 15. Jahrhunderts.* Munich, 1975.

Scheible, H. "Melanchthon zwischen Luther und Erasmus," *Renaissance und Reformation: Gegensätze und Gemeinsamkeiten.* Wolfenbüttel, 1987: 155–180.

Schmelzer, H. *Petrarcas Verhältnis zur vorausgehenden christlichen Philosophie des Abendlandes.* Bonn, 1911.

Schmitt, Ch. *Cicero Scepticus.* The Hague, 1972.

——— *Aristotle and the Renaissance.* Cambridge, Mass., 1983.

Seifert, A. *Logik zwischen Scholastik und Humanismus: Das Kommentarwerk Johann Ecks.* Munich, 1978.

Seigel, J. E. *Rhetoric and Philosophy in Renaissance Humanism: The Union of Eloquence and Wisdom, Petrarch to Valla.* Princeton, 1968.

Sharratt, P. "Peter Ramus and the Reform of the University: The Divorce of Philosophy and Eloquence?" *French Renaissance Studies 1540–1570: Humanism and the Encyclopedia.* Edinburgh, 1976: 4–20.

Smolinsky, H. "Der Humanismus an den theologischen Fakultäten des katholischen Deutschland" in *Der Humanismus und die oberen Fakultäten.* Ed. G. Keil et al. Weinheim, 1987: 21–42.

Sperl, A. *Melanchthon zwischen Humanismus und Reformation.* Munich, 1959.

Spitz, L. *The Religious Renaissance of the German Humanists.* Cambridge, Mass., 1963.

——— "Humanism and the Reformation" in *Transition and Revolution. Problems and Issues of European Renaissance and Reformation History*, ed. R. Kingdon. Minneapolis, 1974: 153–167.

——— "Humanism and the Protestant Reformation" in *Renaissance Humanism.* Ed. A. Rabil. Philadelphia, 1988: 380–411.

——— "The Course of German Humanism" in *Itinerarium Italicum: The Profile of the Italian Renaissance in the Mirror of Its European Transformations. Dedicated to Paul Oskar Kristeller on the Occasion of His 70th Birthday*, eds. H. Oberman and T. Brady (Leiden, 1975) 371–436.

Stern, Leo, "Philipp Melanchthon—Humanist, Reformator, Praeceptor Germaniae" in *Philipp Melanchthon.* Ed. W. Ellinger. Göttingen, 1961: 1–72.

Stupperich, R. *Melanchthon.* London, 1966.

Tate, J. B. *Ensayos sobre la historiografía peninsular del siglo XV.* Madrid, 1970.

Tinkler, J. F. "Erasmus' Conversation with Luther," *Archive for Reformation History* 82 (1991): 59–81.

Tracy, J. "Humanism and the Reformation" in *Reformation Europe. A Guide to Research.* Ed. S. Ozment. St. Louis, 1986.

Trinkaus, Ch. "A Humanist's Image of Humanism: The Inaugural Orations of Bartolommeo della Fonte," *Studies in the Renaisance* 7 (1960): 90–147.

——— *In Our Image and Likeness: Humanity and Divinity in Italian Humanist Thought*, 2 vols. Chicago, 1970.

——— *The Poet as Philosopher: Petrarch and the Formation of Renaissance Consciousness.* New Haven, 1979.

——— "Italian Humanism and Scholastic Theology" in *Renaissance Humanism.* Ed. A. Rabil, III: 327–348. Philadelphia, 1988.

——— "Humanistic Dissidence: Florence versus Milan, or Poggio versus Valla?" in *Florence and Milan: Comparisons and Relations.* Ed. S. Bertelli et al. Florence, 1989: 17–40.

——— "Lorenzo Valla's Anti-Aristotelian Natural Philosophy," *I Tatti Studies* forthcoming.

Trusen, Winfrid. "Johannes Reuchlin und die Fakultäten" in *Der Humanismus und die oberen Fakultäten.* Eds. G. Keil et al. Weinheim, 1987: 115–158.

Vasoli, C. *La dialettica e la retorica dell'umanesimo.* Milan, 1968.

——— "The Origin of Renaissance Philosophy: Scholastic Thought and the Needs of a New Culture" in *The Cambridge History of Renaissance Philosophy.* Eds. Ch. Schmitt and Qu. Skinner. Cambridge, 1988: 57–74.

Vickers, B. "Rhetorik und Philosophie in der Renaissance" in *Rhetorik und Philosophie*. Eds. H. Schanze and J. Kopperschmidt. Munich, 1989: 121–158.

Waswo, R. "The 'Ordinary Language Philosophy' of Lorenzo Valla," *Bibliothèque d'Humanisme et Renaissance* 41 (1979): 255–271.

Wesseler, M. *Die Einheit von Wort und Sache: Der Entwurf einer rhetorischen Philosophie bei Marius Nizolius.* Munich, 1974.

Witt, R. "Medieval 'Ars Dictaminis' and the Beginnings of Humanism: A New Construction of the Problem," *Renaissance Quarterly* 35 (1982): 1–35.

Zika, Ch. "Agrippa of Nettesheim and His Appeal to the Cologne Council in 1533: The Politics of Knowledge in Early 16th Century Germany" in *Humanismus in Köln.* Ed. J. Mehl. Cologne, 1991: 119–174.

Notes

1. The Protagonists and the Issues

1. This chapter expands on my article "*Et cum theologo bella poeta gerit:* The Conflict between Humanism and Scholasticism Revisited," *Sixteenth Century Journal* 23 (1992) 713–726.

2. Mutianus Rufus to Urbanus Rhegius, *Briefwechsel*, ed. C. Krause, in *Zeitschrift des Vereins für hessische Geschichte und Landeskunde* NF Supplement IX (1885) 325.

3. Trans. G. Bull (Penguin Classics, repr. London, 1988) 68.

4. English translation by H. Nachod in *The Renaissance Philosophy of Man*, ed. E. Cassirer et al. (Chicago, repr. 1975) 47–133. For a more detailed discussion of Petrarch's views see below, Chapter 2. On Petrarch's epistolary style see R. Witt, "Medieval 'Ars Dictaminis' and the Beginnings of Humanism: A New Construction of the Problem," *Renaissance Quarterly* 35 (1982), esp. 28–35.

5. For a recent review of modern interpretations see D. Quint, "Humanism and Modernity: A Reconsideration of Bruni's *Dialogues*," *Renaissance Quarterly* 38 (1985) 423–445. See below Chapter 3 for a more detailed discussion of the *Dialogues*.

6. Cornelius Agrippa, *Apologia adversus calumnias propter declamationem de vanitate scientiarum . . .* (n.p. 1533) C i verso.

7. See *Stephan Hoest, Reden und Briefe*, ed. and trans. F. Baron (Munich, 1971): in praise of *via antiqua* pp. 146–63; in praise of *via moderna* pp. 164–179; and for Hoest's humanistic ideas, p. 41.

8. LB X 1334 A–B; compare Allen Ep. 1529:30–31.

9. Cornelius Agrippa, *Apologia* C i verso.

10. Jacob Locher, *Vitiosa sterilis Mulae ad Musam roscida lepidate praedicatam comparatio* (Nürnberg, 1506). An illustration shows a scholastic doctor collect-

ing mule dung and a crow (a common simile for scholastic theologians) declaring "I have eaten the turds" (A iii recto); elsewhere Locher ridicules scholastic questions: they fret about "whether Adam, the first man, shat in the garden of paradise" (B ii recto).

11. Nesen in *Epistola de magistris nostris*, ed. H. de Vocht, *History of the Foundation and the Rise of the Collegium Trilingue Lovaniense* (Louvain, 1951–1955) 1:595; Reuchlin in *Defensio contra calumniatores suos Colonienses* (Tübingen, 1513) C i recto; Ulrich von Hutten, *Opera*, ed. E. Böcking (Leipzig, 1859–70) 1:197; Eobanus Hessus in *Epistolae illustrium virorum* (Haguenau, 1519) y ii recto.

12. *Lamentationes obscurorum virorum* in Hutten's *Opera*, ed. Böcking, Suppl. I: 339, 355.

13. Reported by Erasmus, Allen Ep. 1192:33–34.

14. *De tralatione Bibliae* (Paris, 1525) 82 verso. The terms he uses are *sciolus, homuncio, philosophaster, translationista*.

15. *Vallum humanitatis* (Cologne, 1518) A vi recto.

16. Hutten, *Opera*, ed. Böcking, Supplement I:313.

17. See "Requête de Noël Béda au Parlement de Paris contre les lecteurs royaux," ed. J. Farge in *Le parti conservateur au XVI siècle: Université et Parlement de Paris à l'époque de la Renaissance et de la Réforme* (Paris, 1992) document 7.

18. Aurelio Brandolini, "Epitome in sacram Hebraeorum historiam," MS Bibl. Vat. Ottob. Lat. 438 4 recto—4 verso.

19. *Apologia earum rerum quae illi obiiciuntur* (n.p. 1516?) a iv verso

20. Eck in *Verlegung der Disputation . . .* (1528) p. 110 quoted by Smolinsky 32 n.44; Hutten, ed. Böcking 1:178.

21. *De tralatione Bibliae*, 58 recto.

22. *Annotationes in annotationes Erasmi* (Paris, 1520) DD ii recto.

23. *In materia theologiae dicat et scribat theologice*. V. Beltrán de Heredia, ed., *Cartulario de la Universidad de Salamanca* VI (Salamanca, 1973) 32. This was Juan Arrieta's comment on Erasmus' writings when they were investigated by theologians assembled at Valladolid in 1527.

24. *Ad . . . Wimpinam pro defensione sacre theologie* [Leipzig, c. 1500] A iv verso.

25. Prooemium in librum secundum, p. 3 in the Padua edition of 1734.

26. *Briefwechsel*, ed. C. Krause in *Zeitschrift des Vereins für hessische Geschichte und Landeskunde* NF Supplement IX (1885) 352.

27. *Partitiones dialecticarum libri IV* (Lyons, 1554) in the prefatory letter to Barth. Petreius, p. 3.

28. Allen Ep. 1126:331–33; compare Ep. 1469:245–246: "They declare us heretics because some stupid Carmelite or lawyer brought up on Baldo knows no Latin."

29. "Coloquio del porfiado" 94 verso.

30. *Opera quae praecipue adversus horum temporum haereses conscripsit* (Louvain, 1550) 171 recto.

31. *Correctorium circa quattuor libros Sententiarum*, ed. H. Rückert (Tübingen,

1973) 1:6. Agrippa of Nettesheim even alleged that Hoogstraten declared it "heretical to take refuge in the Bible; and another had no scruples to preach that custom must be observed rather than Holy Writ" (*Responsio* C v recto). Ignatius of Loyola later argued in similar fashion. Rather than going to the Bible directly, it was better to approach it through the medieval interpreters. "The scholastic doctors . . . have a clearer understanding of Holy Scriptures," he said in his *Spiritual Exercises* (trans. A. Mottola, Garden City, 1964, p. 140).

32. Hutten exclaimed in his preface to *Nemo:* "When I think how the theology taught in the last three hundred years has affected the Christian religion!" (Böcking, ed. I:182).

33. *Vallum humanitatis*, B i verso.

34. *Letters of Obscure Men*, ed. H. Holborn in *On the Eve of the Reformation* (New York, 1964) 196, 198; Allen Ep. 456:226–227. G. Ritter, *Die geschichtliche Bedeutung des deutschen Humanismus* (2nd ed. Darmstadt 1963), speaks of financial competition ("wirtschaftlicher Konkurrenzkampf,"p. 15) when it came to examination fees, participation in banquets, and scheduling of private lectures to conflict with public lectures.

35. CWE 7:338. The dialogue was published under Konrad Nesen's name but was reportedly a collaboration between his brother Willem and Erasmus.

36. *La Farce des théologastres*, ed. C. Longeon (Geneva, 1989) lines 6–13, 493–495 (with a pun, *en bonne foy n'estes que garçons heretiques*).

37. In Jan. 1521; quoted by V. García de la Concha, "La impostación religiosa de la Reforma humanística en España" in *Nebrija y la introducción del Renacimiento en España*, ed. V. García de la Concha (Salamanca, 1983) 126.

38. *Briefwechsel*, ed. Krause 52.

39. *Epistola apologetica* (Antwerp, 1530) E ii recto—verso.

40. *Historia utriusque captivitatis propter verbum Dei* (1522) B ii verso. Compare Eck in a letter of 1540 to Contarini: "Erasmus and the Lutherans encourage students to focus on literature (they call it *bonae literae*) and thereby ruin both philosophy and theology" (in W. Friedensburg, "Beiträge zum Briefwechsel der katholischen Gelehrten Deutschlands im Reformationszeitalter," *Zeitschrift für Kirchengeschichte* 19 (1899) 253–258. The quotation appears on p. 256). See also Béda in *Annotationes* b viii verso: "It is no secret how much Erasmus helped Lefèvre and Luther."

41. *De incertitudine et vanitate scientiarum . . .* (Cologne, 1531) Y iii verso.

42. See the translation of the text in Breen, *Christianity and Humanism*; the passage quoted appears on p. 67. The oration has been incorrectly ascribed to Melanchthon. See E. Rummel, "Epistola Hermolai nova ac subditicia: A Declamation Falsely Ascribed to Philip Melanchthon," *Archive for Reformation History* 83 (1992) 302–305.

43. Breen p. 27.

44. Breen p. 38.

45. Breen p. 53.

46. *Apologia* K v verso.

47. See his *Methodus*, ed. H. Holborn (Munich, 1933) 151: "Let there be no impious curiosity. Some mysteries you will be allowed to see precisely because you have reverently averted your gaze." For repeated assertions by Erasmus that he was submitting his findings to the teaching authority of the Church see, for example, his apologia *Manifesta Mendacia*, ed. E. Rummel in *Nederlands Archief voor Kerkgeschiedenis* 70 (1990) 212, 213, 215.

48. "Humanism as a Value System with Reference to Budé and Vives" in *Humanism in France at the End of the Middle Ages and in the Early Renaissance*, ed. A. H. T. Levi (Manchester, 1970) 212. For Erasmus' Christian humanism, see also below, Chapter 6.

49. C. Augustijn, " Humanisten auf dem Scheideweg zwischen Luther und Erasmus" in *Humanismus und Reformation*, ed. O. H. Pesch (Freiburg, 1985) 125; L. Spitz, *The Religious Renaissance of the German Humanists* (Cambridge, Mass. 1963) 289–290. See also G. Ritter, *Die geschichtliche Bedeutung* 60; H. Smolinsky, "Der Humanismus an den theologischen Fakultäten des katholischen Deutschland" in *Der Humanismus und die oberen Fakultäten*, ed. G. Keil et al. (Weinheim, 1987) 21–42, esp. 25–26.

50. J. Overfield, *Humanism and Scholasticism in Late Medieval Germany* (Princeton, 1984) 330.

51. While appreciating the complexity of the concepts, S. Ozment nevertheless notes that "humanism and scholasticism do have definable distinguishing characteristics," which he discusses in "Humanism, Scholasticism, and the Intellectual Origins of the Reformation" in *Continuity and Discontinuity in Church History*, ed. F. Forrester Church and T. George (Leiden, 1979) 138 and ff.

52. Pierre Cousturier, *De tralatione* 99 recto.

53. Allen Ep. 1162:49–50; compare line 182: *rhetorum est omnia fucare, fingere, mentiri*.

54. See F. Pijper, *Disputationes contra Lutherum* (The Hague, 1905) 81; Cousturier, *Antapologia* (Paris, 1526) aa1 verso–aa2 recto; Mutianus Rufus, *Briefwechsel*, ed. Krause, 352.

55. *Gothic Architecture and Scholasticism* (Latrobe 1951) 34. Petrarch ridicules this tendency in his polemic against Jean de Hesdin: "Worried that he might not appear sufficiently scholastic, he inserted chapters and paragraphs and long quotations from outside sources . . .—the labor made him sweat in the middle of winter" (*Contra cuiusdam Galli calumniam* 2, p. 142).

56. *Vallum humanitatis* B iii recto. See J. F. Tinkler, "Erasmus' Conversation with Luther," *Archive for Reformation History* 82 (1991) 71: "Humanists regularly draw attention to the disorder, incoherence, and contradictions of their writings."

57. *Briefwechsel*, ed. Krause 352.

58. L. Spitz, "The Course of German Humanism" in *Itinerarium Italicum: The*

Profile of the Italian Renaissance . . ., eds. H. Oberman and T. Brady (Leiden, 1975) 409.

59. H. B. Gerl, *Philosophie und Philologie* (Munich, 1981) 32–33.

60. Ch. Trinkaus "A Humanist's Image of Humanism: The Inaugural Orations of Bartolommeo della Fonte," *Studies in the Renaissance* 7 (1960) 90–147; the quotation appears on p. 123, n.86.

61. *Adversus quosdam litterarum humaniorum vituperatores oratio* (held in Venice, 1555) in *Orationes XXIII* (Venice, 1576) 26.

62. *Contra vanam curiositatem: Ein Kapitel der Theologen zwischen Seelenwinkel und Weltall* (Zurich, 1974).

63. Carvajal sneers at Erasmus' claims (LB X 1675A–1677D) in his reply, *Dulcoratio amarulentiarum Erasmicae responsionis . . .* (Paris, 1530) 42 verso—43 recto; Wimpina wrote in *Apologeticus in Sacre Theologie defensionem* (Leipzig, 1500) that he had "strayed into that field and composed some three thousand verses" (A v recto).

64. Epilogue to Aristotle's *Physics* (1518). Similar efforts to free students from "vain and useless sophisms" were under way in Vienna, where Konrad Pschlacher produced a new edition of Petrus Hispanus in 1512.

65. See Arno Seifert, *Logik zwischen Scholastik und Humanismus: Das Kommentarwerk Johann Ecks* (Munich, 1978). He concludes:"An Ecks Beispiel zeigt sich, wo die scholastische Selbstreform sich auf diesem Wege vom militanten Humanismus trennte" (p. 35). He calls the reforms "Fassadenrenovierung" (ibidem).

66. Mutianus Rufus, *Briefwechsel*, ed. Krause, 325–326; *Dialogus bilinguium et trilinguium* CWE 7:341 and n42; Agrippa, *Apologia*, C i recto, alleging that the critique of his *De incertitudine* was written not by the theologians, but *per Busconem aliquem poetastrum, cui fingere et mentiri in professo est, aut per alium quempiam scholasticum parasitum.*

67. Ch. Trinkaus, "Humanistic Dissidence: Florence versus Milan, or Poggio versus Valla?" in *Florence and Milan: Comparisons and Relations*, ed. S. Bertelli et al. (Florence, 1989) 21.

68. 5.2.36

69. *Apologeticus*, ed. A. de Petris (Rome, 1980) 11. The image goes back to Jerome, who had to defend himself against the same charge when he revised the Vulgate (see PL 23:448C).

70. *Collationes* (Antwerp, 1529) a7 recto

71. Pio in *Responsio accurata et paraenetica* (Paris, 1529) 29 recto; Ferber von Herborn in *Paradoxa seu theologicae assertiones* (Paris, 1534) 28 verso.

72. CWE 23:36, 25, 34.

73. *Renaissance Thought* (New York, 1961) 114.

74. See also his slightly modified view in a more recent article, "Scholastik und Humanismus an der Universität Heidelberg," in *Der Humanismus und die oberen Fakultäten*, ed. G. Keil et al. (Weinheim, 1987) 10.

75. "Humanism and the Protestant Reformation," in *Renaissance Humanism*, ed. A. Rabil (Philadelphia, 1988) III:393.

76. "Es dürfte feststellen, dass es in Deutschland eine generelle Feindschaft zwischen Humanisten und Scholastiker nicht gab" ("Johannes Reuchlin und die Fakultäten," in *Der Humanismus und die oberen Fakultäten*, 115); J. D'Amico writes less categorically in "Humanism and Pre-Reformation Theology" in *Renaissance Humanism* III:367–368: "There were points of conflict [between humanists and scholastics], but in general there were fewer than historians have maintained." See also his account of the debate in *Renaissance Humanism in Papal Rome* (Baltimore, 1983) 144–147.

77. J. Overfield, *Humanism and Scholasticism in Late Medieval Germany* (Princeton, 1984) 329.

78. "Die Opposition gegen die Scholastik bildet ein von Italien her übernommenes Leitmotiv, besonders des deutschen Frühhumanismus" (L. Boehm, "Humanistische Bildungsbewegungen und mittelalterliche Universitätsverfassung: Aspekte zur frühneuzeitlichen Reformgeschichte der deutschen Universitäten," in *The Universities in the Late Middle Ages*, ed. J. IJsewijn (Louvain, 1978) 315–346); the quotation appears on p. 320.

79. "The Clash of Humanists and Scholastics: An Approach to Pre-Reformation Controversies," *Sixteenth Century Journal* 4 (1973): 2, 5.

80. See P. O. Kristeller, "Scholastik und Humanismus an der Universität Heidelberg," in *Der Humanismus und die oberen Fakultäten*, 11: "Die Theologen waren an den italienischen Universitäten kaum vertreten." J. D'Amico, "Humanism and Pre-Reformation Theology," 367: "Scholasticism had a much stronger position in Northern European universities than in Italy, and humanists had to deal with professional theologians in their areas of strength."

81. Kristeller, *Renaissance Thought*, 113.

82. Erasmus (Allen Ep. 142:132–134) attacks this separation: "Nor do I think that Theology, the Queen of all disciplines, will be offended if she is attended and served with due respect by her handmaid, Grammar."

83. Allen Epp. 2932:28–29 and 2315:300–301 of 1534 and 1530 respectively.

2. Paradigms of the Debate

1. *Gorgias* 456, 463.

2. *Sophist* 268.

3. *Euthydemus* 276 B–C.

4. *Euthydemus* 278, 288.

5. Ficino's ambivalence is noted by J. Hankins, *Plato in the Italian Renaissance* (Leiden, 1990) II:271. See also P. O. Kristeller, "Florentine Platonism and Its Relations with Humanism and Scholasticism," *Church History* 8 (1939) 201–211.

6. *Opera* (Basel 1576; repr. Turin, 1962) II:1297.
7. *Opera* II:1302.
8. *Opera* II:1286, 1317.
9. CWE 24:297.
10. CWE 23:68.
11. *Ratio* in *Ausgewählte Werke*, eds. A. and H. Holborn, (Munich, 1933) 304:11–12, 188:2–3.
12. For a more detailed discussion see below Chapter 6. The quotation comes from Eobanus Hessus' *Dialogi tres* (Erfurt, 1524) B iv recto.
13. Petrarch in *Familiari* 16.14.12, *Contra medicum* 54; Bruni in his *Dialogues*, ed. Griffiths et al. in *The Humanism of Leonardo Bruni* (Binghamton, 1987) 67–69; Vives, *In pseudodialecticos*, ed. and trans. Ch. Fantazzi (Leiden, 1979) 51:12–13, 71:23–73:2.
14. *De incertitudine*, D iii verso–D iv recto.
15. Cited by C. Gilly, "Das Sprichwort 'Die Gelehrten die Verkehrten' oder der Verrat der Intellektuellen im Zeitalter der Glaubensspaltung," *Forme e destinazione del messaggio religioso. Aspetti della propaganda religiosa nel Cinquecento*, ed. A. Rotondo (Florence, 1991) 254.
16. *De tralatione*, 99 recto.
17. *Disputationes contra Lutherum*, ed. F. Pijper (The Hague, 1905) 52–3, 80.
18. For the fortuna of Lucian in Renaissance Europe see Ch. Robinson, *Lucian and His Influence in Europe* (London, 1979), Ch. Lavergnat-Garnière, *Lucien de Samosate et le Lucianisme en France au XVIe siècle* (Geneva, 1988).
19. Pirckheimer's *Epistola apologetica* is prefixed to his edition of *Piscator* (n.p. 1517).
20. CWE Ep. 550:9–12.
21. Quoted by Ch. Lavergnat-Gagnière, *Lucien de Samosate* 72 n67.
22. Ibidem 73, n71; 78 n88.
23. Loeb edition V:67, VII:111, II:281.
24. G. Pontano, *Dialoge*, ed. H. Kiefer (Munich, 1984) 70, 72.
25. Quoted by Emilio Mattioli, *Luciano e l'umanesimo* (Naples, 1980) 131.
26. Alber quoted by C. Gilly, "Das Sprichwort," 268; Sepúlveda and Petrus Canisius quoted by Ch.Lavergnat-Gagnière, *Lucien de Samosate*, 144 n37, 149 n61.
27. Eobanus Hessus, *Dialogi tres*. See also below Chapter 4.
28. See Ch. Robinson, *Lucian and His Influence in Europe* (London, 1979), 123–125.
29. Juan Luis Vives, *Somnium*, ed. and trans. E. V. George (Greenwood, 1989), from which I quote in the following.
30. Robinson, *Lucian*, 97–98: "This kind of application of the Lucian texts . . . was in part responsible for the hardening of conservative opinion against the Greek . . . it becomes common for writers of both extreme Catholic and extreme Protestant persuasion to use Lucian as a symbol of lack of respect for metaphysical values of any kind, to the point of atheism."

31. Marius Nizolius, *De principiis veritatis*, ed. Qu. Breen (Rome, 1956) II 66–67. For a more detailed discussion of this work see Chapter 7.
32. LB VI:926–928, 943–944.
33. *Epistolae divi Pauli apostoli* (Paris, 1515) 203 verso.
34. Masson, ed. F. Pijper in *Disputationes contra Lutherum* (The Hague, 1905) 66.
35. For uses of Jerome and Augustine see below Chapter 5. Buschius (*Vallum humanitatis* H ii verso) accused the scholastics of collecting from the Fathers only "what appears to be said against the *studia humanitatis*; what is said in their favor *passim* and recurs so often that even a blind person could see it, they suppress on purpose."
36. *Confutatio sophistices et quaestionum curiosarum* (Sélestat, 1520). The quotation from the preface appears on sig. a iv verso.
37. Ibidem, e iii recto–verso.
38. For accounts of Petrarch's attitude toward scholasticism see Ch. Trinkaus, *The Poet as Philosopher: Petrarch and the Foundation of Renaissance Consciousness* (New Haven, 1979); E. Kessler, *Petrarca und die Geschichte* (Munich, 1978), esp. 132–140; P. O. Kristeller, "Petrarca, der Humanismus und die Scholastik" in *Petrarca*, ed. A. Buck (Darmstadt, 1976) 261–281; H. Schmelzer, *Petrarcas Verhältnis zur vorausgehenden christlichen Philosophie des Abendlandes* (Bonn, 1911); and notes below.
39. The translation of quotations in this chapter is mine; I used the Latin text, ed. L. M. Capelli (Paris, 1906). There is also an English translation in *The Renaissance Philosophy of Man*, ed. E. Cassirer et al. (Chicago, 1975). Other works of Petrarch quoted in the following footnotes are cited according to the following editions: his letters, in my translation, from the Latin text, ed. V. Rossi in *Le familiari* (Florence, 1933–1942); the apologia *Contra medicum*, in my translation, from the Latin text, ed. P. G. Ricci (Rome, 1978); *Rerum memorandarum libri*, ed. G. Billanovich (Florence, 1943).
40. *Opera* (Basel, 1554) 880.
41. *Familiari* 1.2.18, 1.7.1, see 16. 14.10; *De sua ignorantia* 68, 90.
42. *Familiari* 12.3.10, 17.1.5 (loquacity); *Familiari* 1.2.19, *De sua ignorantia* 68, 72 (clamor); *Familiari* 16.14.12; *Contra medicum* 54; *Familiari* 1.2.18 (sophists).
43. *Familiari* 1.7.13–14; see *Contra medicum* 52, 53.
44. *Familiari* 12.3.10.
45. *Familiari* 17.1.8.
46. *Familiari* 17.1.10, citing Cicero *Tusc. Disp.* 2.4.11–12.
47. *De sua ignorantia* 29.
48. *Familiari* 10.5.8, *De sua ignorantia* 30, quoting Job 28:28. Several scholars have regarded this as an allusion rather than an exact biblical quotation (for example, Rossi in the *Familiari* n67 *ad locum*, H. Nachod in his translation of *De sua ignorantia* in *The Renaissance Philosophy of Man* [Chicago, 1975] 65, n41), but while modern editions of the Bible have *timor dei*, fear of God,

the passage is quoted in the form *pietas est sapientia* in patristic writings, as in Augustine's *Enchiridion* (PL 40:231; see 44:211).

49. See F. X. Murphy, "Petrarch and the Christian Philosophy" in *Francesco Petrarca: Citizen of the World*, ed. G. Billanovich et al. (Padova, 1980); P. de Nolhac, *Petrarque et l'Humanisme* (Paris, 1907) I:104, II:208, 216, 224; P. P. Gerosa, *Umanesimo Cristiano del Petrarca* (Turin, 1966) 161.

50. *De sua ignorantia* 69.

51. *De sua ignorantia* 70, 29.

52. *Familiari* 12.3.10; *Scaber factus Aristoteles* (*De sua ignorantia* 21).

53. *De sua ignorantia* 30.

54. *De sua ignorantia* 40.

55. Ibidem.

56. *De sua ignorantia* 44.

57. *De sua ignorantia* 41, cf 77.

58. *De sua ignorantia* 78; cf Augustine *Enarratio in Ps.* 77.27.

59. *Non ex singulis vocibus . . . sed ex perpetuitate atque constantia* (*De sua ignorantia* 52), quoting Cicero, *Tusculanae disputationes* 5.10.31.

60. *De sua ignorantia* 56.

61. *Revixisse et Christianum factum* (*De sua ignorantia* 79).

62. *De sua ignorantia* 66.

63. *Familiari* 16.14.12: *neque enim Dei amatores sed cognitores [sunt]*.

64. *Rer. mem.* 1.19.4; compare Augustine, *Sermo* 293.2 (PL 38:1328) similarly PL 44:595) referring to John the Baptist as "on the borderline between the Old and the New Testament."

65. Ch. Trinkaus, "Italian Humanism and Scholastic Theology," in *Renaissance Humanism*, ed. A. Rabil (Philadelphia, 1988) 3:329.

66. See P. O. Kristeller, "Petrarch's Averroists," *Bibliothèque d'Humanisme et Renaissance* 14 (1952) 59–65.

67. For our subject J. L. Connolly, *John Gerson, Reformer and Mystic* (Louvain, 1928), is still the best account; see also L. P. Pascoe, *Jean Gerson: Principles of Church Reform* (Leiden, 1973), especially pp. 89–104.

68. *Oeuvres complètes*, ed. P. Glorieux (Paris, 1960–1973) 10.257. In the following, references are to volume and page of this edition. On the debate over the ranking of disciplines see below, Chapter 5.

69. 3.245: "Excessive zeal in seeking to obtain the fundamentals from pagan philosophers is vain curiosity and dangerous for the study of theology. It must be avoided because it takes away penitence and faith."

70. "Clarity and teaching that is easily understood nauseate them. They consider nothing to be profound or subtle unless they do not understand it, or understand it only with the greatest of difficulty and discomfort after spending a great deal of time on it" (3.248).

71. 3:230; sim. 240.

72. For example, at 3:233.

73. *De mystica theologia*, ed. A. Combes (Verona, 1958) 77, 79.

74. LB IX 919B. The fact that Noël Béda, the syndic of the faculty, had earlier on sternly directed him to read Gerson (Allen Ep. 1579: 159–160) adds poignancy to Erasmus' retort.

75. See *Chartularium Universitatis parisiensis*, eds. H. Denifle and Ae. Chatelain (Paris, 1897) IV:203, where the faculty is called upon to condemn articles *auctoritate doctrinali*. In 1414 Charles VI congratulated the faculty on its learning and its international prestige: *magistros theologos . . . in omni sanctarum literarum eruditione precipuos esse constat, quos vel fallere vel falli posse nemo facile judicaverit . . . ipsa quandoque Romana sedes, et olim et nuper, si quid apud eos ambiguum in doctrina Christiane religionis obtigeret, certitudinem ab ipso consilio fidei Parisius existente postulare nec puduit nec piguit.*

76. C. Prantl, *Geschichte der Logik im Abendlande* (Leipzig, 1947) IV:151.

77. Quoted by S. Ozment, "Scholasticism and the Intellectual Origins of the Reformation" in *Continuity and Discontinuity in Church History*, eds. F. Forrester Church and T. George (Leiden, 1979) 135.

3. The Debate as Epideictic Literature

1. Latin text in *Epistolario di Coluccio Salutati*, ed. F. Novati (Rome, 1905) IV:169–205, which I quote in the following.

2. For recent literature on this and some of the other works discussed in this chapter see Ch. Trinkaus, "Italian Humanism and Scholastic Theology," in A. Rabil, *Renaissance Humanism* (Philadelphia, 1988) III: 327–348.

3. Latin text of *Lucula Noctis*, ed. E. Hunt (Notre Dame, 1940), which I quote in the following. For biographical information on Dominici see P. Denley, "Giovanni Dominici's opposition to humanism," *Religion and Humanism*, ed. K. Robbins (Oxford, 1981) 103–114.

4. Page 22; see also p. 81: *ad quorum eversionem necesse est scire illorum doctrinas.*

5. Page 136, see also p. 278: *ad illorum errorem extirpandum venenum aliquando legunt.*

6. Pages 42, 61, 70.

7. The Latin text of Salutati's reply is in Novati (see n. 1 above) IV:205–239. The quotations in this paragraph appear on pp. 215–216.

8. Text in G. Griffiths et al., eds. *The Humanism of Leonardo Bruni* (Binghamton, 1987) 63–84, which I quote in the following notes. For a recent interpretation and biographical references see D. Quint, "Humanism and Modernity: A Reconsideration of Bruni's *Dialogues*," *Renaissance Quarterly* 38 (1985) 423–445.

9. In the following I quote from the translation of Qu. Breen in *Christianity and Humanism* (Grand Rapids, 1968).

10. English text in CWE 23, 16–122, from which I quote in the following.

11. As Erasmus explained in the preface, CWE 23:16.

12. The dialogue appeared in a book entitled *Theologica Emphasis* ([Basel: Io. Bergmann], 1496), which I quote in the following.

13. The epistle is dated 1506 and was published in *Commentaria epistolarum conficiendarum* (Pforzheim, 1508), from which I quote in the following.

14. The dialogue appears in Mair's commentary on the Sentences, *In Primum Sententiarum* (Paris, 1510). The Latin text is in J. Mair, *History of Greater Britain*, ed. A. Constable (Edinburgh, 1892) Appendix II, 425–428.

15. See A. Broadie, *The Circle of John Mair: Logic and Logicians in Pre-Reformation Scotland* (Oxford, 1985).

16. *Boccaccio on Poetry*, trans. Charles G. Osgood (New York, 1956) 20.

17. In explaining the prerequisites of piety, for example, he supplies a numbered list: "firstly a knowledge of God, secondly a knowledge of self," (p. 62). Of a similar cast is his rigid distinction between degrees of obligation in determining the propriety of an action: concession, advice, command, precept, and so on (p. 139). At times, his argumentation tastes of the textbook: *Hec consequentia non dubitatur, cum media, sine quibus finis imperatus non potest haberi, sub fine simul mandari dicantur* (p. 40). He uses the technical terms and the pedestrian style often ridiculed by humanists, as, for example, in his conclusion concerning God's knowledge: *Ex hiis elicitur clare una verissima disiunctiva, que copulative realiter equipollet, videlicet: solus Deus de creaturis habet scientiam, vel scientia Dei et scientia nostra non sunt eiusdem generis* (p. 195).

18. On this feature see D. Marsh, *The Quattrocento Dialogue: Classical Tradition and Humanist Innovation* (Cambridge, Mass., 1980), especially pp. 14–16, 31 (concerning Bruni's *Dialogues*) and 40–42 (on Poggio and Valla).

19. Text ed. B. Kieszkowski (Geneva, 1973).

20. Trans. and ed. G. Griffiths et al. (see above note 8) 213–214. See also J. Hankins' remarks on the polemic between Bruni and Alonso of Cartagena, ibidem 201–208.

21. The Latin text of Alonso's response is in A. Birkenmajer, "Der Streit des Alfonso von Cartagena mit Leonardo Bruni Aretino," *Beiträge zur Geschichte der Philosophie des Mittelalters* 20–25 (1920): 162–186, which I quote in the following. On Alonso of Cartagena see Ottavio di Camillo, *El humanismo castellano del siglo XV* (Valencia, 1976), especially chapters 5 and 6; J. Seigel, *Rhetoric and Philosophy in Renaissance Humanism* (Princeton, 1968) 123–133; N. G. Round, "Renaissance Culture and Its Opponents in 15th Century Castile," *Modern Language Review* 57 (1972) 204–215; J. Lawrance, "Humanism in the Iberian Peninsula" in *The Impact of Humanism on Western Europe*, eds. A. Goodwin and A. MacKay (London, 1990) 223–227.

22. G. Gentile, *Storia della filosofia italiana* (Florence, 1969) 317, a view supported by most modern scholars but contested by di Camillo, who characterizes Alonso as a progressive thinker (see *El humanismo* 150 nn19 and 26; 215).

23. *Razones fermosas*, that is, beautiful, agreeable, excellent reasoning. The text of Alonso's preface to his translation is in M. Menéndez y Pelayo, *Historia de las ideas estéticas en España* (Buenos Aires, 1889) I, Appendix II, 597–603. The quotation appears on p. 602.

24. Ibidem, p. 599: "Aristotiles . . . compuso un libro que se llama de la Retórica, en que escribió muchas y nobles conclusiones pertenecientes a esta arte, de las cuales así por teólogos como por juristas son muchas en diversos lugares allegadas cada una a su propósito."

25. Text quoted by di Camillo, *El humanismo* 149, n24.

26. Ibidem 150 n26.

27. Text in L. Dorez and L. Thuasne, *Pic de la Mirandole en France (1485–1488)* (Paris, 1897, repr. in Pico's *Opera omnia*, Turin, 1972). The passage quoted is at II:421.

28. Ibidem II:440. The Latin text and a French translation of Pico's *Apologia*, defending his conclusions, and Garcia's reply are in H. Crouzel, *Controverse sur Origène à la Renaissance: Jean Pic de la Mirandole et Pierre Garcia* (Paris, 1977). Garcia's comments have special significance in light of Pico's claim that in his *Conclusiones* he had been "imitating the style of the most famous disputants in Paris" (*Opera omnia* I:63).

29. The preface is not included in Crouzel's text. I am translating the text in the facsimile edition of the *Opera omnia* (Turin, 1972) I:125. There is a modern edition of the preface, ed. J. V. De Pina Martins (Lisbon, 1963), but I have not been able to see it.

30. *Opera omnia*, I:118.

31. The Latin text is in the facsimile of the Basel 1573 edition of Gianfrancesco Pico's *Opera omnia* (Turin, 1972). The quotations are from p. 27.

32. The text of the letter is in Birkenmajer, "Der Streit des Alfonso," p. 193.

33. *Epistolario* IV:127, 129, quoted and discussed by Ch. Trinkaus, "Humanistic Dissidence: Florence versus Milan, or Poggio versus Valla," in *Florence and Milan: Comparisons and Relations*, ed. S. Bertelli et al. (Florence, 1989) 22–23.

34. M. O'Rourke Boyle, *Rhetoric and Reform: Erasmus' Civil Dispute with Luther* (Cambridge, Mass., 1983) 158.

35. Quoted by Boyle, *Rhetoric and Reform*, 161.

4. The Debate at the Universities

1. The literature on university reforms is extensive. A good general bibliography can be found in *Rebirth, Reform and Resilience: Universities in Transition, 1300–1700*, eds. J. Kittelson and P. Transue (Columbia, 1984). For summaries of relevant developments see also T. Heath, "Logical Grammar, Grammatical Logic, and Humanism in Three German Universities," *Studies in the Renaissance* 18 (1971) 9–64; J. M. Fletcher, "Change and Resistance to Change: A Consideration of the Development of English and German Universities during the Sixteenth Century," *History of Universities* 1 (1981) 1–36; L. Boehm, "Humanistische Bildungsbewegung und Mittelalterliche Universitätsverfassung: Aspekte zur früh-neuzeitlichen Reformgeschichte der

deutschen Universitäten" in *The Universities in the Late Middle Ages*, eds. J. IJsewijn and J. Paquet (Louvain, 1978) 315–346; and J. Overfield, *Humanism and Scholasticism in Late Medieval Germany* (Princeton, 1984), chapter 2. For references to literature on individual universities see notes below.

2. J. Fletcher ventures this comment in *The History of the University of Oxford*, vol. 3, ed. J. McConica (Oxford, 1986) 159: "Most northern universities accepted the criticism of Renaissance scholars, abandoned the intensive study of logic and most of the works of the medieval logicians, introduced classical literature and Greek, and used declamations in addition to the traditional disputations."

3. Summaries with extensive quotations are in E. Friedberg, *Die Universität Leipzig in Vergangenheit und Gegenwart* (Leipzig, 1898), who copied the originals in the Dresden Hauptstaatsarchiv (Locat. 10596) "as far as the manuscripts, which are almost completely illegible and partly discoloured, could be deciphered" (p. 95). The references on the following pages are to the pages in Friedberg. Interestingly, all but two of the submissions are in German, perhaps for the benefit of the Duke. Dr. theol. Magnus Hundt, however, insisted on writing in Latin, "lest the rude Teuton and Saxon style nauseate many" (p. 109). See also Overfield's discussion of the submissions, 222–235.

4. Friedberg, p. 145; similar complaints pp. 147, 111, 117, 129.

5. Ibidem 123, 127.

6. Ibidem 148, 131; Andreas Boner speaks of "secret conspiracies," p. 145.

7. Ibidem 113; see pp. 112, 137, 139, 145.

8. Ibidem 102; see 146–148.

9. My translation from the Latin in *Selections from Conrad Celtis (1459–1508)*, ed. L. Forster (Cambridge, 1948) 22.

10. Quoted by Ch. Nauert, "Humanists, Scholastics, and the Struggle to Reform the University of Cologne, 1523–1525," *Humanism in Cologne*, ed. J. Mehl (Cologne, 1991) 63. See also Overfield, *Humanism and Scholasticism* 322–325.

11. Nauert speaks of a "serious institutional problem for which the faculty and the city council shared responsibility, the granting of university prebends in the city's collegiate churches to persons who were neither willing nor able to deliver the lectures that were supposed to be supported by these benefices" (Nauert, "Humanists," in *Humanism in Cologne* 69).

12. *Opera* II:1141–1142 (facsimile edition, Hildesheim, 1970), quoted by Ch. Zika, "Agrippa of Nettesheim and His Appeal to the Cologne Council in 1533: The Politics of Knowledge in Early 16th Century Germany," in *Humanism in Cologne*, 135, n40.

13. The quotations in this passage come from the *Acta facultatis artium* III:99 verso-100 recto. See *Urkundenbuch der Universität Heidelberg*, ed. E. Winkelmann (Heidelberg, 1886) II, no. 705. For a general survey, see N. Ham-

merstein, "The University of Heidelberg in the Early Modern Period: Aspects of its History as a Contribution to its Sexcentenary," *History of Universities* 6 (1987–7) 105–134.

14. *Urkundenbuch*, I:218; see Overfield, *Humanism and Scholasticism*, 314–316.
15. See E. Kleineidam, *Universitas Studii Erffordensis* II (Leipzig, 1969) 227–257.
16. *Dialogi tres* (Erfurt, 1524) B iii verso. The references in the following paragraphs are to this edition.
17. *Briefwechsel*, ed. C. Krause in *Zeitschrift des Vereins für hessische Geschichte und Landeskunde* NF Supplement IX (1885) 324.
18. On the conflict see J. Overfield, *Humanism and Scholasticism* 173–185.
19. See n38 below; the conflict is described in Overfield 185–206.
20. *Briefwechsel*, ed. Krause 325, 328.
21. *The Complete Works of Thomas More* (New Haven, 1986) vol. 15, ed. D. Kinney, from which I quote in the following.
22. Ibidem 145, 147. In spite of such efforts on behalf of humanistic studies, Fletcher concludes that Oxford remained static by comparison with universities on the Continent, and that there was on the whole an "absence of any serious attempt to modify its structure or curriculum by radical statutory change" (*History of Oxford University* III:156).
23. On Erasmus' controversies with the Louvain theologians, see E. Rummel, *Erasmus and His Catholic Critics* (Nieuwkoop, 1989) I: passim, II:1–22.
24. See Luis Gil, "Nebrija y el menester del gramático," in *Nebrija y la introducción del Renacimiento en España*, ed. V. García de la Concha (Salamanca, 1983) 64; F. Rico, *Nebrija frente a los bárbaros* (Salamanca, 1978).
25. Allen Ep. 1909:233–47. On the conditions at Paris see J. Farge, *Orthodoxy and Reform in Early Reformation France* (Leiden, 1985).
26. *Advertissements sur la censure qu'ont faicte les bestes de Sorbonne* (n.l. 1547) A5 verso-6 recto. I used the copy in the Bibliothèque Nationale, Paris. The pamphlet was at one time attributed to Guillaume Farel, but more recently F. Higman has made a case for Calvin's authorship. See "Un pamphlet de Calvin restitué à son auteur," *Revue d'histoire et philosophie religieuse* 60 (1980) Part I:167–180, Part II:327–337.
27. Dullard is quoted by Farge, *Orthodoxy and Reform* 170; Erasmus's remark comes from CWE Ep. 64:87–90.
28. J. Farge, *Orthodoxy and Reform* 53.
29. See Paul Grendler's forthcoming book on Italian universities in the Renaissance.
30. Quoted by E. Gallina, *Aonio Paleario* (Sora, 1989) II:744; see also 743–44 for Paleario's claim that he was the first to introduce humanistic studies in Lucca (primus in hac urbe barbarorum claustra fregi) and 758, where he describes the reaction of the "sophists, who groan like owls drawn into the light."

31. *Dyalogus recommendacionis exprobracionisque poetices* [Leipzig 1494]. See G. Bauch, *Geschichte des Leipziger Frühhumanismus* (Leipzig, 1899) 39–43.

32. The list of "useful" authors he gives, which includes Pliny and Aristotle, shows that the debate was not about poetry in the modern sense but about the humanities or classical learning in general.

33. See Bauch, *Geschichte des Leipziger Frühhumanismus* 59–65.

34. *Pro concordia dialecticorum et oratorum . . .*, excerpts in J. Riegger, *Amoenitates Litterariae Friburgensis* (Ulm, 1775) II:194–196.

35. Ibidem II:344.

36. Ibidem II:254.

37. Ibidem II:275.

38. The Latin text of the mock-confession, entitled *Jacobus Vuimphelingus Selestatinus Jacobo Philomuso poete laureato presens confessionale dicat*, is in J. Schlecht, "Zu Wimphelings Fehden mit Jakob Locher und Paul Lang" in *Festgabe Karl Theodor von Heigel . . .*, ed. Th. Bitterauf (Munich, 1903) 240–243.

39. *Contra turpem libellum Philomusi theologie scholastice et neotericorum defensio* (Nürnberg, 1510) B i recto; he made exceptions, however, for Virgil and the Christian poet Baptista Mantuanus.

40. *Jacob Wimpfelings Briefwechsel*, ed. O. Herding (Munich, 1990) 687; see also his letter to Erasmus, CWE Ep. 224. Both statements appeared as prefaces to Schürer's 1511 edition of Erasmus' *Praise of Folly*.

41. Leipzig, c. 1500.

42. *Laconismus tumultuarius . . . in defensionem poetices . . .* (Leipzig, 1500) c i verso–c ii recto. The following quotations also come from this edition.

43. The quotations are on c v verso and b iv verso; references to the barbarous speech of theologians are found on a v verso, c vi recto, b i verso; to their pride on a v recto.

44. *Responsio et Apologia Conradi Wimpine contra laconismum . . .* (Leipzig, 1502). The following quotations come from this edition.

45. *De studio humanarum disciplinarum et laude poetarum* [Freiburg: F. Riederer, 1496].

46. See above, Chapter 3.

47. Quoted by Overfield, *Humanism and Scholasticism* 186.

48. *Vitiosa sterilis Mulae ad Musam roscida lepiditate praedicatam Comparatio* (Nürnberg, 1506), from which I quote in the following.

49. A iv recto, B ii recto-verso.

50. Listed in Schlecht, "Zu Wimpfelings Fehden" 243–245.

51. See n39 above. The quotations in this paragraph appear at C i recto-verso, C ii verso. We have already noted Wimpheling's ambivalence. Here his role as controversialist obliged him to defend scholasticism in a categorical manner. Elsewhere he showed an awareness of its faults, questioning the usefulness of the scholastic method inasmuch as it was "full of knots and Aristo-

telian phrases, not to speak of obscure distinctions, quiddities, relations, formalities, and other such stuff, which, however much they prove a man's intellectual acumen, do not move him to piety, devotion, and a Christian life" (*Briefwechsel*, ed. O. Herding 812; similarly 864–866).

52. CWE Ep 347:110, 279, 273–274, quoting Jerome's commentary on Ezechiel PL 25:236D-237A and Augustine's *De doctrina Christiana* 2.31.

53. CWE Ep. 347:348–357.

54. Text in *Dialogus de trium linguarum et studii theologici ratione*, ed. F. Pijper in *Disputationes contra Lutherum* (The Hague, 1905). The references in the following are to pages in this edition.

55. See Eugène Marcotte, *La nature de la théologie d'après Melchior Cano* (Ottawa, 1949); A. Lang, *Die Loci Theologici des Melchior Cano und die Methode des dogmatischen Beweises* (Hildesheim, 1974).

56. *De locis theologicis* 2. proem; 8.1–2 (pp. 2–4, 232–235 in the Padua edition of 1734).

57. *Opusculum de dignitate sacerdotum* f iv recto-verso, g i recto, g ii recto. Compare Guillaume Fichet on the predominant views at Paris: "They despise anyone among us who is skilled in both disciplines. As a result no one has appeared at Paris . . . who combines rhetoric with philosophy and teaches it" (preface to his *Rhetorica* of 1471, quoted by Saccharo 119, n483).

58. *Vallum humanitatis*, F i recto.

59. *Opera* I:356.

60. *Decretales* of Gregor IX, I, tit. VI, cap. xxxiv (Friedberg II, col. 80). I owe this reference to James Farge.

61. *Carmen patheticum fratris Wigandi*, n. p., n.d. The copy I saw in the Herzog August Bibliothek, Wolfenbuettel (41.3 Quod) was bound with Brant's defense of Mary ([Oppenheim]: J. Kobel, 1503).

62. *Ad praestantem . . . Wimpinam pro defensione sacre theologie et theologice veritatis* [Leipzig, c. 1500] A ii recto and A iii recto (grammaticista illa cum theologis disceptatio).

63. *Illustrium virorum epistolae* (Haguenau, 1519) z ii recto.

64. CWE Ep. 347:167.

65. *Hasardi Angiani Apologia* (Louvain, 1520) b iii verso.

66. CWE Epp. 182:125–130, 337:881–883; similarly Ep. 326:94.

67. MS Bibl. Vat. Ottob. lat. 438, fol. 3 recto–4 recto; see Henricus Glareanus' remark: *magisterium venditur* (Herminjard I. 38, note 2).

68. Ibidem, 4 recto; the pun *doctus/doctor* is also used by Vives *Contra pseudodialecticos*, ed. Ch. Fantazzi (Leiden, 1979), 74–76; see Brunfels, *Confutatio sophistices* (Selestat, 1520) a iii recto: *Cuique etiam mediocriter docto theologum esse liceat.*

69. Ibidem 5 recto. See Guillaume Budé, who speaks of "ung cercle des ars liberaulx et sciences polytiques appellée encyclopedie . . . ayant les dictes ciences et disciplines connexité mutuelle" (quoted by N. Kenny, *The Palace of Secrets*, Oxford, 1990, p. 15).

70. *Apologia earum rerum quae illi obiiciuntur ad . . . Franciscum Ximenez* (n.d., n.p). I used the copy in the British Museum Library. The quotation comes from an autograph letter by the author to the Bishop of Málaga on the page facing a i recto.

71. Ibidem a i recto, a iv verso.

72. Quoted by F. Olmedo, *Nebrija (1441–1522): Debelador de la barbarie* (Madrid, 1942) 43.

73. *Laconismus tumultuarius* a iv verso.

74. Herminjard I:11, 12; *Illustrium virorum epistolae* q iii verso, s i verso.

75. *Destructio Cabalae* 4.6.

76. *Defensio contra calumniatores suos Colonienses* (Tübingen, 1513) D ii verso.

77. Ibidem L i recto; Tongeren was Master of Arts (1486); he taught in the theological faculty at Cologne.

78. *Epistolae obscurorum virorum*, ed. F. G. Stokes (London, 1909) I.5.

79. Ibidem II.38, Demetrius Phalerus to Ortvin Gratius.

80. *Apologia* B ii verso.

81. *Illustrium virorum epistolae* y1 recto.

82. *De fructu qui ex doctrina percipitur*, ed. and trans. F. Manley and R. Sylvester (New York, 1967) 118–119.

83. *Antapologia* 153 recto.

84. The document is printed in H. de Jongh, *L'ancienne faculté de théologie de Louvain* (repr. Utrecht, 1980) 3*–4*.

85. CWE Ep. 643:11

86. Allen Ep. 1581:21.

87. Preface to *Annotationes* aa1 verso–aa2 recto.

88. *Annotationes* A i verso. See R. Cameron, "The Attack on the Biblical work of Lefèvre d'Etaples, 1514–1521," *Church History* 38 (1969) 9–24.

89. *Antapologia* 62 recto, 58 recto; *De tralatione* 99 recto.

90. LB IX 922 C–D.

91. J. Farge, *Le parti conservateur au XVI siècle: Université et Parlement de Paris* (Paris, 1992), document 7: A, B.

92. Quoted by Boehm, "Humanistische Bildungsbewegung und mittelalterliche Universitätsverfassung" in *The Universities in the Late Middle Ages*, ed. J. IJsewijn and J. Pacquet (Louvain, 1978) 335.

93. *Contra turpem libellum* a iv verso. It should be noted, however, that at the beginning of the century teachers of poetry often also taught in the higher faculties (see T. Heath "Logical Grammar, Grammatical Logic, and Humanism in Three German Universities," *Studies in the Renaissance* 18 [1971] 32, 37). At Ingolstadt, Celtis was the first *poeta* who did not do so.

94. Johann Eck, *Oratio . . . pro venerando patre Stephano priore Eberspergio* (1512) c ii recto; see also D i recto: *Theologia alias omnes scientias longo intervallo post se dimittens . . . ad aeternae felicitatis sedes foelicissime sola deducit.*

95. *Apologeticus* B vi verso, B i recto-verso, B iii recto.

96. *Vitiosa sterilis Mulae ad Musam . . . comparatio* A iii verso, B i verso, B ii verso-B iii recto.

97. This work appeared in *Farrago miscellaneorum Conradi Wimpinae Fagis* (Cologne, 1531). The quotation is on 163 verso.

98. *Contra turpem libellum* A ii recto, D ii verso.

99. Quoted by Luis Gil, "Nebrija y el menester del gramático" 129–130.

100. *Oratio de variarum linguarum cognitione paranda* (Leipzig 1518). The quotations in this paragraph appears on sigs. B i verso, D ii verso, E iii recto.

101. *Dialogus de tribus linguis,* ed. Pijper 82–83.

102. H. de Jongh, *L'ancienne faculté de théologie de Louvain* 21*–24*; see 237 n5.

103. I.17, ed. Stokes.

104. Quoted by Boehm, "Humanistische Bildungsbewegung" 341.

105. Polich in *Laconismus* a iv recto; Buschius in *Praestabili et rare eruditionis viro Martino Mellerstat . . .* (Leipzig 1502) A iii recto; Murmellius in *Didascalici libri duo* (Cologne, 1510) a iii verso; More, ed. Kinney, 141.

106. CWE Epp. 347:168–169, 182:149, 373:147–158, 1062:50–52.

107. CWE Ep. 1062:65–87.

108. *Oratio,* in *History of the Foundation and the Rise of the Collegium Trilingue Lovaniense, 1517–1550,* ed. H. de Vocht (Louvain, 1951–1955). The passage quoted is at I:537.

5. Biblical Scholarship

1. *Maclean's,* Nov. 18 1991, p. 13.

2. The passage, from Wimpheling's *Castigationes locorum in canticis ecclesiasticis et divinis officiis depravatorum* (Strasbourg, 1513), is quoted in J. V. Riegger, *Amoenitates Litterariae Friburgenses* (Ulm, 1775) 343.

3. PL 28:1186A, PL 29:557B–559A, PL 23:448C.

4. *Opera* I:897, 385.

5. *Adversus suae novae Psalterii traductionis obtrectatores apologetici libri V,* ed. A. de Petris (Rome, 1980) 11; the Jerome passage quoted is PL 23:448C.

6. MS Vat. Ottob. Lat. 438 3 recto, 5 verso, 6 recto.

7. Quoted T. Heath, "Logical Grammar, Grammatical Logic, and Humanism in Three German Universities," *Studies in the Renaissance* 18 (1971) 30.

8. *The Colloquies of Erasmus,* trans. C. R. Thompson (Chicago, 1965) 81.

9. *Vita S. Nicolai* in *Flores et Elegantiae ex diversis libris Hochstrati . . . collectae* (s.l., s.d.) I iv verso, d i verso.

10. E. Rummel, trans., *Scheming Papists and Lutheran Fools* (New York, 1993) 57, 62, 63.

11. *Responsio* C v recto.

12. *De tralatione Bibliae* 46 recto, 63 verso.

13. *The Works of Sir Thomas More,* ed. D. Kinney (New Haven, 1986), vol. 15, p. 226.

14. *Collationes*, in the introduction A4 verso; in the text a7 recto, a4 recto, c8 recto.

15. V. Beltran de Heredia, ed., *Cartulario de la Universidad de Salamanca* VI:29, 53, 99, 112, 85.

16. Stunica, *Annotationes* A i verso.

17. In E. Rice, *The Prefatory Epistles of Jacques Lefèvre* (New York, 1972) 425 (to Louis Guillart).

18. *Prefatory Epistles*, ed. Rice 197.

19. CWE Ep. 373:44–46.

20. PG 161:625D, 626C.

21. *Opera* I:800a.

22. *Apologia* b i recto; the biblical quotations come from Luke 11:43 and 14:7.

23. *De tralatione* 57 verso–58 recto.

24. Béda in *Annotationes* 4 recto–verso; Stunica in *Annotationes* A i verso.

25. On the role attributed to Jerome in the revision of the Vulgate see E. Rice, *Saint Jerome in the Renaissance* (Baltimore, 1985) 173–199.

26. PL 28:505A, 603A.

27. PL 28:1142A, 1474B.

28. PL 28:1391A–1394A, PL 29:557B–559A.

29. PL 29:424A, PL 28:182A–183A.

30. PG 161:627D–630C, 640B.

31. Valla, *Antidotum primum*, ed. A. Wesseling (Amsterdam, 1978) 111–112.

32. Ibidem 112.

33. Brandolini 5 verso; Manetti (ed. A. de Petris) 3.

34. *Prefatory Epistles*, ed. Rice 299.

35. *Scholia* on Jerome's preface to the Gospels (Basel, 1536) 31; *Apologia* in *Ausgewählte Werke*, eds. A. and H. Holborn (Munich, 1933) 170:11–12.

36. CWE Ep. 337:758–771; Jerome PL 28:182A.

37. CWE Ep. 337:816–828, 843–863.

38. Jerome PL 28:1474B, see also 1172A–B.

39. *De tralatione* 49 recto, 54 verso. Compare 34 verso, 40 verso.

40. Ibidem 22 verso, 34 verso.

41. Ibidem 65 recto–verso.

42. *Annotationes* a iii recto.

43. Ibidem a i verso.

44. See J. Bentley, *Humanists and Holy Writ* (Princeton, 1983) 169; E. Rummel, *Erasmus' Annotations on the New Testament* (Toronto, 1986) 152–160.

45. Quoted by J. D'Amico, *Theory and Practice in Renaissance Textual Criticism* (Berkeley, 1988) 153.

46. See, for example, G. Lloyd Jones, *The Discovery of Hebrew in Tudor England: A Third Language* (Manchester, 1983); *Le temps des Réformes et la Bible*, eds. G. Bedouelle and B. Roussel (Paris, 1989); I. Rashkow, "Hebrew Bible Translations and the Fear of Judaization," *Sixteenth Century Journal* 21

(1990) 217–234; H. Oberman, *Roots of Antisemitism in the Age of the Renaissance and Reformation* (Philadelphia, 1983); idem, "Discovery of Hebrew and Discrimination against the Jews: The *Veritas Hebraica* as Double-Edged Sword in Renaissance and Reformation," in *Germania Illustrata*, eds. A. Fix and S. Karant-Nunn (Kirksville, 1992) 19–34.

47. Steuco's book was entitled *Veteris Testamenti ad Hebraicam veritatem recognitio* (Venice, 1529). See R. Delph, "Italian Humanism in the Early Reformation: Agostino Steuco (1497–1548)" (PhD. diss., University of Michigan 1987, now being revised for publication) 26.

48. Pico's and Reuchlin's cases were complicated by the fact that their interest extended to the Cabala.

49. Quoted by Oberman, "Discovery of Hebrew and Discrimination" 32.

50. CWE Ep. 798:25–28.

51. *Prefatory Epistles*, ed. Rice 196, 354.

52. Ibidem 484; see also 440 (Address to the Reader in Lefèvre's commentary on the Gospels).

53. J. Olin, *Catholic Reform from Cardinal Ximenes to the Council of Trent 1495–1563* (New York, 1990) 62.

54. *Apologia* a iii recto, a iv verso, a iii verso.

55. CWE Ep. 373:16–17, LB VI ***1 verso, 2 recto, 4 recto.

56. Quoted by T. M. Centi, "L'attività letteraria di Santi Pagnini (1470–1536) nel campo delle scienze bibliche," *Archivum fratrum Praedicatorum* 15 (1945) 26.

57. *Prefatory Letters*, ed. Rice 295.

58. CWE Epp. 347:185–186, 304:101–102, 347:192–194, LB IX 435C.

59. *Collationes* c5 verso.

60. *Antapologia* 116 verso, 136 verso; *De tralatione* 59 recto, 60 verso.

61. *Paradoxa seu theologicae assertationes divinis eloquiis . . . roboratae* (Paris, 1534) 51 recto.

62. *Introducciones Latinas* (s.l. [1488]), in the dedicatory letter to Queen Isabel, a i verso. Similarly, Celtis in *Oratio* (held at Ingolstadt, 1492) says that theologians neglect Jerome and Augustine, "the leaders of our faith," because they cannot understand them (*Conradus Celtis Protucius. Oratio*, ed. H. Ruprich, Leipzig, 1932, p. 9).

63. Quoted by G. Lloyd Jones, *The Discovery of Hebrew in Tudor England: A Third Language* (Manchester, 1983) n20.

64. *Epistola apologetica* (n.p. 1517) b vi recto–b vii recto; an anonymous mock petition to the Pope expresses similar thoughts, and is likely Pirckheimer's work. See E. Rummel, "A Little-Known 'Petition' and 'Papal Rescript': From the Pen of Willibald Pirckheimer?" *Archive for Reformation History* 85 (1994): 309–316.

65. Both texts have been edited by A. and H. Holborn (Munich, 1933) 150–162 (*Methodus*) and 175–305 (*Ratio*), from which I am quoting.

66. Holborn 151–152.

67. *De tralatione* 63 recto–verso.
68. E. Rummel, trans., *Scheming Papists* 57.
69. *Salibus cribratus dialogus*, ed. Böcking, Supplement I 306–307.
70. CWE Ep. 149:51–55, see Ep. 337:733–735.
71. *Oratio de variarum linguarum cognitione paranda* (Leipzig, 1518) A ii verso. The other quotations in this paragraph come from the same edition.
72. *Apologia* C i recto–verso, C iii verso.
73. R. Wakefield, *On the Three Languages*, ed. and trans. G. Lloyd Jones (Binghamton, 1989) 59, 62, 64.
74. *Clavis Scripturae* (Basel, 1580) a3 verso–a4 verso.
75. *Sermo habitus apud iuventutem academiae Wittebergensis*, ed. H. Stupperich (Güterloh, 1951) III:30–42. English translation in *A Melanchthon Reader*, ed. R. Keen (New York, 1988) 47–57.
76. *Sermo*, ed. Stupperich III:30, 40; the translation is mine.
77. *Schriften* 30:565. See H. Junghans, "Der Einfluss des Humanismus auf Luthers Entwicklung," *Lutherjahrbuch* 37 (1970) 37–101.
78. Masson in *Dialogus*, ed. Pijper 48; Titelmans in *Collationes* a8 verso.
79. de Vocht I:540.
80. *Oratio* B v verso–B vi recto, C1 verso–2 recto.
81. *Dialogus*, ed. Pijper 56, 63–64.
82. *Annotationes* 24 verso.
83. Quoted by Erasmus LB IX 657D. His suggestion that the apostles had learned Greek from the common people and therefore "spoke like sailors and cart-drivers" was met with great indignation (see Allen Ep. 1304:142).
84. Jerome in Ep. 22.30, Origen PG 14:185A, 825B.
85. *De genealogia* 14.12; *De otio religioso*, ed. G. Rotondi (Citta del Vaticano, 1958) 105.
86. Brandolini 2 verso; Valla *Opera* I:821a, 809b.
87. Brandolini 3 verso; Erasmus LB IX 777C.
88. *Apologia* i iv verso.
89. LB VI **3 verso.
90. Breen 17, 18, 29.
91. *Apologeticus*, ed. de Petris 52, 127, 129.
92. Brandolini 7 verso–8 recto.
93. On Cortesi, see J. D'Amico, *Renaissance Humanism in Papal Rome* (Baltimore, 1983) 76–81, 148–152.
94. I quote from *In Sententias*, a variant title for Cortesi's work (Basel: Froben, 1513) B1 verso, A2 recto–2 verso, A6 verso.
95. The following quotations appear on d4 recto–verso.
96. *De tralatione* 66 recto–70 recto.
97. Alberto Pio, *Responsio accurata et paraenetica ad Erasmi Roterodami expostulationem* (Paris, 1529) 29 recto.
98. *Antibarbarians* CWE 23:32, Allen Epp. 1581:391–392, 1607:18–19.
99. LB VI **3 verso.

100. See the examples in E. Rummel, *Erasmus' Annotations on the New Testament* (Toronto, 1986) 104–105.
101. CWE 28:390; *aptum et decorum* were the buzzwords used by Cicero and Quintilian in describing the ideal speech.
102. CWE 28:388, 447.
103. Allen Epp. 1661:8–12, 3127:48–50; compare Epp. 1479: 176–178, 1496: 183–184, 1755:20–22.
104. CWE 28:447; LB IX 530B.
105. CWE 28:373.
106. CWE 28:389 and C. Reedijk, *The Poems of Desiderius Erasmus* (Leiden, 1956) number 15.
107. CWE 28:393, 381–383, LB VI **4 recto.
108. CWE 28:400.

6. The Debate and the Reformation

1. B. Moeller, "Die deutschen Humanisten und die Anfänge der Reformation," *Zeitschrift für Kirchengeschichte* 70 (1959) 54.
2. *Epistolae aliquot eruditorum virorum* (Basel, 1520) 152 (Pirckheimer), 172 (Buschius). Similarly, Hermann of Neuenahr, drawing a comparison between Erasmus and Reuchlin, concluded that both men had fallen into the hands of theologians, which was "like falling into the hands of robbers" (ibidem 28). See also Agrippa of Nettesheim, *Responsio* C vi recto: "Tell me, professors of theology at Louvain and Cologne, what glory have you gained from attacking Reuchlin . . . what advantages from attacking Erasmus, Lefèvre, and Petrus Ravennas?"
3. CWE Ep. 1161:9–10.
4. *Epistolae aliquot eruditorum virorum* (Basel, 1520) 158–159 (Zasius to Beatus Rhenanus).
5. CR I, Ep. 43.
6. Moeller, "Die deutschen Humanisten" 52.
7. *Correspondance de Martin Bucer*, ed. J. Rott (Leiden, 1979) Ep. 3:54–55; Zwingli, *Werke* (Leipzig, 1911) vol. 7, Ep. 60, p. 139:16–17.
8. Allen Epp. 1300:53–55, 1345:39, 1659:80–87, see also 1664:65–70 and 1805:49–63.
9. Hutten in CWE Ep. 1161:23.
10. Budé, *Opera omnia* I:174; Agrippa in *Apologia* D v verso.
11. See WABr III, Ep. 596:21–25.
12. Even after the "institutionalization" of humanism at Lutheran universities (see M. Fleischer, "The Institutionalization of Humanism in Silesia," *Archive for Reformation History* 66 (1975) 156–173), theologians carefully guarded their professional identity as distinct in task and status from that of humanists. See S. Ozment, "Humanism, Scholasticism, and the Intellectual Origins of the Reformation" in *Continuity and Discontinuity in*

Church History, eds. F. Forrester Church and T. George (Leiden, 1979) 136; see also J. Kittelson, "Humanism in the Theological Faculties of Lutheran Universities during the Late Reformation," in *The Harvest of Humanism in Central Europe: Essays in Honor of Lewis W. Spitz*, ed. M. Fleischer (St. Louis, 1992) 139–178. William Bouwsma, however, puts more emphasis on the humanist ingredient: "The deepest assumptions of earlier humanist culture found theological expression in the Protestant Reformation" ("Changing Assumptions in Later Renaissance Culture," *Viator* 7 [1976] 439). See also "Renaissance and Reformation: An Enquiry into Their Affinities and Connections" in *Luther and the Dawn of the Modern Era*, ed. H. Oberman (Leiden, 1972) 127–149.

13. CWE Ep. 1127A:77–78, 59–61; see similar remarks in a letter to Melanchthon, Ep. 1113:40–41.

14. CWE Epp. 1443:77–78, 23–25; Ep. 1135:46–48.

15. R. Stupperich, *Melanchthon* (London, 1966) 66; W. Maurer, "Melanchthon als Humanist" in *Philip Melanchthon*, ed. W. Ellinger (Göttingen, 1961) 116–132: "der Abgrund ist unüberbrückbar aufgerissen zwischen humanistischer Bildungs- und reformatorischer Gnadenreligion" (123). Conversely, S. Ozment, "The Intellectual Origins" 134: "The breach that later opened between Luther and Erasmus in 1525 did not end the collaboration between humanists and Protestant reformers, and this famous confrontation should not be taken as symptomatic of a larger incompatibility, much less divorce, between humanism and Protestantism."

16. F. Heer, *Die dritte Kraft: Der Humanismus zwischen den Fronten des konfessionellen Zeitalters* (Frankfurt, 1959) 221.

17. CWE Ep. 1352:39–43.

18. Allen Ep. 1496:50–51; see W. Maurer, "Melanchthon's Anteil am Streit zwischen Luther und Erasmus," *Archive for Reformation History* 49 (1958) 89–115; for the most recent summary of the conflict and bibliographical references see C. Augustijn, *Erasmus: His Life, Works, and Influence* (Toronto, 1991), chapter 11.

19. See LB X 1286E; Augustijn, *Erasmus* 141.

20. Quoted in Allen's headnote to Ep. 1496.

21. On the rhetorical nature of the treatise see C. Augustijn, "Le dialogue Erasme-Luther dans l'*Hyperaspistes* II," in *Actes du colloque international Erasme*, ed. J. Chomarat et al. (Geneva, 1990) 171–184; M. O'Rourke Boyle, *Rhetoric and Reform* 133–134; F. Tinkler, "Erasmus' Conversation with Luther," *Archive for Reformation History* 82 (1991) 59–81.

22. The exceptions are scholars who had formed bonds of friendship with both men, but their decision was personal and social rather than intellectual. A case in point is Melanchthon, who had to choose between two mentors and rationalized his decision in the often quoted "De Erasmo et Luthero Elogion" (a remark first published in 1522): "In theological matters we have two principal requirements: firstly, . . . evangelical and Christian teaching,

unworldly and divorced from all human reasoning. This is what Luther teaches . . .; secondly, good morals and civility. This is what Erasmus teaches; but so did the pagan philosophers" (CR XX:700). See H. Scheible, "Melanchthon zwischen Luther und Erasmus," *Renaissance und Reformation: Gegensätze und Gemeinsamkeiten* (Wolfenbüttel, 1984) 155–180.

23. J. Tracy, "Humanism and the Reformation," in *Reformation Europe: A Guide to Research*, ed. Steven Ozment (St. Louis, 1986) 33–57. For another survey of the relationship between humanism and the Reformation see P. Matheson, "Humanism and Reform Movements," in *The Impact of Humanism on Western Europe*, eds. A. Goodwin and A. MacKay (London, 1990) 23–42.

24. *Briefwechsel*, ed. Krause, Ep. 645.

25. *Der Briefwechsel des Beatus Rhenanus*, eds. A. Horawitz and K. Hartfelder (Leipzig, 1886) 9, 590.

26. J. Kittelson, *Wolfgang Capito: From Humanist to Reformer* (Leiden, 1975) 127; see 238.

27. Quoted by Mutianus, *Briefwechsel*, ed. Krause Ep 633 (June 1520).

28. W. P. Fuchs, "Willibald Pirckheimer," *Jahrbuch für Fränkische Landesforschung* 31 (1971) 16.

29. He wrote a preface to Emser's *Canonis missae contra H. Zwinglium defensio* (1524); see J. Knepper, *Jacob Wimpheling (1450–1528)* (Freiburg im Breisgau, 1902) 320.

30. For recent works see A. Rabil, "Desiderius Erasmus," in *Renaissance Humanism: Foundations, Form, and Legacy* (Philadelphia, 1988) II:216–264; and C. Augustijn, *Erasmus: His Life, Works, and Influence* (Toronto, 1991), esp. chapters 9–11. Both works have extensive bibliographical information. Also of relevance is C. Augustijn's "Humanisten auf dem Scheideweg zwischen Luther und Erasmus," in *Humanismus und Reformation: Martin Luther und Erasmus von Rotterdam in den Konflikten ihrer Zeit*, ed. O. H. Pesch (Freiburg, 1985) 119–134.

31. CWE Ep. 64:97–101, 84–85.

32. Allen Ep. 1794:27–34.

33. CWE Ep. 61:133–137.

34. In his *Lectures on Corinthians* Colet wrote: "If any should say, as is often said, that to read heathen authors is of assistance for the right understanding of Holy Writ, let them reflect whether the very fact of such reliance being placed upon them does not make them a chief obstacle to such understanding . . . the gospel truth is understood by grace . . . to have recourse to other means is mere infatuation" (ed. and trans. J. H. Lupton, London, 1874, 110–111).

35. *Poems*, ed. Reedijk, no. 15:15–17.

36. CWE Epp. 177:112–113; 188:13–14 (preface to his translations from Euripides).

37. CWE Ep. 164:50.

38. See Chapters 3 and 5.

39. Holborn 190:12–18, 193:6, 24–28, 295:1–5.
40. LB IX 262D–E, LB VI **3 verso.
41. 207–208 verso.
42. LB IX 1069D, 870D.
43. ASD IX–1 256:575–258:605; likewise, LB X 1262A–B.
44. LB V 1171F.
45. ASD IX–1 291:226–228, 418:964–966; Allen Epp. 1644:15–17, 2615:42–45, LB X 1268E.
46. *Colloquies*, ed. Thompson, 270; *De sarcienda ecclesiae concordia*, trans. R. Himelick in *Erasmus and the Seamless Coat of Jesus* (Lafayette, 1971) 86.
47. Holborn 178–180.
48. Most relevant to our discussion among recent Melanchthon studies is A. Sperl, *Melanchthon zwischen Humanismus und Reformation* (Munich, 1959); W. Maurer, *Der junge Melanchthon zwischen Humanismus und Reformation* (Göttingen, 1967). See also P. Joachimsen, "*Loci Communes*. Eine Untersuchung zur Geistesgeschichte des Humanismus und der Reformation" in *Gesammelte Aufsätze*, ed. v. N. Hammerstein (Aalen, 1970) 387–442.
49. *Melanchthons Werke in Auswahl*, ed. R. Stupperich (Gütersloh 1951–1975) III:10–21.
50. CR I 9, 24.
51. Stupperich III:31, 38, 32, 34.
52. Stupperich III:38, 33, see also 40, 70.
53. Stupperich III:58.
54. Stupperich III:58, 59.
55. Stupperich III:58–59, 61.
56. Establishing the classical pedigree of his work, he writes in a letter to Johannes Hess (CR I 147) that he "followed the counsel of the orators who direct us to sum up the basic concepts of the disciplines."
57. *Summa* I.1.8.2: "The *locus* 'from authority' which is based on divine revelation is most efficacious. And sacred doctrine uses human reasoning not to prove faith ... but to make manifest certain matters transmitted through doctrine."
58. PL 210:621A.
59. Stupperich II:1, 3.
60. Ibidem: "The authors of old adopted [the system of *loci*], but with economy and in a straightforward manner; among the more recent writers, [Johannes] Damascenus and [Peter] Lombard did so, but both ineptly." The works of neither man have much similarity to Melanchthon's *Loci*, however, and he is eloquently silent about Isidore of Seville's *Sentences*, which bear a closer structural resemblance.
61. CR XXI, 334. He mentions Origen's *Peri Archon*, "so entitled because he presents in order the principal *loci* of Christian doctrine and attempts to explain them"; *De fide ad Petrum*, a work often ascribed to Augustine; and an unspecified work of Gregory of Nyssa, perhaps his *Oratio catechetica magna*.

62. CWE 27:212.
63. Holborn 158–159.
64. Holborn 291. The heading "on ceremonies" has been excised, and the heading "piety" was made more specific: "obligation (*pietas*) toward parents or children."
65. Stupperich I:184, 7 ff.
66. CR I 575.
67. CR XX 702–4.
68. Stupperich III:139, 143.
69. CR I 575.
70. CR I 576, 607.
71. CR I 575 (*theologica . . . omittere malim*); I 606 (*nihil minus cogitans quam quod postea evenit . . .*).
72. "Ist Melanchthon als Theologe anzusehen?": K. Aland, "Die theologische Fakultät Wittenberg und ihre Stellung im Gesamtzusammenhang der Leucorea während dem 16. Jahrhundert" in *450 Jahre Luther Universität* (s.l. 1952) I: 174, quoted and discussed by L. Stern, "Philipp Melanchthon—Humanist, Reformator, Praeceptor Germaniae," *Philipp Melanchthon*, ed. W. Ellinger (Göttingen, 1961) 34–35.
73. CR I 722: *Ego mihi conscius sum, non ob aliam causam unquam tetheolokenai nisi ut vitam emendarem.*
74. See A. Sperl, *Melanchthon zwischen Humanismus und Reformation* (Munich, 1959) 163, 168.
75. English translation of Burchard's *Reply to Pico* in Qu. Breen, *Christianity and Humanism* 52–68. On the attribution of this text to Melanchthon see above, Chapter 1, n.42. There is no modern edition of F. Titelmans' *Collationes quinque super epistolam ad Romanos* (Antwerp, 1529), which prompted a polemical reply from Erasmus. On the controversy see E. Rummel, *Erasmus and His Catholic Critics* (Nieuwkoop, 1989) II:15–22.
76. Text in Breen, *Christianity and Humanism* 11–38. Barbaro answered Pico with a brief note and a more elaborate letter. Burchard rewrote the latter. The quotation in this paragraph appears on p. 25 of Breen's translation.
77. For the Latin text of Burchard's prefatory letter see E. Rummel "*Epistola Hermolai nova ac subditicia*" 303–304. The passage quoted is on p. 304.
78. Allen Ep. 2206:115.

7. Humanist Critique of Scholastic Dialectic

1. C. Prantl, *Geschichte der Logik im Abendlande* (Leipzig, 1927) IV:151, calls humanism a "belebender Hauch"; Ch. Schmitt noted in *Aristotle and the Renaissance* (Cambridge, Mass., 1983) 21: "If historians of logic and science uniformly decry the humanization of logic as a disaster, literary and cultural historians tend to see it as a fine thing." On the subject of humanistic dialectic see the relevant articles in *The Cambridge History of Renaissance Philosophy*,

eds. Ch. Schmitt and Qu. Skinner (Cambridge, 1988): C. Vasoli, "The Origin of Renaissance Philosophy: Scholastic Thought and the Needs of a New Culture" (57–74); E. Ashworth, "Traditional Logic" (147–172); L. Jardine, "Humanistic Logic" (173–198). Among the wealth of literature the following may be cited as of particular relevance to our subject: C. Vasoli, *La dialettica e la retorica dell'umanesimo* (Milan, 1968); A. Seifert, *Logik zwischen Scholastik und Humanismus. Das Kommentarwerk Johann Ecks* (Munich, 1978); A. Perreiah, "Humanistic Critiques of Scholastic Dialectic, *Sixteenth Century Journal* 13 (1982) 3–22; E. Kessler, "The Transformation of Aristotelianism during the Renaissance" in *New Perspectives on Renaissance Thought*, ed. J. Henry and S. Hutton (London, 1990) 137–147. For literature on individual humanists see notes below. P. Mack's *Renaissance Argument: Valla and Agricola in the Traditions of Rhetoric and Dialectic* (Leiden, 1993) became available only when this book was already in production.

2. Pierre Galland, the Paris master who defended Aristotelianism against Ramus' criticism, observed that the humanists reviled Aristotle but nevertheless retained his system (*Contra novam academiam Petri Rami oratio*, Paris, 1551, 9 recto). On the polemic see W. Ong, *Ramus, Method and the Decay of Dialogue* (Cambridge, Mass., 1958) 39–40 and Ch. Schmitt, *Cicero Scepticus* (The Hague, 1972) 92–102.

3. The *Summulae Logicales* of Peter of Spain, the textbook most widely used in the late Middle Ages and early Renaissance, states at the outset: *dialectica probabiliter disputat de principiis scientiarum* (facsimile of 1572 ed., Hildesheim, 1981) 2.

4. Prantl IV:1.

5. CWE 27:126–127; see H. Oberman on the use of the metaphor "labyrinth," "labyrinthine" in connection with the scholastic method, "Initia Calvini: The matrix of Calvin's Reformation" in *Mededelingen der Koninklijke Nederlandse Akademie van Wetenschappen* 54–55 (1991) 20–21.

6. On this subject see Perreiah, "Humanistic Critiques" 13 and his introduction to Paulus Venetus, *Logica Parva* (Munich, 1984) 19 and 30, n8.

7. For the history of the text see G. Zippel's introduction to his edition of *Laurentii Valle Repastinatio dialectice et philosophie* (Padua, 1982), 2 vols. In the following I quote from the third redaction of the work, entitled *Retractatio totius dialectice cum fundamentis universe philosophie*, the text of which is in the first volume of Zippel's edition. For critical analyses of Valla's dialectic see, for example, H. B. Gerl, *Rhetorik als Philosophie: Lorenzo Valla* (Munich, 1974); L. Jardine, "Lorenzo Valla and the Intellectual Origins of Humanist Dialectic," *Journal of the History of Philosophy* 15 (1977) 143–164; R. Waswo, "The 'Ordinary Language Philosophy' of Lorenzo Valla," *BHR* 41 (1979) 255–271; L. Jardine, "Dialectic or Dialectical Rhetoric? Agostino Nifo's Criticism of Lorenzo Valla," *Rivista critica di storia della filosofia* 36 (1981) 253–270; E. Kessler, "Die Transformation des aristotelischen *Organon* durch L. Valla," in *Aristotelismus und Renaissance*, ed. E. Kessler et al. (Wies-

NOTES TO PAGES 156–159

baden, 1988) 53–87; Monfasani, J., "Lorenzo Valla and Rudolph Agricola," *Journal of the History of Philosophy* 28 (1990) 181–200; Ch. Trinkaus, "Lorenzo Valla's Anti-Aristotelian Natural Philosophy," *I Tatti Studies* forthcoming.

8. Ch. Trinkaus, *In Our Image and Likeness* (Chicago, 1970) I:150; Kessler 55; Waswo 257.

9. Tertullian, *Exhortatio castitatis* 6.

10. Zippel 277:24–278:5.

11. In the following I quote from the facsimile of the Cologne 1539 edition (Nieuwkoop, 1967). For recent literature on the dialectic of Agricola see M. Nikolaou, *Sprache als Welterschliessung und Sprache als Norm: Uberlegungen zu R. Agricola und J. Sturm* (Munich, 1984); L. Jardine, "Distinctive Discipline: R. Agricola's Influence on Methodical Thinking in the Humanities" in *Rodolphus Agricola Phrisius, 1444–1485*, ed. F. Akkerman and A. J. Vanderjagt (Leiden, 1988) 38–57; Ong, *Ramus, Method* 95–130; A. Faust, "Die Dialektik R. Agricolas: Ein Beitrag zur Charakteristik des deutschen Humanismus," *Archiv für Geschichte der Philosophie* 34 (1922) 118–135; T. Heath, "Logical Grammar, Grammatical Logic and Humanism in Three German Universities," *Studies in the Renaissance* 18 (1971) 9–64. Wood Bouldin, "Rodolphus Agricola's Scholastic Theory of Humanistic Rhetoric" (paper given at the Sixteenth Century Studies Conference, Philadelphia, 1991). See also W. Risse's preface to Agricola's *De inventione dialectica* (Hildesheim, 1976).

12. I quote from the translation of Ch. Fantazzi in *Juan Luis Vives: In Pseudodialecticos* (Leiden, 1979). The quotation appears on p. 30. On Vives' critique of traditional dialectics see most recently C. G. Noreña, "Agricola, Vives and the Low Countries," in *Erasmus in Hispania, Vives in Belgia*, eds. J. IJsewijn and A. Losada (Louvain, 1986) 99–118.

13. Dialectic is discussed in Book III of this work. In the following I quote the text in Vives, *Opera Omnia*, ed. F. Fabian y Fuero (Valencia, 1785; repr. Farnborough, 1964) VI:110–151. The quotations in this paragraph appear on pp. 120, 151.

14. It survives today in a single copy at the Bibliothèque Nationale in Paris. For a summary of the contents see Vicente Muñoz Delgado, "Nominalismo, lógica y humanismo" in *El Erasmismo en España* (Santander, 1986) 109–174.

15. Text in *Opera Omnia* III, 68–82, 82–120.

16. The text I use is in CR XIII:514–751. This is the definitive version (Wittenberg, 1547) which superseded the earlier versions, *Compendiaria dialectices ratio* of 1520 and *Dialectices libri quattuor* of 1528.

17. For the history of the editions see W. Ong, *Ramus and Talon Inventory* (Cambridge, Mass., 1958). Ong's *Ramus, Method* is still the standard book on the subject, but for more recent examinations of Ramus' dialectic see N. Bruyère, *Methode et dialectique dans l'oeuvre de La Ramée* (Paris, 1984); A. Grafton and L. Jardine, *From Humanism to the Humanities* (Cambridge, Mass., 1986),

240

chapter 7; P. Sharratt, "Peter Ramus and the Reform of the University: The Divorce of Philosophy and Eloquence," in *French Renaissance Studies 1540–1570*, ed. P. Sharratt (Edinburgh, 1976) 4–20; J. Freedman, "The Diffusion of the Writings of Petrus Ramus in Central Europe, c. 1570–c. 1630," *Renaissance Quarterly* 46 (1993) 98–152.

18. My references are to the Latin text, ed. Qu. Breen (Rome 1956), 2 vols.; there is a German translation by K. Thieme (Munich, 1980). For biographical data on Nizolius see Breen's introduction to the text and his article "Marius Nizolius: Ciceronian Lexicographer and Philosopher," *Archive for Reformation History* 46 (1955) 69–87. For other literature see the following notes.

19. Quoted by P. Rossi, "Il 'De Principiis' di Mario Nizolio" in *Testi umanistici su la retorica*, ed. Eu. Garin et al. (Rome, 1953) 88.

20. For evaluations of Nizolius see M. Wesseler, *Die Einheit von Wort und Sache: Der Entwurf einer rhetorischen Philosophie bei Marius Nizolius* (Munich, 1974) 23–24.

21. Ockham, *In librum praedicamentorum Aristotelis* chapter 7, h i verso (facsimile ed., Ridgewood, 1964): *Queritur utrum predicamenta . . . sint decem et non plura nec pauciora.*

22. Abelard in *De partibus categoricorum;* cf Kneale 206.

23. In the story as told by the Greek historian Herodotus, the man whose horse neighed was to be given the kingship; Darius' servant saw to it that his master's horse neighed at the right moment.

24. The quotation is from *De veritate* question 1, article 1, in the translation of R. W. Mulligan (Chicago, 1952) 3–9.

25. Pierre Galland, *Contra novam academiam Petri Rami oratio* (Paris, 1551) 8 recto-verso; on the polemic see Ong, *Ramus* 39–40 and Ch. Schmitt, *Cicero Scepticus* (The Hague, 1972) 92–102.

26. Ong, *Ramus* 172.

27. *Animadversiones* (facsimile ed. Stuttgart, 1964, with an introduction by W. Risse) 21, 65–66.

28. *Dialecticae institutiones,* 1543 (facsimile edition, with introduction by W. Risse, Stuttgart, 1964) 5.

29. Ibidem 48 recto, 57 recto.

30. A case in point is the theory of commonplaces. Nizolius points out what he considers the flaws in Aristotle's treatment of individual *topoi*, but his objections address the presentation rather than concepts themselves. "The treatment is so obscure," he complains, "and so topsy-turvy and without any true system or order" (II.129). Accordingly, he does not discard the theory of commonplaces but recommends to his readers "to take the doctrine of invention from Cicero and other orators rather than from Aristotle and the dialecticians" (II.130).

31. II.79.

32. *Opera* VI:130, 132.

33. As discussed by Aristotle in the *Posterior Analytics* 72b, 99b.
34. *Opera* VI:119, 69, 70, 77.
35. CR XIII 598 (Melanchthon makes this remark concerning his treatment of syllogisms).
36. Ibidem 586.
37. Ibidem 656; the area in which Aristotle went wrong, according to Melanchthon, was metaphysics. "In this area, let us follow the doctrine handed down by God through illustrious witnesses" (ibidem).
38. Ibidem 641.
39. "More could have been enumerated," he says, for example, about the postpraedicamenta (561).
40. Ibidem 616.
41. *Opera* I: 907; see Gerl 125, who shows that Valla used the terms rhetoric and dialectic interchangeably.
42. *Orator* 69, *De optimo genere oratorum* 2.121, and so on.
43. Zippel 168:19–22 (quoting Quintilian, *Institutio Oratoria* 7.3.2–3).
44. Zippel 172:29–173:4; see also next note.
45. Zippel 244:14–27; the section on *loci* is taken from Quintilian, *Institutio oratoria* 5.8–10.
46. But it appears in handbooks published after Valla—that is, he brought it to the attention of humanists.
47. See 2.4, pp. 198–99.
48. 1.1, p. 1; see 2.2, p. 198.
49. The text of the *Oratio in laudem philosophiae* is in the second volume (separate pagination) of the Cologne 1539 edition (facsimile ed. Nieuwkoop, 1967). The passage quoted appears in that volume on p. 151.
50. *Contra pseudodialecticos* 111, 150.
51. *Opera* VI:149; III:120.
52. *Ars disserendi* in *Dialecticae partitiones* (1543) fol. 5—this is a Ciceronian definition also used by Agricola 2.2, p. 156; the French definition comes from Ramus' *Dialectique* of 1555 (see Ong, *Ramus* 347).
53. The various passages are quoted by Ong, *Ramus* 160–161.
54. *Rhetoricae distinctiones in Quintilianum*, ed. and trans. J. J. Murphy (DeKalb, 1986) 86.
55. Galland, *Contra novam academiam*. The quotations in this paragraph appear on 13 verso, 16 verso–17 recto.
56. The quotations in this paragraph are from *Dialecticae institutiones* 20 recto, 27 recto, 29 verso, 36 verso.
57. "The first general principle of truth and of the right way of philosophizing is, as we believe, a knowledge and familiarity with Greek and Latin, in which practically everything that is worth noting is written and handed down" (I 22). "The second principle of truth is a knowledge of the precepts and writings which are handed down in the books of grammar and rhetoric, without which all learning is unlearned, and all erudition inerudite" (I 23).

58. Just how difficult it is to put Valla's remarks into context is clear from the radically different interpretations of R. Waswo, H.-B. Gerl, and E. Kessler. Waswo notes with resignation that this is "as explicit a statement as Valla was ever able to give" and "his final inference here remains, it seems to me, ambiguous" (265, 627). Gerl does not quite commit herself and merely notes that Valla comes up against the limits of what language can express: "Hier stosst Valla an die Grenze der sprachlichen Vorstellungskraft" (221). On the basis of some generous paraphrasing of Valla's words she postulates: "Damit hat Valla die von der Scholastik aufgestellte Trennung von Inhalt, Erkenntnis und Zeichen überwunden" (223). Kessler makes the same claim, but with less plausibility. He boldly labels Valla's theories "Ockhamist"— "konsequente Anwendung der schon von Ockham formulierten logischen Bestimmung des Transcendentalen" (65).

59. CR IX 693, 699; XI 440.

60. Horace, *Ars poetica* 1.15, quoted by Valla, Zippel, 148:22.

61. *Aristotelicae animadversiones* 10 verso, 6 verso.

62. *Animadversiones* 22 verso.

63. Ibidem 11 verso.

64. *Animadversiones* 26 recto; *Dialecticae institutiones* 30 recto. The full passage on the two methods is translated by Ong, *Ramus* 245–246.

65. In the French edition of 1555, the two methods appear as "méthode de la nature" and "méthode de prudence" respectively, although Ramus also used the combination "méthode de la nature et de doctrine"—the difference being between the simple natural method imitated by art and the contrived method of the speaker who must use cunning in addressing an audience of nonscholars. On the difficulties with Ramus' concept of method see Ong, *Ramus* 228–247.

66. Considerations of consistency eventually led Ramus to suppress the method of prudence as a "cryptic" method, which has no universal applicability since it is adjusted to specific circumstances (see *Dialectica* 1549, p. 139: quae pro conditione personarum, rerum, temporum, locorum, consilium disponendi dabit).

67. Pierre Galland, 46 verso; Adrien Turnèbe, quoted by Ong, *Ramus* p. 237.

68. Galland 53 recto–verso.

69. Leibniz mentions "the distinguished philosopher" Viotti repeatedly, for example in his *New Essays on Common Understanding* 4.12 para. 6, and in a letter to Jacob Thomas in April 1669 (*Philosophical Papers and Letters*, ed. L. E. Loemker, p. 95) which was appended to the Nizolius edition. For Viotti see W. Risse, *Die Logik der Neuzeit* (Stuttgart, 1964) I:261–262.

70. In the following I use the Braunschweig 1685 edition. The passages quoted in this paragraph appear on a4 recto, f4 verso and pp. 8–9, 13, 63, 57. (The prefatory material in this edition has signatures only; the text is paginated).

71. Ibidem pp. 146, 154. Compare Nizolius' emphasis on reexamining tradition. He urged scholars to "rely more on arguments and reasoning than

on authorities and preconceived notions." Their "five senses, intelligence, thought processes, memory, applications, and experience are to be their masters and teachers" (I 27).

Conclusion

1. The "missing link," as W. Risse says: "Hier liegt, bisher nicht recht gewürdigt, das 'fehlende Glied' in der Entwicklung des menschlichen Geistes vom antik-mittelalterlichen zum modernen Denken" (*Die Logik der Neuzeit,* I:13, Stuttgart, 1964).

Index

Abelard, Peter, 160
Academicians, 167, 173
Adrianus, Matthaeus, 94, 116
Aegidius, 48, 60
Agricola, Rudolf, 25, 71, 134, 156–158, 163–165, 170–172, 175–176, 180, 182–184, 191
Agrippa of Nettesheim, Cornelius, 3, 9, 10, 13, 22, 66, 98, 128
Aland, K., 146
Alanus of Lille, 143
Alberti, Leon Battista, 26
Albertus Magnus, 12, 48, 60, 76, 81
Alberus, Erasmus, 26
Alcala, 71, 82
Aleandro, Girolamo, 8, 9
Alexander Gallus (Alexandre de Ville-Dieu), 80
Alexander of Hales, 48, 81
Alonso of Cartagena, 56–59, 61
Ambrose, St., 136
Appel, Nicolaus, 65
Arabic, 108
Arator, 87
Ariston of Chios, 27
Aristotle, Aristotelianism, 2, 4, 11, 12, 22, 25, 26, 28, 30, 32–34, 44, 45, 49, 51, 56, 57, 59, 60, 67, 75, 77, 80, 81, 112, 115, 128, 136, 141, 153, 156–169 passim, 176, 177, 180, 182, 189, 190, 191, 194
Ath, Jan Briart of, 71
Athanasius, St., 98
Augsburg, 29, 130, 136
Augustijn, C., 10

Augustine, St., 29, 31–33, 73, 79, 80, 89, 98, 102, 114–119, 130, 136
Averroes, Averroists, 28, 31, 111

Baden, 132
Baechem, Nicolaus, 5, 9, 11, 97–81, 111
Baptista, Mantuanus, 77
Barbaro, Ermolao, 2, 9, 41, 45–6, 48, 55, 119, 120, 147–151
Barbosa, Arius, 87
Barinus, Jacobus, 73
Basel, 108; Council of, 132
Batmanson, John, 98
Batt, Jakob, 46–47
Bebel, Heinrich, 41, 47–51, 54, 55
Béda, Noël, 6, 71, 83, 89, 91, 100, 106, 118
Bede, the Venerable, 48
Bernard of Clairvaux, St., 32
Berquin, Louis, 8, 72
Bessarion, Joannes, 99, 102, 103
Biel, Gabriel, 7
Boccaccio, Giovanni, 42, 45, 51, 54, 119
Boethius, 43, 165
Bolgar, R. R., 10
Bonaventure, St., 81
Brabant, 5, 128
Brandolini, Aurelio, 6, 86, 97, 103, 119, 120
Brant, Sebastian, 84
Briçonnet, Guillaume, 109
Brulifer, Stephen Pillet, 79
Brunfels, Otto, 29–30, 133
Bruni, Leonardo, 2, 3, 22, 147, 151–152

245

Bucer, Martin, 127, 132, 139
Buchwald, Sigismund, 69, 70
Budé, Guillaume, 109, 128
Burchard, Franz, 9, 147–152
Bureau, Nicolaus, 123
Buridan, Jean, 79
Burleus, Gualterus, 79
Buschius, Hermannus, 6, 8, 12, 65, 83, 89,
   93, 127, 132

Caesarius, Johannes, 191
Calvinists, 40
Canisius, Petrus, 26
Cano, Melchior, 7, 82
Capito, Wolfgang, 29, 132
Ca(r)melite, 97–98. *See also* Baechem,
   Nicolaus.
Carvajal, Luis, 13
Castellio, Sebastian, 40
Castiglione, Balthasar, 3
Cato, 44
Catullus, 75
Celtis, Conrad, 65–66, 93
Chrysostom, John, St., 98, 136
Church Fathers. *See* patristics.
Cicero(nian), 15, 28, 29, 32, 33, 44, 46,
   56, 57, 66, 122–125, 162, 169, 172, 175,
   176, 189, 194
Claymond, John, 124
Clement of Alexandria, St., 136
Clement VII, Pope, 111
Clichtove, Josse, 99
Colet, John, 135
Cologne, 6, 25, 65–66, 69, 87, 89, 127,
   132, 140
Conradi, Tilman, 1, 70
Cordus, Euricius, 70
Cousturier, Pierre, 5, 6, 22, 89, 90, 98,
   100, 105–106, 111, 113, 122–123
Cranston, David, 49–50
Cyprian, St., 136

D'Ailly, Pierre, 38
Dante, Alighieri, 45, 54
Demosthenes, 124
Deza, Diego de, 71
dialectic: and rhetoric, 159, 168–177; and
   theology, 183–186; practical application
   of, 187–189
Diogenes, 44
Dionysodorus, 20
Dominici, Giovanni, 43–44, 52–54

Dorp, Maarten von, 13, 71, 80, 81, 85, 94,
   111
Douglas, Gawain, 49–50
Dullard (Dullaert), Jan, 72
Durandus, Guilelmus, 141
Dürer, Albrecht, 127

Eck, Johann, 6, 13, 25, 91
England, English, 135
Epicurus, Epicureans, 44, 167
Erasmus, Desiderius, 4, 5, 8, 9, 10, 13, 15,
   16, 18, 21, 22, 25, 26, 28, 30, 39, 41, 46,
   50, 51, 54–56, 61–62, 67, 71, 72, 80, 81,
   85, 86, 89–91, 94, 97–100, 103–11, 112,
   114, 119, 123–124, 126–130, 132,
   134–140, 143–144, 146, 147, 151, 155
Erfurt, 2, 9, 67–70, 132
Estienne, Robert, 109, 111, 114
Euthydemus, 20, 21

Ficino, Marsilio, 21
Flaccius Illyricus, Matthias, 115
France, French, 26, 87, 141
Franck, Sebastian, 40
Frankfurt, 132
Freiburg, 13, 75, 132
Freige, Johann Thomas, 159, 162
Fonte, Bartolommeo della, 12
Fuchs, W., 133

Galland, Pierre, 174, 188
Gansfort, Wessel, 108
García, Pedro, 59
Gentile, G., 56
George of Trebizond, 191
Gerl, H.-B., 12
Germany, German, 6, 17, 22, 23, 26, 45,
   70, 79, 87, 115, 127, 131, 141
Gerson, Jean, 34–39
Glareanus, Henricus, 132
Göbler, Justus, 147
Gordon, Ch., 96
Gorgias, 19–21
Gotha, 9, 13
Gratius, Ortvinus, 5, 113, 127
Greek. *See* languages, study of.
Gregory, St., 32
Grey, Thomas, 134
Guarini, Guarino, 24

Hasard, Jacques, 85
Hebrew, 108–118. *See also* languages,
   study of.